Palgrave Socio-Legal Studies

Series Editor
Dave Cowan
University of Bristol Law School
Bristol, UK

The Palgrave Socio-Legal Studies series is a developing series of monographs and textbooks featuring cutting edge work which, in the best tradition of socio-legal studies, reach out to a wide international audience.

More information about this series at
http://www.palgrave.com/gp/series/14679

Dave Cowan • Helen Carr • Alison Wallace

Ownership, Narrative, Things

palgrave
macmillan

Dave Cowan
School of Law
University of Bristol
Bristol, UK

Helen Carr
Kent Law School
University of Kent
Canterbury, UK

Alison Wallace
Centre for Housing Policy
University of York
York, UK

Palgrave Socio-Legal Studies
ISBN 978-1-137-59068-8   ISBN 978-1-137-59069-5   (eBook)
https://doi.org/10.1057/978-1-137-59069-5

Library of Congress Control Number: 2018942877

Cover illustration: ultrapro

Printed on acid-free paper

This Palgrave Macmillan imprint is published by the registered company Springer Nature Limited
The registered company address is: The Campus, 4 Crinan Street, London, N1 9XW, United Kingdom

Preface

This is a book about "shared ownership", a peculiar compromise and an invention, both in label and in design. However, although shared ownership forms its substantive subject matter, the book ranges across various methodological pre-occupations of ours—legal consciousness, actor–network theory, property—and diverse interdisciplinary approaches to property, ownership, home, and things. Despite the evident complications and ambitions inherent in that range, our arguments are quite simple, and can be boiled down to some basic propositions. First, and foremost, we argue that binary constructions of ownership/renting, and social/private, are simply inapposite to describe and represent the everyday lives, experiences, and crisis points of buyers. In this rendering, property is porous and fluid, flexible and accommodating. Secondly, although shared ownership can be presented as quite a simple device—you buy a percentage share of a dwelling, and rent the rest—it is much more complex, and, indeed, as we were told, we still are not entirely sure what the status is of shared owners (at least legally speaking). That status, however, is one which travels, and changes as it travels. Thirdly, we argue for the importance of what Daniel Miller wonderfully calls "stuff". In our study, stuff ranges from the formal (such as the lease, which underpins the shared ownership relation) to a particular outfit (operationalised by one of the people to whom we spoke to divide herself off from the other). Indeed, we argue, perhaps counter-intuitively, that stuff has a legal consciousness.

In pursuing these three propositions, we draw on around 95 interviews, including 70 with buyers themselves and 22 with eminent players (policy-makers, shared owners, and others), and three focus groups with our case study housing associations at the end of our project; observation data with housing associations; archival texts going back to the "start" of shared ownership; and other texts, such as advertising materials. All of these materials are brought to bear in our analysis. The purpose of a preface, though, other than to set out our stall, is to thank those who have contributed to this text. We decided to give our shared owner participants names, in part to humanise them, as opposed to the dehumanising codes that are often ascribed to data in socio-legal research. We "meet" them in the chapters of this book. However, these are not their real names. We thanked them in person and subsequently, but we thank them formally here. We wish also to thank our housing association participants, without whom this whole study would have been impossible. When we approached them with the subject of our study—"Shared Ownership – Crisis Moments"—rather than back away, they engaged with us, assisted us all along the way, and were wonderfully generous with their time. Their dedication to shared ownership should come across in the text. And, finally, we thank those we have labelled "eminent players", who are mostly not named. They do include Sir John Stanley, however, who we would not have been able to anonymise and who played a central role in the formation and propagation of the shared ownership concept. He gave a considerable amount of his time to this project, for which we are grateful.

As researchers, we came to the project from different, complementary angles. Dave and Helen had worked together for some time on and off. They had tried to get a research proposal off the ground with doctrinal lawyers, and had made a number of unsuccessful grant applications. Alison wanted to run a shared ownership project, but had similarly been unsuccessful. It was serendipitous that we came together, and that we put together a project application which the Leverhulme Trust funded under RPG-2013-255. The Trust proved to be a most forgiving and amazing research funder, which left us to get on with our work, requiring the bare minimum by way of reporting. We are in their debt. Our close working relationship, which developed over the course of this project, and its outputs quite simply would not have been possible without their input. The University of Bristol Law School also provided funding for the extra archival research that forms parts of Chaps. 2 and 3. This has been a project in which the team's particular skill sets have been worked (to the bone, at times), and we hope that you enjoy this "product".

We are grateful to our academic colleagues for sharing their time with us, listening to our presentations at various meetings and conferences (SLSA, LSA, ALPS, Onati), making valuable comments, and enabling us to develop our arguments more sharply. In particular, Antonia Layard and Becky Tunstall made comments on an early draft of this book, which caused us to go back over it and redraw it; Colin Perrin, Emilie Cloatre, Alex Marsh, and Sally Wheeler also helped with the development of the opening chapter. Over many years, Antonia Layard has offered both discussion and critique of many of the ideas which appear in this book – we express our gratitude for that engagement in addition to her reading of the draft. Parts of Chaps. 3 and 4 have appeared in research articles published in *Housing Studies* (Chap. 3) and *Journal of Law and Society* (Chap. 4), albeit with rather different framings. We are grateful to these journals for publishing those papers and also for our use of that material.

Finally, Dave wishes to add a dedication. This is the first time he has written with the name "Dave" on the front cover. He has always been David, for his Dad's sake. However, Dad passed away in January 2016, between the end of our fieldwork and the writing of this book. His children did his bidding by singing the Kaddish. Dave wishes to dedicate this book to Norman Cowan, of blessed memory, who finally found peace.

Canterbury, UK   Helen Carr
Bristol, UK   Dave Cowan
York, UK   Alison Wallace
June 2017

Contents

List of Figures

1

Ownership, Narrative, Things

This is a book about the everyday life of "shared ownership", a peculiar pragmatic invention, both in label and in design. Although it is much messier than this, the marketing slogan for shared ownership is that it involves "part buy, part rent". However, although shared ownership forms its substantive subject matter, the book ranges across, and makes a contribution to, various methodological pre-occupations of ours—legal consciousness, actor–network theory, property—and diverse interdisciplinary approaches to ownership, home, and things. In this chapter, we set out how we bring these diverse pre-occupations together and introduce this thing called "shared ownership".

Despite the evident complications and ambitions inherent in our methodological range, our arguments in this book are quite simple, and can be boiled down to three basic propositions. First, and foremost, we argue that apparently binary constructions of homeownership and renting, and social and private housing, are simply not useful to describe and represent the everyday lives, experiences, and crisis points of shared ownership. In our rendering, property is porous and fluid, flexible and accommodating. It is consistently inconsistent, and this is reflected in our data. Listening to a shared owner describe how they felt out of control at different times and for different reasons—whether that be as a result of dripping water or problematic neighbours—but then subsequently say that they felt like an owner because they were in control represented a kind of compartmentalisation of their identities, and we argue that this was more than a compartmentalisation to the extent that it represented a fluidity inherent in the nature of ownership.

The original version of this chapter was revised. An erratum to this chapter can be found at https://doi.org/10.1057/978-1-137-59069-5_9

Part of our research has been to ask how the shared ownership label came into being in the first place, and became blackboxed over time, the process that is ascribed to the complex internal workings of systems or products that, over time, become seemingly self-evident and no longer attract attention. Similarly, we have asked how housing associations (which provide most shared ownership) have integrated shared ownership into their housing management portfolio, alongside their rented products. And finally, we asked how buyers experience shared ownership, from learning about it, to buying it, to engaging in it as part of their everyday lives. It is these three inquiries which animated our understandings in this book. What underpins our analysis is an attempt to appreciate the hold that ownership has in the everyday lives of policy-makers, housing providers, and buyers. In the first part of this chapter, we consider the relevant parts of the literature on property and ownership, and argue for an interactive, mutually constituting triptych of law–property–society.

The second proposition is that, although shared ownership can be presented as quite a simple device—you buy a percentage share of a dwelling, and rent the rest—it is much more complex, and, indeed, as we were told, we are still not entirely sure what the status is of shared owners (at least legally speaking). That status, however, is one which travels, and changes as it travels. It was an innovation, designed in the 1970s, to address a particular moment in the ongoing housing crisis through the creation of an intermediate tenure, with the purpose of enabling those on marginal incomes to get "a foot on the ladder" (an expression about which we have much to say). In the second part of this chapter, we introduce shared ownership and its status within social housing provision, and draw attention to certain ruptures at the heart of social housing in England (the location of our study).

Like anything relatively new and innovative, shared ownership makes people think, and it brings out into the open what they think it is. It makes people think about how it is going to be structured, financed, and produced. It makes people think about how they are going to sell it and, in so doing, distil what is a rather complex legal arrangement into a marketing slogan. It makes organisations that provide it think about how they are going to manage it. It makes those who buy it think about what they are buying and what they think they are. In other words, something like this that is new requires a range of rather ordinary organisations and ordinary people to address really basic, but important, questions. At points of crisis, these answers may well become crystallised, or alter as a result of interactions with others. This is not to suggest that such an innovation provides a kind of "state of nature", in which primary understandings are developed. However, what we have found is that these thoughts, the questions raised, and their answers have consequences, and the purpose of this book is to unwrap those consequences.

Thirdly, we argue for the importance of what Daniel Miller (2010) wonderfully calls "stuff", but to which we refer simply as things (there is no particular significance to this change other than that the latter more easily embraces both human and non-human actors). In our study, things range from the formal (such as the lease, which underpins the shared ownership relation) to the maxidress (operationalised by one of the people to whom we spoke to divide herself off from the other) to other actors (either as a group, such as "owners" or "social" renters, or as individuals). Indeed, we argue, perhaps counter-intuitively, that all things are imbued with and are repositories of a legal consciousness. This idea of the legal consciousness of things—which, properly, is a footnote in that literature—requires some extrapolation, which is the purpose of the third part of this chapter.

We are constantly being shaped and mediated by an infinite series of devices, from papers or bricks to computers and microchips; or, in this study, from documents to feature walls, water as it drips through your ceiling, and flowers that you place outside your front door. Bruno Latour's classic, ironic, and pseudonymous study of the "sociology of the door closer" (Johnson 1988) emphasises this problematic of a sociology which rejects, or minimises the significance of, the material. Zooming out from this discussion of the piston automatic door closer, he argues (1988: 303): "The label 'inhuman' applied to techniques simply overlooks translation mechanisms and the many choices that exist for figuring or de-figuring, personifying or abstracting, embodying or disembodying actors." The dividing line between people and things is negotiable and negotiated, and in action. Miller (2010: 96) plays on the meaning of the word "accommodating" to the same effect, arguing that it involves a "sense of an appropriation of the home by its inhabitants", and that it also implies "the need to change ourselves in order to suit our accommodation". So, in short, things are more than the object of ownership stories; they are also about producing networks, relations, and events, questioning what goes as unseen and unquestioned in the constitution of everyday life (Cloatre and Cowan forthcoming).

In the fourth and fifth parts of this chapter, we set out our various datasets and the structure of this book, respectively. These parts enable you to orient yourself within our framing and the book itself.

Law–Property–Society

The mutually constituting law–society relationship has considerable heritage in socio-legal studies. It represents a break from the problematic "Law and ..." scholarship in which law takes the front seat, driving our ideas about society. We have inserted property in the middle in part because that is the subject of our study, and in part also because of property's mediating influence between law and society. In this part, we develop this proposition through a consideration of three different sets of literature. The first set is what might be termed the standard literature on ownership in law. This is well travelled, and so we do no more than highlight its contours. It is important for our study because our data challenges the pre-established conceptions about property boundaries and exclusion. The second set is literature taken from housing research. As we discuss this research, a key binary unfolds between owning and renting. It is not one which has a strict basis in property law, but one which has taken hold in law–property–society. This relates to our subject of study—the location of shared ownership within this idea of tenure. A succession of moves ended with the production of the label "shared ownership" and its relation with ownership, but this was not a pre-given. In the third part, we present our perspective on this literature, linking it with recent property scholarship.

Ownership

The classic lawyer's exposition of ownership is that ownership is "the greatest possible interest in a thing which a mature system of law recognizes" (Honore 1961). Further, "ownership ... and similar words stand not merely for the greatest interest in things in particular systems but for a type of interest with common features transcending particular systems". That focus on the "thing" is important because ownership is the relationship between the person and the thing. These common features include a bundle of 11 leading incidents and correlative obligations. As Honore put it,

> No doubt the concentration in the same person of the right (liberty) of using as one wishes, the right to exclude others, the power of alienating and an immunity from expropriation is a cardinal feature of the institution. Yet it would be a distortion – and one of which the 18th century, with its overemphasis on subjective rights, was patently guilty – to speak as if this concentration of patiently garnered rights was the only legally or socially important characteristic of the owner's position. (Honore 1961: 113)

Nevertheless, he regarded the right to exclusive possession of a thing as "the foundation on which the whole superstructure of ownership rests". Yet if the right to exclude was the foundation, he noted that the right to use "at one's discretion has rightly been recognized as a cardinal feature of ownership". This way of framing the concept of ownership as a matter of common sense and common knowledge is one which appears to be a particular trope of jurisprudential scholarship about ownership. This transcendental common-sense truth suggests that it is a kind of blackboxed idea. That is, we know instinctively what it means; it's obvious. It is no longer controversial.

This kind of common-sense reasoning also underpins a second branch of scholarship, which suggests that the chief incident of property, perhaps that which enables us to refer to a thing as "mine", relates to exclusivity of possession—our ability as an owner to keep somebody else off our property; what Blackstone (1765: Book 2, Chap. 1; see also, Hume 1740 [2004]) in his *Commentaries on the Law of England* described, in tune with the natural lawyers' conception of dominion, as "that sole and despotic dominion which one man [sic] claims and exercises over the external things of the world, in total exclusion of the right of any other individual in the universe". Morris Cohen (1927: 12), for example, recognised that, in law, what is significant is not our relation with the thing, but our relation with others in relation to the thing. The thing lacks relevance; what is important is that "the essence of private property is always the right to exclude others". The modern origin of this line of analysis appears to be a supposed deficiency with the bundle of rights theory. As Penner (1996, 1997: 1) puts it, ownership lacks an identity as a legal concept: "[I]t doesn't effectively characterise any particular sort of legal relation." Rose (1985, 1994: 17) adds the significant point (for our analysis—see below) that the law works through possession, and that possession speaks and needs to be interpreted like a text.

For some law and economics scholars, this fairly simple and monochrome claim that rights to property depend on exclusivity provides the foundation stone of property and ownership. Indeed, its simplicity is the crucial component because, as Merrill and Smith (2001: 389) suggest, it "allows the owner to control, plan and invest, and permits this to happen with a minimum of information costs to others. … [People] know that, unless special regulations or private contracts carve out some specific use rights, the bright-line rules of trespass apply." Thus, the law's "halfhearted commitment to truth seeking", as Valverde (2003: 5) rather nicely puts it, is facilitated because ownership itself is largely irrelevant for property law; all that matters is to protect a claim to exclusivity. All that matters is the boundary that must not be crossed. This bracketing of property is independent of context (Blomley 2014: 135), but also by its very nature produces an inside and an outside.

The coldness of this exclusion analysis is confronted by an almost contrasting perspective, which is much warmer in that it reacts against that exclusion thesis, suggesting a wider frame of analysis and labelling itself "progressive". Again, it is based on a common-sense understanding; this time about the social, and the ways in which property is necessary for the survival of that social. As Nedelsky (1990) argues, boundaries are constructs, just like the bounded self, and, further, individual boundedness is a capacity produced by law and the disciplines, whereas autonomy is a capacity which can be developed through constructive relationships as opposed to protection from intrusion. A group of scholars have developed a basis for understanding property, as Underkuffler (2016: 17) has put it, "anchored … in what are believed to be the underlying and avoidable theoretical mega-questions that property involves". The exclusion thesis is critiqued on the basis that there are "internal tensions within this conception and the inevitable impacts of one person's property rights on others make it inadequate as the sole basis for resolving property conflicts or for designing property institutions. For those tasks, we must look to the underlying human values that property serves and the social relationships it shapes and reflects" (Alexander et al. 2008/2009: 743).

This alternative thesis is best described as a law in context thesis, and, in our view, suffers from many of the problems of such an approach; that is, it risks placing law first as the determining force. So, for example, it understands the significance of property as enabling the flourishing of human life. From this perspective, the values promoted by property include "life and human flourishing, the protection of physical security, the ability to acquire knowledge and make choices, and the freedom to live one's life on one's own terms. They also include wealth, happiness, and other aspects of individual and social well-being" (Alexander et al., *id.*). The thesis then seeks to find, or inculcate, these values in law. The thesis has led to an explosion of thinking about the relation between property and community, without necessarily recognising the latter as both a governing and a limiting concept (see Rose 1999).

Rather different versions of property and ownership have emerged from critical socio-legal scholarship around the idea of belonging. Our work shares much with these understandings. Beginning with an idea of property as propriety, Davina Cooper (2007), for example, builds on her data about a particular school in England, to argue that, in that context, property practices have "five intersecting dimensions: (1) belonging, (2) codification, (3) definition, (4) recognition, and (5) power" (628). Belonging, for Cooper, has both a subject and an object element, but also "as a relationship of connection, of part to whole" (629). In that second sense, it offers a constitutive relationship of part to whole (630). Keenan (2013: 481) develops this thesis by arguing that belonging "must also be structured in such a way that the relation of belonging is conceptually, socially and physically supported or 'held up'. By this, I mean that those relations are recognised, accepted and supported in ways that have a range of effects and consequences."

In our study, these ideas of spaces of belonging, holding up, and the inseparability of subject from object powerfully tie in with our methodological understandings about the co-constitution of legal consciousness and the interrelation of actors (see, more generally, Keenan 2015). Furthermore, beginning as they do from situated, interactive, and dynamic understandings of everyday life in particular settings, they emphasise the limitations in the "law first" property literature. This is the point made by Nicholas Blomley. Despite all this property and ownership literature, quite disarmingly, he notes (2016: 225),

[T]here is very little scholarship on the work of the everyday property boundary. Empirically speaking, we simply do not know enough about lay conceptions and practices of property. This is a curious omission. Property scholarship of various complexions makes strong claims concerning property's lived effects and ethical dispositions, yet spends little time documenting property's lived world, including critical sites such as the boundary. This, perhaps, reflects the disposition of many lawyers to eschew research on the everyday.

A focus on ideas of property ownership that are grounded in everyday experience offers something radically different, dynamically relational, layering the rhetorical power of ownership (van der Walt 2009: 31; Fox O'Mahony 2014). Rather than focus on the narrow person–thing relation, analyses which focus on belonging have an affective dimension through which identity is produced. So, for example, the ideas of elective and selective belonging are significant for us, because they denote the ways in which identities come to be framed around things, as well as differentiate the self from others (see, in particular, Benson and Jackson 2017; Savage et al. 2004; Watt 2009).

Ownership: A Housing Studies Perspective

The exclusion perspective to ownership is reflected in some housing studies literature, reflecting its particular rhetorical potency (Atkinson and Blandy 2007, 2016). However, this literature also recognises that property and ownership are governing tools (what the lawyers think about as the "proper" in "property": see, for example, Rose 1994: 58–61; Davies 1997). Scholars have recognised that ownership talk engages with such aphorisms and metaphors, so its status has become normalised. Gurney (1999a: 1706), for example, argues "that metaphor and analogy are discursive practices which socially construct a housing tenure knowledge and that this is both stereotypical and prejudiced". Reporting on his fieldwork he notes in a table the aphorisms used to "hold up" a particular version of ownership.

Table 1. Some common housing tenure aphorisms
An Englishman's home is his castle.
It's yours at the end of the day.
If it's yours [then] you [can] do more to it.
It's an investment for the future.
Renting's [just] money down the drain.
Rent[ing']s [just] dead money.
Note: These expressions are examples of aphorisms reported in the St. George fieldwork which were recorded verbatim, on more than 12 separate occasions and (on each occasion) in different households.

A key point of departure for Gurney in this analysis was that ownership as a tenure could not be considered in isolation but by way of comparison and contrast with the perceived attributes and experiences of other tenures, principally renting (see also Murie and Williams 2015).

Gurney's analysis of metaphor and analogy also presaged a more policy-oriented analysis (Gurney 1999b). This analysis demonstrated how individual property ownership has become, over time, *the* goal of UK housing policy, to the extent that the housing policy of David Cameron's government after the 2015 election could be described as mono-tenurial. Ownership was pursued because of its ethico-moral values of self-reliance and self-responsibility, which chimed with the liberal and neoliberal state rationality, but it also chimed with a housing welfare state which became fixated on housing debt as a governing tool (Smith 2015; Kennett et al. 2013).

From the 1970s onwards, there have been a range of empirical and conceptual appreciations of ownership, which, perhaps oddly, have largely escaped interrogation in the almost endless literature about property and ownership produced by legal scholars. Any brief summary of the housing literature would in itself not do justice to the carefully nuanced positions which have been developed. However, for the purposes of this book, two points of departure in this literature are significant. The first recognises that "homeownership" has been promoted as a natural desire in policy literature; the second draws on empirical data about households' experiences of ownership. As regards the former, as Murie et al. (1976: 171) put it:

Even the use of the English language is affected in government statements. "Despite the continuing growth of <u>home</u> ownership, there are still over 8 million rented <u>dwellings</u>." Owner occupiers have homes, tenants have dwellings. Council tenants have homes when they are being urged to buy them. The use of the emotive word in the one context rather than the other reflects the attitudes of those making the statements. (Original emphasis)

In housing policy documents in the post-war period, homeownership was said to be a "basic and natural desire" (DoE 1977: 50), or a "deep and natural desire ... to have independent control of the home that shelters him and his family" (DoE 1971). In their 1995 White Paper, the DoE argued the case for homeownership in these terms:

> A high level of home ownership, alongside a healthy rented market, is good for the country and good for the individual. 80% of people favour home ownership over other forms of tenure. They value independence and control over their own home. Buying a home is often cheaper than renting. Home owners know that in later life, when the mortgage has been paid off, they will have the security of an asset which will help maintain their living standards. (DoE 1995: 12)

As Gurney (1999b: 173) puts it, that White Paper expresses the notion of home through "ideas of love, warmth, comfort, pride, independence and self-respect", and ties it inextricably to ownership.

Others have sought to demonstrate that desires for homeownership satisfy a craving for ontological security (Saunders 1990). Saunders (1990: 84) makes the following strong claims for ownership from his questionnaire data:

> Two principal motives are mentioned time and time again when people are asked why they prefer to own rather than rent their homes. One is financial – buying is seen as cheaper in the long run, or rent is seen as a waste of money, or rising prices are seen as a means of saving for the future or accumulating capital. The other has to do with the sense of independence and autonomy which ownership confers – the freedom from control and surveillance by a landlord and the ability to personalize the property according to one's tastes.

King (2010: 5–6) makes similar strong claims in respect of the right of local authority occupiers to buy their homes:

> It let many working-class households use their dwelling as they saw fit for the first time. Instead of being constrained by the landlords, they could now paint their dwelling how they liked, change it, improve it or even leave it be, and it was their problem and not an issue for others to interfere in. The [right to buy] allowed households to be independent and act in the responsible manner that they were always capable of if only they had been allowed to.

These strong claims have been disputed in the literature from a variety of perspectives. For example, there is a reflective strain of work about ownership which recognises its social and geographical stratification and its differentiation in substance and form. In a classic study of low-income homeownership in inner-city Birmingham (Karn et al. 1985), it was argued that buyers were faced with coerced choice, but their positions had been made worse by owning, which was a "squalid trap" (106). The ideas underpinning "filtering theory"—that building, for example, executive homes enables those at the marginal ends of tenure to improve their housing situations, and that households get a rung on the ownership ladder and pull themselves up—were far too simplistic in a context of building societies' preference for lending to particular ethnic groups and types of property. That study was in a context of redlining and discriminatory practices of banks and building societies. Homeownership as a tenure reflects diverse, fragmented experiences (Forrest et al. 1990: 2). Gender, ethnicity, and disability, for example, all impact on the experience of ownership (see Dowling 1998; Bowes and Sim 2002). In this literature, the focus is less on the promotion of homeownership as a choice than on the balance between that exercise of choice and the constraints on its exercise. Piketty (2015) makes this point well: "[E]xtreme inequalities in monetary resources always tend to generate inequalities in basic social and political capabilities and status."

A further set of research about ownership reflects on the experience through a rather closer analysis of tenure than appears in more mainstream legal analyses. Here, the focus is on long leaseholds and the realisation that these might not bring the sense of control over one's own destiny which exists with much freehold land. Generally in the UK, the outright ownership of flats is not possible because it would give rise to the problem of enforcing the relationship between the flat owners. The solution consistent with the law of property is that flat owners usually take under long tenancy agreements of say 99 or 999 years. For property lawyers, they are long leaseholders (the "long" being added, one might suppose, to differentiate such leaseholders from the private rented sector), but for the householders themselves, they more usually perceive themselves to be owners (see Blandy and Robinson 2001; Cole and Robinson 2000; Robertson 2006; Carr 2011). This complexity is manifested often in a lack of control exercised by the tenant-owner in what they are able to do to their property, the sometimes inadequate management of common parts, and the payment of often considerable sums for repairs to those parts and not at a time of their choosing. Additionally, there are particular problems when the length of the agreement runs down (see Birch 2017). Statute has provided complex solutions to these problems, as well as mechanisms of resolving problems through tribunals as opposed to courts. However, as Carr (2011: 540) points out:

[L]easeholders are permanently disappointed that their status fails to deliver the ownership and control that they expect. …'That disappointment reflects the economic vulnerability of this form of tenure.

Finally, a significant stream of work emphasises the opportunity for capital gains to be made from ownership, not least for low-income households, which frequently have no other wealth or financial assets (Saunders 1990; King 2010). Despite calls to highlight other attributes of ownership, ownership has been said to be an important way for low-income households to accumulate any assets (Herbert et al. 2013). However, evidence of lower-income homeowners accumulating significant wealth is also limited, as they remain in ownership for shorter periods, are less likely to trade up, refinance to lower interest rates less frequently, and rather than transcend inequalities in the labour market, it can accentuate wealth inequalities, as more affluent owners gain the most (Boehm and Schlottmann 2008; Burridge 2010; Hamnett 1999).

Ownership Talk

By way of contrast with all that common sense and knowledge about ownership discussed so far, our argument is that ownership actually has no fixed and stable meaning, other than that which is produced. To the extent that stability is perceived, this is produced and reproduced through discursive work. Indeed, it is an actant almost precisely because of that lack, as it makes a difference in a particular course of action; it renders seemingly heterogeneous things durable (Latour 2005: 71). It operates as a "material semiotic" (Law and Mol 1995: 280–1), by which we mean that it is produced by actors, whether human or non-human, working together, folding their understandings around each other. As a result, it is both complex and contradictory, situational and cultural, and not dephysicalised (on which, see Graham 2011: especially Chap. 5). It is performed and in process; indeed, it is a process in its own right (Rose 1994; Blomley 2003, 2016). Ownership, like its bedfellow, legality, works "as both an interpretive framework and a set of resources with which and through which the social world (including that part known as the law) is constituted" (Ewick and Silbey 1998: 23).

Ownership talk refers to the narratives that are produced about ownership through interactions between things. The kind of legal and common-sense versions of property and ownership are just as important as our own talk in producing it. After all, both the exclusion and progressive versions of property depend, at some level, on empirical truths about both law and the world around us. They present different versions of those apparent truths as realities, but, as with legal techniques, they produce boundaries (perhaps paradoxically) which require testing and further thought. Indeed, in a range of brilliant work, drawing on a potent mix of performativity and assemblage theory, Blomley (2003, 2014, 2016) argues that they don't stand up to such testing and further thought.

One of Blomley's points is that boundaries are creations, so, as one set of his stories suggested, they can be "a subtle, learned, and improvised set of communications, understandings, and actions, that unfold over and help constitute a boundary relationship" (2016: 238). But these boundaries are made and re-made. He argues, in a critique of the progressive version of property, that "[p]roperty claims are continuously remade and re-enacted, and, as such, open to surprise and complexity, yet also capable of fixity and sedimentation" (2014: 25).

One key to Blomley's analysis rests on his engagement with the way in which Carol Rose (1994) regards property narratives as significant. As Rose (*id.*: 6) puts it, "[N]arrative matters: stories, allegories, and metaphors can change minds. Through narratives, or so it is said, people can create a kind of narrative community in which the storyteller can suggest the possibility that things could be different and perhaps better (or, alternatively, worse)." In a brilliant essay on original property stories told by some of the great early legal scholars, she asks why these scholars needed to tell stories about the creation of property systems. Her answer (*id.*, 41–2), following a thought experiment, is that "those tales are moral ones all the same, just as much as Aesop's fables, speaking to and constituting a kind of moral community and urging that community to change its ways".

Our focus on Blomley's work is also because he rightly argues that property is a "complex combination of things and people" (2014: 25). This combination shifts in different contexts and over time. This involves unbracketing, so to speak, the objectification of property so that rather than focus on the thing (property), we think about what makes up this thing. The work in producing the property bracket "entails the attempt to extricate agents and entities from the relational networks that give them meaning" (Blomley 2014: 142). This chimes with our study, in which we are concerned with how the shared ownership "assemblage", to use that ugly word, is both produced and co-constituted by some of the key players.

The notion of things requires some extrapolation here. Circulating ideas about property and ownership are things for us. Atkinson and Blandy (2016: 9) talk about tessellated neoliberalism, in which ideas about the private home, political life, and the economy expand outwards from the micro-scale of a multitude of owned homes. These ideas resonate with work that has begun to question the objectification of the market in the home, and regard emotions as things which both shape the market and the home (Wallace 2008; Christie et al. 2008; Easthope 2004, 2014; Jorgensen 2016). This book and our research took shape at a time when the social project of property ownership has been replaced by its financialisation; when, rather than being about the social aspiration and conditioning of the middle classes, ownership has become stratified between the financially privileged and the others, the sub-primes and financially excluded (Forrest and Hiroyama 2015), who are unable to rely on "the bank of mum and dad" (to use that redolent aphorism). This kind of emotional market is about the excluded and the effects of such exclusion on them.

In the particular context of this study, emotion is also about the production of home in ownership. These two words home and ownership are often elided, both grammatically and in our normal property talk (as if a place that is not owned cannot be home: Easthope 2014). It provides an affective dimension to property (Giuliani 1991; Easthope 2004), which is commonly said to depend on the control one has over where one lives.

In this sense, rather than focus on the exclusivity of possession, that is, against outsiders, the affective dimension of property commonly relates to control over the interior of the property. Drawing on a Bourdieusian sociology, Miller (2010: 53) argues that objects make people—"[T]he whole system of things, with their internal order, makes us the people we are. And they are exemplary in their humility, never really drawing attention to what we owe them." They are powerful precisely because they are invisible.

We argue also that documents produce property. This almost goes without saying to lawyers, but it is precisely because of that comment that it needs to be said. Freeman and Maybin (2011: 165) argue that inscription into a document "is a practised thing … a conduit or corridor, something through which other things (power, meaning) flow". A document functions as "a technique for inter-esting" (160; see also Latour and Woolgar 1986: 45–50); documents "anticipate and enable certain actions by others – extensions, amplifications, and modifications of both content and form" (Riles 2006: 21). Further,

> the document is a translation that also translates. It is intrinsic to those communicative processes in which actors inhabiting different social worlds first enter into relations with each other and then begin to recast or reconstruct themselves, their interests and their worlds. This means simply that the document connects actors and coordinates their actions. (Freeman and Maybin 2011: 165)

The standardisation of things, in particular, makes possible an array of new techniques (McKenzie 2006). And the standardisation of *legal* documents allow things to become crucial technologies in private legal infrastructures as "devices through which particular technical, institutional, political, legal, and economic arrangements fain solidity and durability" (Riles 2011: 46). These documents are powerful by their absence and by the fact that their standardisation can lead to what Radin (2012) describes as normative and democratic degradation. In our study, the lease is a crucial thing because it made shared ownership possible. It was a translation that also translates and is a technology around which interested parties congregate. Our work takes on the insights of Caroline Hunter's brilliant authoethnography (2015). Sitting as a tribunal judge, she was asked to adjudicate on whether terms of a lease, encrusted with time, enabled one leaseholder to put up solar panels on "their" home. The lease, so often apparently passive, had to speak and to be translated, exercising power through making others (human and non-human) possible and actively do things.

Shared Ownership: A Snapshot

In this part, we provide a short snapshot of shared ownership, which prefaces the longer examination in Chap. 2. It is two dimensional, and designed to provide some context for this chapter on two levels. Firstly, we explain the basics and hint at the complexity of shared ownership, locating it within "social housing"; secondly, we discuss in outline the providers of shared ownership—housing associations—and draw attention to the complexity and contradictions of their operation. We expand on these points throughout this book.

The Basics

Across the globe, as wealth is being concentrated, cities and states with high-value areas are struggling to think about the best strategies to accommodate low- and no-income households, at the same time as the social state (to the extent that it existed) is being contracted (Sassen 2014: 15). It is a time for solutions to the problems caused by private markets, which mean that many, who need to live in a particular place, cannot afford to do so (Forrest and Hiroyama 2015). They cannot afford to rent (particularly as the state has withdrawn or restricted the subsidy) and feel insecure. They cannot afford to buy. Cities are becoming segregated enclosures. In the US, New South Wales, the

Netherlands, and Spain, for different reasons and at different times, the innovative solution has been to create forms of intermediate ownership (see, e.g., Elsinga et al. 2015; Teruel 2015; Mercer 2016). In the UK, intermediate forms of tenure crystallised as a particular policy formation in the 1970s, when borrowing for ownership was scarce and expensive, and house prices were out of reach of most. One form developed at this time was "shared ownership".

The number of shared ownership properties currently held as such is uncertain. In 2016, it was said that there were 175,000 shared ownership properties in England, representing 0.8 per cent of all housing (Savills 2016). On 19 January 2017, there were 25,000 further shared ownership properties under construction and there was said to be a "combined ambition to lift delivery of shared ownership units to 39,000 homes per year" (Apps 2017). Many billions of public and private funds have been levered into the development of shared ownership, in part because its design was (and is) to provide accommodation to people who are unlikely to obtain social rented housing and cannot afford what has come to be called private ownership.

Although shared ownership is a complex product, which has been re-launched numerous times using different labels,[1] it has been reduced to a simple slogan, "part rent, part buy". It has been promoted as a low-cost home-ownership product, and the ownership element has consistently been emphasised. In essence, a person is said to buy a share of a property from a provider, usually no less than 25 per cent, and they pay rent on the other share. The property itself is either a house or an apartment, often located in an estate or block which has multiple different tenures usually collected together. For example, a block of flats might be built shared ownership flats located together, private and other social housing located separately.

The part bought is usually purchased with a proportionately small deposit (such as 5 per cent of the share value) and the aid of a mortgage over the rest of the share. There are a smaller range of mortgage lenders willing to provide mortgages on shared ownership and the cost of the mortgage product sold can be more expensive than for a traditional ownership mortgage. The rent, and increases in rent, is usually capped at a particular level (around 3 per cent above the retail price index). The buyer's ability to afford the ongoing costs is subject to checks by the housing and mortgage provider. The key point about the purchase is that, at the outset, the costs of the mortgage and rent are usually cheaper in aggregate than the costs of renting a property in the private rented sector. The rent does increase in value and increases annually, and over time becomes more expensive.

---

[1] Indeed, the label "shared ownership" is a re-launch in itself, as discussed in Chap. 2.

The main unknown cost at the outset is the cost of "service charges" to which the buyer signs up and must pay. These charges reflect the proportionate share of the costs of managing the property, which are passed on to the buyer by the property manager (which is usually either the social housing provider or a managing agent). These costs tend to be larger in blocks of flats where there are common spaces and things, such as lifts and roofs, to service. They can be estimated at the outset, but such charges can never be precisely ascertained in advance because management and maintenance charges, by their nature, vary over time depending on the kinds of unforeseeable events (leaking roof, out-of-order lift) and differential charging (e.g. between managing agents) which can occur.

Over time, the buyer can increase their stake in the property, by buying additional shares up to 100 per cent (a process called staircasing), at which point they will be entitled to a conveyance of the entire legal interest in the property. Staircasing, however, is a relatively coarse-grained process, as the buyer has to buy relatively large chunks of additional equity, often in a rising market, as opposed to acquiring an extra 1 or 2 per cent at a time. Nevertheless, the shared ownership bargain is predicated on the buyer increasing their stake over time. Shared ownership generally works best when the buyer staircases up. Increases in rent can weight the bargain (which, initially, can be favourable to the buyer) against the buyer over time because of above-inflation rent increases. However, increases in house prices can make the acquisition of extra shares in the property unaffordable to buyers on marginal incomes

The buyer formally obtains a lease for their purchase, and it is that document which governs the relationship between the buyer and the provider, but also accommodates the interest of any lender. It is what might be called a non-standard "full repairing" lease—that is, the buyer is responsible for all repairs and service charges attributable to the property, irrespective of the proportion of the share that they have bought.

At heart, there is a paradox in shared ownership: there is nothing "shared" or "ownership" about it at all. Hence, there is some discursive work achieved in the label. The buyer enters into a relationship with a housing association, which provides the property, but that is a relationship of domination in that it is governed formally by a lease that is pre-drawn and to which the buyer has no choice but to submit. Since 1981, there has been a model lease. It is not ownership—and certainly not in Honore's sense of being the greatest possible interest in the thing that English law understands. As legal scholars Susan Bright and Nicholas Hopkins have suggested (2011), it is like the Emperor's new clothes—the label is not even recognised in the English system of land law. Yet, it does have a definition as forming part of "social housing" because the Housing and Regeneration Act 2008 so defines that term as including "low-cost homeownership":

(1) Accommodation is low-cost homeownership accommodation if the following conditions are satisfied.
(2) Condition 1 is that the accommodation is occupied, or made available for occupation, in accordance with—
    (a) shared ownership arrangements,
    …
(3) Condition 2 is that the accommodation is made available in accordance with rules designed to ensure that it is made available to people whose needs are not adequately served by the commercial housing market.
(4) "Shared ownership arrangements" means arrangements under a lease which—
    (a) is granted on payment of a premium calculated by reference to a percentage of either the value of the accommodation or the cost of providing it, and
    (b) provides that the tenant (or the tenant's personal representatives) will or may be entitled to a sum calculated by reference to the value of the accommodation.

So, shared ownership is a construct, partly social and partly legal, to take advantage of a particular set of characteristics in the housing market and versions of truth in the policy-making community.

The Providers

The provider of shared ownership was initially local government, but it was enthusiastically adopted from the late 1970s by a group of housing providers, to which we refer in this book as "housing associations". Housing associations are a heterogeneous group of providers of low-cost housing for people broadly in need of it. Although rather broadbrush, housing associations as bodies have developed at different times for different purposes. The early ones, like almshouses and other small providers, are not relevant to this book. Two particular growth periods for housing associations were the late Victorian period and the 1960s. The organisations established in the former period were built around certain key individuals and organisations, such as the Peabody Trust, Guinness

Trust, Octavia Hill, a pioneer philanthropist. In the 1960s, as a response to a particular deficit of decent-quality, low-cost housing in certain parts of London, a number of local associations grew up around, for example, Notting Hill and Shepherds Bush in West London, fuelled by capital grants from central government (the story is told best by McDermont 2010).

Over time, these organisations have become the dominant suppliers of social housing in England, particularly as local government largely stopped building new properties in the 1980s and much of its stock was sold either to residents or to housing associations (Pawson and Mullins 2010). The reasons for this transfer of assets is complex, but a particularly significant factor after 1988 was the ability of housing associations to mix public money given by way of grant with private finance levered from the market (see, e.g., Malpass 2000b; McDermont 2010).

Housing associations are not-for-profit institutions, a large proportion of which are registered charities, but many are now so large that they could be floated on the stock market as FTSE 100 companies. They can have group structures and well-designed business plans; they have annual glossy accounts. They can be entrepreneurial organisations, with innovative strategies for developing their business. They have put in place various strategies pioneered by the private sector, from 0800 numbers to report repairs through to strategies designed to incentivise their occupiers to self-govern (Flint 2002, 2004; McKee 2011). They have agglomerated, merged, and produced even bigger organisations. No longer do their organisations bear the names which identify their origins—these organisations have names such as Gentoo, Curo, or Places for People, which are products in their own right, dreamed up by branding and marketing agents.

They are diversifying organisations (Mullins et al. 2014), partly as a result of the withdrawal of state support for social housing and partly as a result of an entrepreneurial drive combined with the logic of the market (Morrison 2016; Tang et al. 2017); and, following a government announcement in 2015 that it was reducing rents, some even stopped (or threatened to stop) developing social rented housing (Murtha 2015). This widely reported story reflects tensions within the housing association sector, which have been present since the move to mixed funding regime—the extent to which the sector is self-governing or influenced or led by central government; perhaps, today, the better expression is the extent to which it works alongside government for mutual interest.

However, the more significant side of this particular story has been the lurch to risk and commercialism at the expense of balancing what has been described as "social purpose" (Manzi and Morrison 2017). So, it has been said that the commercial logic has taken root through an increased reliance on property sales income as a proportion of turnover; an increased exposure to market risk, including "fundamental restructuring and develop[ing] new business models"; and changing the socio-economic composition of their residents (*id.*, 8–9).

The Legal Consciousness of Things

In our inquiries, we have been particularly influenced by two aspects of social theory. First and foremost, our inquiry is an inquiry about the hegemony of ownership, and why people want to engage in it despite the apparent paradox that there is no such thing as shared ownership. In these circumstances, it was perhaps natural that the first perspective was that of legal consciousness. We discuss what this means both in general and for our study in the first section. We then go on to argue that, while liberating, legal consciousness studies require what we think of as a methodological footnote, one which enables things to take centre stage, not just people. We then go on to discuss the significance of narrative for this study.

The Study of Legal Consciousness

There have been many attempts at defining legal consciousness, but perhaps the one with the most utility for our study is captured by Simon Halliday and Bronwen Morgan in their classic study of environmental dissidents: "[T]o study legal consciousness is to study the taken-for-granted and not-immediately noticeable: the background assumptions about legality which structure and inform everyday thoughts and actions" (Halliday and Morgan 2013: 2). Legal consciousness research radically re-shapes socio-legal research so that the focus is on the everyday, the mundane, actions and omissions.

In most legal consciousness studies, there is a significant shift from law to legality. Rather than understanding legality as a formal thing with a separate existence, legality (or, as we prefer to think about it, legalities) emerges from what people say and do, and, just as importantly, what they don't say and don't do. This is a radical position in so much as it extends beyond the invocation of formal law with official sanctions; as Ewick and Silbey (1998: 22) put it, "[P]eople may invoke and enact legality in ways neither approved nor acknowledged by the law."

This shift is significant for our study because the specific formal law on shared ownership is both limited and what exists can be found in diverse locations. We discuss specific challenges and interpretations—or translations—in

Chap. 3. However, these are challenges on specific points. We have noted above how shared ownership is part of the statutory formulation of social housing. It is excluded from much of the complicated law on enfranchisement (where a leaseholder buys a freehold or other superior interest) so that the actual bargain is reflected, and other bits and bobs can be found in legislation from Stamp Duty (a tax paid on the purchase of land) to the right to buy one's home. Much of this is marginal and incorporated into working practices. There is *no* recognition of such a thing as shared ownership otherwise in the law of property. It is not one of the accepted tenures and does not exist in the Law of Property Act 1925 nor in the Land Registration Act 2002.

Very little of this specific formal law actually permeates our study. What is relevant, however, for our study is the formulation of the underpinning document—the lease—as this is the most tangible thing available to the players in the shared ownership relation. It might not be understood, and its terms might not be appreciated, but that is not the point. This book (and the study of legal consciousness) is not a sort of test of legal knowledge or capability. It is a study of the meaning which people give to these things, and how these things exert agency, in the everyday lives of shared ownership. The idea of ownership is another thing, in particular its significance in modern social life as a kind of social marker, to which we assert legalities beyond formal law. As Silbey (2005: 346) suggests: "Because law is both an embedded and an emergent feature of social life, it collaborates with other social structures ... to infuse meaning and constrain social action. Furthermore, because of this collaboration of structures, in many instances law may be present although subordinate."

Legal consciousness studies are based on stories—indeed, stories are their essence. In their study of acts of resistance, Silbey and Ewick (2003: 1331) argue, "The meaning of what seem like petty acts lies in their narratives. The process through which an event is made into a story is sociologically significant in and of itself. We argue that all stories are social events. In other words, stories are not just about social reality; 'social reality happens in stories.'" Stories bind together the key methodological tools—schemas and resources. But, as Patricia Ewick (2008: 87) argues, stories do so much more:

> *Narrative* is also a powerful technique of legitimation. By presenting events in the form of a story, depictions of the world are embedded in plots that unfold in a particular and inevitable chain of events leading to a moral claim about meaning. ...
>
> It is the narrative form, rather than the content of any particular story, that constitutes the principal means through which narratives operate ideologically. ...
> Well-plotted stories cohere by relating various (selectively appropriated) events

and details into a temporally organized whole. The coherent whole, the configuration of events and characters arranged in believable plots, pre-empts alternative stories. The events seem to speak for themselves. Narratives also sustain power relations to the extent that they conceal the social organization of their production and plausibility. Narratives embody general understandings of the world that by their deployment and repetition come to constitute and sustain the lifeworld. Yet because narratives depict specific persons existing in particular social, physical, and historical locations, those general understandings often remain unacknowledged. By failing to make these manifest, narratives draw on unexamined assumptions and causal claims without displaying these assumptions and claims or laying them open to challenge or testing.

Stories, then, produce versions of the world and truth; what is important is their construction, as Ewick says, "their unexamined assumptions and causal claims", as well as what they don't say.

Against Typologies, Towards Things

Much legal consciousness scholarship starts with fitting a dataset into a typology, or set of orientations, outlined by Ewick and Silbey: "before the law", "with the law", and "against the law". These orientations derive from a particular philosophical position, in seeking to mediate between the dualism of structure and agency by arguing for their mutuality, their co-constitution. Drawing on scholarship in cultural studies, they argue that "consciousness is understood to be part of a reciprocal process in which the meanings, given by individuals to their world become patterned, stabilized and objectified" (1998: 39). Stabilisations can occur through the use of schemas (which point "to the power of naming as a fundamental aspect of social action" (40)) and resources (which are, of course, differently distributed). They claim that legality is a structural component of society:

> Legality is not inserted into situations; rather, through repeated invocations of the law and legal concepts and terminology, as well as through imaginative and unusual associations between legality and other social structures, legality is constituted through everyday actions and practices. (43)

This work, along with its predecessors (especially Bumiller 1988; Sarat 1990; Merry 1990), has been both liberating and constraining.

It is liberating in changing the focus of socio-legal scholarship away from a top-down institutionalism; no longer is formal law our starting and end point. If we are true to the concerns of legal consciousness scholarship, law is but one structuring device of everyday life, but by far and away not the only such device. If one grows one's understanding of legality in everyday life from the bottom up, then one's focus shifts from the abnormal to the everyday, the mundane; as Ewick and Silbey observe, "[C]onsciousness is produced and revealed in what people *do* as well as what they *say*" (46), as well as what people don't do and don't say. This liberation has a concomitant effect on the types of method employed. If legality emerges in this way, so that it is mutually constitutive with social relations, law and legality do not themselves come first in this study. Indeed, from this perspective, shared ownership provides an interesting subject because it is itself characterised by the lack of a formal specific law; there are general principles of law, to be sure, but there is no such thing recognised in property law as "shared ownership". So, in getting to grips with shared ownership, one is reliant on the ways in which it is interpreted and narrated by its key actors.

It is constraining, we argue, in two ways: categorisations and the legal consciousness of things.

On Categorisation

While the Ewick and Silbey typology has been particularly powerful, most research has tended to fit data into that typology and sometimes shoehorn it; oddly, bearing in mind its postish derivation, it has taken the force of law in itself. When data does not fit, a new category emerges ("under the law" or "dissident collectivism"—Fritzvold 2009; Halliday and Morgan 2013) or discussion occurs about the range of one of the types (usually, "against the law"). In short, the typology has become the primary definer of a particular, emergent sub-discipline. We can certainly agree with Hull (2016: 569) that we need a better understanding of resistant legal consciousness, and a better account of how resistance interacts with the types, and accept that the parameters of power/resistance is one which is perhaps the least well defined in scholarship (Hillyard and Watson 1994). But the broader point we make (with Hull 2016: 567) is that "the existence of that typology has inhibited creative theoretical analysis to some degree".

The Legal Consciousness of Things

Legal consciousness scholarship focuses on what people say and do (or don't); in doing so, we argue, it misses a trick. In this book, we make the (perhaps rather odd) assertion that a broader range of things, including humans, exert legal consciousness. We need to take some time here to unpack this key point for our study.

Our first point is the obvious one: things (human and non-human) do not exist in their own right. Legalities are brought into effect by their interactions, enrolments, and translations with, and by, other things. The chair on the front cover of *The Common Place of Law* has no identity unless one relates it to the snow, the shovel that clears the snow, the human who wields the shovel and does the clearing, as well as the community norm that imposes a sense of legality on the chair itself. The chair itself has no consciousness, but, in anthropomorphic style, it becomes invested with the hopes, fears, anxieties, and consciousness of the entities by and through which it becomes located, apparently soullessly, in the snow. And this consciousness is legal, in the sense that it appropriates a Lockeian version of property that is based on one's own labour (Silbey and Ewick 2003). This claim has proved controversial as an example of legality, because there is no precise method of enforcement of the "right", but, as Silbey (2010: 68) puts it, when drivers disagree, "the disagreement is engaged within commonly exchanged terms and meanings about property, right, trespass, however diverse and ambiguous those meanings". At root, this is about legal culture.

However, the chair is not just a representation of such local laws, meanings, and investments, it is also constitutive of them and hence plays—or played—an active role in its constitution (presumably just as it did, say, 30 minutes before-hand when it was used as a table chair). Recall the door closer example to which we drew attention at the start of this chapter. As Latour (2000: 117; original emphasis) says, "As I see it, things are unfairly accused of being just 'things'", and all things "also means an *assembly* of a judicial nature gathered around a topic, *reus*, that creates both conflict and assent". This is why John Law (1999: 4; original emphasis) refers to this set of ideas as "a *semiotics of materiality*. It takes the semiotic insight, that of the relationality of entities, the notion that they are produced in relations, and applies this ruthlessly to all materials – and not simply to those that are linguistic." When discussing this point with our friend, Colin, he drew a vital connection. He said that the interesting question was why the chair was used in the first place, how it came to act as mediator, and entered into the account (Latour 2005: 79). We have no answer for this question (because we are not told by the authors), but it is a pertinent question in our study (why was a lease used—see Chap. 3). For us, who have never been to New Jersey and who have but one visual representation of the chair, it was both an object which is immutable and one which is mobile—the method of mass communication has made it so (Latour 1987). Presumably, there are many chairs of different shapes and designs—but what, we might ask, if they were all of the same design (like the model lease in our study).

We do not know why chairs became the carrier; they cannot tell us: "This is why specific tricks have to be invented to *make them talk*, that is, to offer descriptions of themselves, to produce *scripts* of what they are making others – humans or non-humans – do" (Latour 2005: 79). Without the chairs, there is simply cleared snow in the street and space which belongs to anybody; the chairs talk for property rights and become a passive intermediary. Yet, there are times, according to Latour, when one can trace the visible connections that make up the object: the moment of innovation in the laboratory; when there is distance in time or space between the users; or by accidents, breakdowns, and strikes (like the door closer). Even when they have "receded into the background for good, it is always possible – but more difficult – to bring them back to light by using archives, documents, memoirs, museum collections etc., to artificially produce, through historians' accounts, the state of crisis in which machines, devices, and implements were born" (Latour 2005: 801).

Similarly, the chief artefact which underpins our analysis in this book—the lease—reflects both these elements. It is the representation of the meaning of shared ownership as property, and ownership; it also has agency in its own right, giving meaning to, as well as structuring, the relationships around it. It is understood as supporting ownership. It produces the well-known Latin expression familiar to buyers—*caveat emptor*, or beware the buyer—and produces action, such as a housing association refusing to help the buyer with an emergency repair because that is their responsibility. On a more mundane plane, it supports assertions of ownership. As this is a study in which the lease plays such a key role, it was incumbent on us to trace its origin, and make visible the connections which both produced it and make it alive. Yet, even as it fades in to the background in the everyday and adopts a passive pose, it is ready to come alive and produce relations. There are other artefacts in our study—such as pot plants, cigarette butts, flowers, drips of water—but the one that we encounter the most is the lease.

Consciousness is an *effect* of the connections, mostly fragile, between things that stabilise at particular moments in time; but, the fragile nature of these connections means that they can spiral off—as John Law (1996) nicely puts it, there is both traduction and trahison, a point forcefully made in Michel Callon's studies (1984, 1986) of the dissolution of one company's vision for the electric car or misbehaving scallops in St. Brieuc Bay.

This leads on to the next point: there is no particular reason why human actors are prioritised in this particular framing of legal consciousness. This is as much an ethnographic point as theoretical, but it bears repetition. In part, the significance of this is that no single entity can necessarily be prioritised analytically, because size is an irrelevance; a simple microbe can exert more influence than the sovereign. This is not to deny that large/small exists, but it is to say that such words explain nothing if we assume that size matters (Callon and Latour 1981: 280). The point is that actors, such as microbes and other things, have causal influence on outcomes.

It is the *associations* between things that matter and the way they produce their own black boxes. So, actors can be "[a]ny element which bends space around itself, makes other elements dependent upon itself and translates their will into a language of its own" (Callon and Latour 1981: 286). It is through such associations that a social is performed (Latour 2000). This focus on associations leads to the rallying call, or slogan, for this kind of scholarship that "you have 'to follow the actors themselves', that is try to catch up with their often wild innovations in order to learn from them what the collective existence has become in their hands, which methods they have elaborated to make it fit together, which accounts could best define the new associations that they have been forced to establish" (Latour 2005: 12).

Such associations are produced by, and produce, translations. Callon (1986) refers to the associations being made as a result of a translator spokesperson of the entities that are constituted; this is "at first an endeavour. Later it may be achieved" (25). Translation has spatial effects in that it produces an entity as indispensable, referred to as an "obligatory point of passage" (26). Thirdly, translation is also what he calls "displacement"—the inscription of things, the movement of materials and money: "Translation cannot be effective, ie lead to stable constructions, if it is not anchored to such movements, to physical and social displacements" (27). There is a temporality to such translations (Grabham 2016), just as there is in legal consciousness. As Ewick and Silbey (1998: 43–4) observe in a rather beautiful analogy, like the change in whale song as a result of the micro-contributions of individual whales, the schemas and resources which make up legality are also continually being produced and worked upon. Likewise, Nielson (2000: 1087), in a situated study of hate speech, makes the point that "people make connections from their past experiences – good or bad – which arise in part for the social positions they occupy – and that these experiences shape their understanding of the law".

So, in our version of legal consciousness, like the whale song, we are adding these various things. These are hardly novel observations in certain parts of the academy, and ones which a brand of housing studies scholarship has recognised (including two journal special issues: Jacobs and Smith 2008; Jacobs and Gabriel 2013); so, we see this more as a methodological footnote to the specific legal consciousness scholarship. After all, there is clearly a relationship between these things and legal consciousness. Both Latour (2005: 7) and Silbey and Cavicchi (2005) have suggested these interactions. There have been a number of insightful studies in which these things have been used in one way or other to work out the effects of the particular kinds of assemblages of law (see, e.g., Valverde 2005; Latour 2010; Van Oorschot and Schinkel 2015; Jacob 2017). Emilie Cloatre's study of the trade-related intellectual property agreements offers a range of valuable insights about law—as she puts it, "[A] broader analysis of legal objects both in their making and their deployment, suggests a revisiting of the boundaries of the law" (Cloatre 2013: 21). This seems to us to re-state the legal consciousness problematic that legality in everyday life produces new and differently constituted boundaries.

Legality, Property, Narrative

The people who you will come to know in this book tell stories about their experiences, histories, and understandings, which are in narrative form and use things to make their point. They make us appreciate that what Silbey and Cavicchi call "legalfacts" are rather loosely shut black boxes, capable of being opened at different times, fluid and in motion. Things such as leases and picture walls are brought together and add texture to legality as it is experienced and thought about (if at all). It is not the stuff on its own that adds this texture, but the kinds of associations that are made, and, significantly for us, the stories or narratives that are told about this weave. As Hurdley (2006: 718) describes, in her sensitive analysis of mantelpieces and things,

> By constructing narratives around visual productions in the apparently private space of the home, people participate in the ongoing accomplishments of social, moral identities. Thus, the practice of producing narratives around objects contributes to the personal work of autobiography and renders objects as meaningful participants in the social work of identity-building.

The narrative format enables stories to be told about law–property–society. Carol Rose argues that property needs storytelling: "The existence of a property regime is not in the least predictable from a starting point of rational self-interest; and, consequently, from that perspective, property needs a tale, a story, a post hoc explanation" (Rose 1994: 38). Property narratives are designed to make clear that property is a good thing or, at worst, a necessary evil (Rose 1994: 287). Atkinson and Blandy's tessellated neoliberalism offers a not-dissimilar version of truth about ownership as being a good thing, a positive contribution produced out of a particular way of thinking. Just as Rose seeks to explain the property stories in Blackstone and Locke, Atkinson and Blandy explain the seemingly inexplicable—the desire for ownership—by reference to our relationship with ideological forces.

And a particular shared ownership story is told about property, in that it is described as "the first rung on the ladder", and that buyers have "a foot on the ladder". These aphorisms and metaphors are particularly powerful and feature in many shared ownership stories, whether it be policy documents (NAO 2006) or individual stories. Over and over again in our study, policy-makers and shared owners explained shared ownership by reference to these linguistic strategies. We argue that they are inherently legal. They divide off tenure, because the ladder represents ownership and not some tenure continuum. They emphasise the marginal status of shared ownership and the hierarchy inherent in ownership itself because we are only talking about its first rung. And that metaphor performs an ethico-moral purpose because of its inherent assumption that there is, or at least in principle can be, steady progress up the ladder as well as the damage of falling off it. Various studies suggest that housing market mobility is not linear and unidirectional, but frequently encompasses different pathways through renting and ownership according to life's transitions (Croucher et al. forthcoming).

Further, as Law (2002: 7) suggests, these kinds of stories (and there are plenty of others told in this book about shared ownership) "collude[] to enact it into being". The many different parts of shared ownership are brought together by the label, the stories, the different ways of envisioning it, the idea that it is a product, this book and our ongoing project. They produce a kind of singularity, where there is "fractional coherence". The stories we were told in the course of our research project were many and different, although they centred around the meanings of ownership. The kinds of narratives we tell, that were told to us, that are inscribed in texts produce their own law–property–society. We find narratives in different places, such as the translation of case notes into computer records or the translation of the aspirations of shared ownership's progenitors into the lease.

Research Methods

In many respects, our research methods can be regarded as the standardised methods of the social sciences. We conducted a literature review, archival research, observation, and semi-structured interviews with a range of (human) participants. However, each of these stages requires a few further words to explain our slightly different approaches. We do not lay claim to anything as grand as a "method assemblage" (Law 2004), but we must recognise, of course, that our methods and writing perform a neatening and tidying of a messy, complex reality. There is a children's book where the central character is a mass of squiggles, and has a ramshackle house; the character meets two other characters, neat and tidy, who make that character and the house neat and tidy; and, at the end of the story, the central character is a nice, roundish, smiling blob in a picture-perfect house (Hargreaves 2014). That blob and picture-perfect house are this output (although we do not claim to any form of perfection—that is just an analogy).

Making Up Literature

Why did we need to conduct a literature review? Alison had undertaken research and written about shared ownership, and remained curious about the experience of a "hybrid tenure". Dave and Helen had puzzled over shared ownership at different times in different projects, and Dave had provided expert witness evidence in a law case which didn't, in the end, see the light of day. We were aware of most of the academic literature about shared ownership, although the project afforded us the opportunity to revisit older evidence produced in the 1970s and 1980s. What we sought to do here, however, was to examine policy and consumer discourse about the "products" and focus on information about shared ownership available online, which, we supposed, would be a significant resource for people considering entering this market. The resources were categorised into three main sources of information: that provided by housing providers directly; commentary by intermediaries, journalists, and so on; and comments from members of online communities. This is "made up" literature in the sense that it makes up its subject/object, shared ownership.

All three sources of information reflected tensions in the provision of shared ownership—making assumptions about ownership, as opposed to renting, and private, as opposed to social—designed to shape perceptions and inform. However, there were some surprises. So, for example, rather than the dry policy-based material that one might find in certain sections of websites, we found glossy marketing materials including aspirational and seductive prose, graphics that promoted the desirability of place, and the qualitative attributes attainable through the purchase of a shared ownership property. We found contradictions about shared ownership between different newspapers, different times in the same newspaper, and even the same newspaper on the same day (apparently unintentionally). Debates about the merit of shared ownership in meeting the needs of people priced out of homeownership, or the more positively presented opportunities that shared ownership provides to access the "property ladder", were set against the negative effects of having limited mobility in some circumstances.

Stakeholder Interviews

We conducted 19 interviews with people who we believed would be stake-holders in our research. For example, we conducted interviews (mostly by telephone) with representatives of building societies, banks, pressure groups, policy-makers, local authorities, housing associations, and all their interlocutors. We conducted a focus group in person with a shared ownership buyers' organisation, and observed one of their meetings. Although we asked certain specific questions of course, we were also interested to find out responses to some generic questions, such as what is shared ownership? We received conflictual responses, often in the same interview.

So, for example, in an interview with a housing manager, we were first told that it was a simple product:

> If you think about it in general terms, it is not a complicated product – you can buy an asset and pay rent; sell it and this is the process; if you want to buy the rest of it [you can].

But, scratch and sniff, and a rather different smell emerged; when we sought to open up that simple box, we were told that it was also rather more complicated:

> What is less clear is what is the legal status of that shared owner – we don't define what that ownership is – we need to get smarter on that – the customer needs to be the legal owner of that share – the law treats them as a leaseholder which means they don't get certain rights – and that needs to be tightened up. The morality [and] practice of it is that we treat them as a pure stakeholder. We just need to make sure legally that it is tight enough.

In this rather disarming comment, the manager drew on a series of buzz-words that are the subject of this book: ownership, legal constructions, customer, "pure" stakeholder, tightening it up.

At the end of our project, we conducted two further interviews with people who had been there "at the beginning". One of those persons was a former chief executive of a housing association. The other was Sir John Stanley, the Housing Minister in the first Thatcher Conservative government elected in 1979—he gave us permission to name him in our writing, in part because it would have been obvious who he was and equally obvious as to his status in the then developing field of shared ownership. Sir John was one of the people who can lay claim to having established shared ownership at the outset.

Archival Work

Our archival research was stimulated by a problem which occurred during the early phases of fieldwork. We found that when we interviewed elite actors who were there or thereabouts in the beginning, different people were said (or claimed) to have invented the idea of shared ownership. At the start of our project, we read that John Coward, a key player in housing associations but who unfortunately passed away at that time, "pioneered the concept" of shared ownership (Daily Telegraph 2013). Others claimed it for themselves or for their organisation. We read that it "began" in Notting Hill in 1979 (Heywood 2016), or in Birmingham in 1975 (Forrest et al. 1984).

We visited the National Archive, London Metropolitan Archive (for Greater London Council records), and the Birmingham Library archive of Birmingham City Council. We generated around 4500 photographs of such documents, the majority of which came from the Housing and Local Government (HLG) series in the National Archive. In a pre-electronic age, inscription of meetings in minutes, memoranda, and legal advice was committed to paper and mostly stored away in archives (Freeman 2008: 15).

Observation and Interviews

Our interview sample was drawn from two housing association shared owner-ship providers that we have called "Greendale" and "Fixham". Alison con-ducted a 3-week period of observation of the management of the shared ownership estate in each housing association, talking to and shadowing employees with shared ownership responsibilities and interactions. Both Greendale and Fixham have provided shared ownership for a lengthy period. Both are stereotypical housing associations. Both might be described as entre-preneurial organisations working at the interface between social and commer-cial practices. The phrase "social business" was regularly used across both study areas to describe this elision.

We conducted 32 interviews with Greendale shared owners and 38 with those in Fixham during 2014–15. The interviews were conducted with shared owners in their homes in London, the South-East, and East of England and were drawn from highly contrasting housing markets. As might be expected, the circumstances of the shared owner buyers also varied considerably from young professionals in central London to lower-income households in areas outside the capital. The owners responded to us following an email (and snail mail, in Greendale) invitation sent by the providers. We emphasised that our research was independent of their association, both in the email invitation and in subsequent correspondence, as well as during the interview. Interviews were between around 45 minutes and 2.5 hours. In this book, rather than give our interviewees codes, we have given them real-life names so that the code does not obscure the narrative, and because names give life to things.

Many spoke enthusiastically about their purchase, conveying a sense of independence and security afforded to them away from former marital homes, family homes, or the private rented sector. Conversely, they also spoke, often in heart-wrenching terms, about the problems they faced in their homes, and their struggles to solve those problems. Despite those problems, many loved their homes in part because they had made them their homes. However, whether the problems were about repairs, improvements, poor-quality new build, the payment of rent, or service charges, they felt those problems at a deep level. We learnt that a packet of tissues was often a good prop, alongside the audio recorder. The appendix provides some basic relevant detail about each of our interviewees (their pseudonym, occupation, time and type of property bought, and a brief summary of their issues, if any).

We were not seeking a representative sample of shared owners, although we understand that our sample is roughly representative of the gender balance among shared owners. In Greendale, 17 of our interviewees were female, 13 were male, and 2 were couples. In Fixham, 24 were female, 9 were male, and 5 were couples. Our sample was obviously drawn from the historic stock of shared owners who had entered the sector over many years, but this gender split generally reflects new entrants to the sector, where women are over-represented, comprising 58 per cent of single-adult households, which in themselves comprise 56 per cent of all new sales (DCLG CORE Sales logs 2015/2016). Couples comprised 28 per cent of new sales, and couples with children only 10 per cent. As regards ethnicity, there is likely to be a story to tell; however, that story is not this research output because, although 11 per cent of new sales have been to owners who identify as non-white, our black and minority ethnic sub-sample was too small to be meaningful.

The topic guide for the interviews was carefully constructed. It took its cue from the description of the interview schedule provided by Ewick and Silbey (1998). It asked general questions about housing pathways, exchange professionals, and descriptions of their areas. It then asked about any general or particular issues which had arisen since they had bought the property. Only towards the end of the interview were buyers asked if they felt like owners or not, and why they felt the way they did. We did not explicitly ask about "crisis moments" (the title of our successful grant application) because we did not wish to impose some pre-defined categorisation on our interviewees. This research was designed, in other words, as an everyday life study. As Ewick and

Silbey (1998: 24–5) put it, "[I]t was the respondents' own understandings and definitions of these concepts – as they might be expressed in their words, revealed in their actions, or embedded in their stories and accounts – that we wanted to hear about."

In most cases, we were able to interview our sample in their homes. Only in around five cases was this not possible and, in those cases, we met at coffee bars or other venues near their places of employment. All bar one of the interviews was conducted face to face. It was important to us that the interview was conducted in the home because we felt that the interviewee would be more expressive in that place, and would feel more in control of the interview process. This location was also instrumental in our data collection, because our interviewees often explained things by reference to the objects around themselves. Thus, tenure was given life through the humble, the mundane, the everyday objects that might otherwise have remained unnoticed. Of course, this was often a co-construction by the interviewee, the researcher, and the objects themselves, albeit one led by the interviewee in the out-of-ordinary interview; but we began to understand during the course of the field-work that the home space and the objects themselves talked as one.

Structure of the Book

Now that we have cleared much of the conceptual and methodological groundwork, we can present the arguments in the specific chapters of this book. Consistent with our methodological positionality, we recognise that this book and all our other interactions around this project are actors themselves.

In the next chapter we provide more detail about shared ownership to set the context for the book. Our argument is that, in the very way in which it is discussed and represented in policy and by policy-makers, it appears as a very simple "product", albeit one which has gone through a series of different iterations—a kind of public relations (PR) mill which goes round and round. That very simple product, at heart, is about low-cost homeownership—to adopt the metaphor, enabling people to "get a foot on the ladder" of homeownership. We tell the story about how shared ownership was made up, how it was re-made and re-made at different times for different purposes. It is this discussion which sets up the rest of the book, for, as we have observed, the label shared ownership is meaningless.

But how did that idea of ownership develop? Indeed, as we have observed above, there is a paradox at the heart of shared ownership that it is not about ownership at all. That is the focus of the discussion in Chap. 3. Here, we draw on our archival work principally to develop a set of narratives about the production of the label, shared ownership, and principally about its central actor, the lease. Both are material semiotics, and both have real power in the sense that they get things moving, they convey ideas, they create its universality.

The story of the lease is, in many respects, *the* story of shared ownership. It is the governing device, the translation through inscription of the ideas of shared ownership into documentary form. It is also so much more than that. It is drawn (as lawyers like to describe the making of such a document) so that it is weighted almost entirely against the buyer's interest. In this chapter, we make good this point and describe how this came about in its earliest incarnations, and the significance of the promulgation of a model lease by the regulator (the then Housing Corporation)—not only this, but also the way it has been translated over time, its modifications, its construction through litigation, and the construction of that litigation.

In Chap. 4, we introduce our participant housing associations, Greendale and Fixham, in more detail. We describe their social business orientation. We describe a particular problematisation, which goes like this: they are organisations which manage social housing that is rented and provided to vulnerable households; they are providing a relatively new product, which is a hybrid of ownership and renting; how should they manage this new stock? Should they manage it as owning or renting, for there is that binary? We think here about the ways in which social housing management has developed over time into, as the Foucauldians put it, a governing, responsibilising machine. Social rented housing, however, must be managed; its residents are often vulnerable and require that management to sustain their occupancy.

Should shared ownership housing be managed in the same way or as something different? Indeed, what is "management" in this context? These are the big questions, which were addressed by Greendale and Fixham, quite consciously, and, in doing so, they constructed, again quite consciously, what ownership means. Recognising that management "produces" shared ownership, and that ownership is situational and interactive, we also consider how our buyer interviewees reacted to their management (and its absence). From this perspective, we are able to argue that ownership is constantly in action and negotiated, arguing that ownership is a social construction, rather than a set of norms or values.

We then move on in Chap. 5 to describe the way in which shared ownership is sold—to coin a horrible word, its productisation. We do so through the marketing literature and compare this with the reasons why our buyers entered the shared ownership market. Through these different narratives of aspiration and hope, and not a little desperation, our buyer participants produced a sense of the social by abstracting themselves from social housing. Unpacking that just a little further, we argue that our buyers generally made clear to us that they were not purchasing social housing, but, in making that clear, and abstracting themselves from social housing, they defined their own sociality. They differentiated themselves from the other. This reflected a difference about tenurial perceptions between the social clientele and their aspirations to ownership. Thus, tenure speaks at this point through an abstraction of self.

In Chaps. 6 and 7, we take on the themes that we have developed in the previous chapters about ownership and sociality to tell some of the stories about the experiences of living in this tenure. We do so in two different ways in these chapters. In Chap. 6, we seek to draw some boundaries to our study, imposing a sense of analysis on our data. In doing so, we also seek to expose the inherent inconsistencies in these stories. They are stories in which our buyers construct themselves mostly as owners, but in which there are what we describe as interrupting issues. These are issues where the buyer was made to stop and think about their tenurial location; this moment's hesitation, though, appeared to be just that, a mere blip in an otherwise often apparently linear story of ownership. In Chap. 7, we tell the story in a radically different way, taking our inspiration from David Engel and Frank Munger's work (2003) on civil rights legislation in the US. Here, we (mostly) let five sets of interviewees tell their stories and impose themselves on this book. We "top and tail" those stories with our own analysis. However, our purpose of framing this chapter like this is to allow our interviewees' narratives to highlight the fluidity, malleability, and permeability of tenure for them as they negotiate tricky moments. They are stories about potted plants, cigarette butts, water penetration and roofs, being a good neighbour, about the market, what has become known as "poor doors" (i.e. spatial divisions between private and social housing: Osborne 2014), and so on. They are also our stories, both in the telling and also because we present our recollections of certain incidents which occurred during our fieldwork. The stories convey the complexities of the relationships involved as well as the kinds of themes which arose across our interviews. Principally, however, the stories also convey the contradictions of everyday life—the ways in which, as owners, our research participants described their sense of control over their space, but yet their stories are also their anger, feelings of powerlessness/lack of control, resistance, and community. And these stories are also stories about translation, about the ways in which, for example, the potted plant became a material translation of the lease, tenure, and relationality, and how it gets others moving around that, performing property.

Concluding Observations

This book is designed to develop an empirically focused set of insights into the idea of ownership, its production and re-production. We argue that apparent binaries between ownership and renting, and social and private, are nothing of the sort, but operate on a continuum. Where one sits on those continua is situated and interactional, and produces a varied and variable legal consciousness in which law–property–society become co-constituted. This relates not just simply to the percentage material interest that owners hold in the property, but also to internal and external sentiments and influences that are brought to bear upon their experience. Therefore, this is not just a legal consciousness of people, but one in which there is a mix of things, and those things are made to speak, although they do not provide a coherent narrative. Therein lies the puzzle of ownership, something which normative prescription cannot satisfy or reflect.

Bibliography

Alexander, G., Panalver, E., Singer, J. and Underkuffler, L. (2009), 'A Statement of Progressive Property', 94(4), *Cornell Law Review*: 743–4.

Apps, P. (2017), '25,000 Shared Ownership Homes Under Construction', *Inside Housing*, 19th January.

Atkinson, R. and Blandy, S. (2007), 'Panic Rooms: The Rise of Defensive Homeownership', 22(4), *Housing Studies*: 443–58.

Atkinson, R. and Blandy, S. (2016), *Domestic Fortress: Fear and the New Home Front*, Manchester: MUP.

Benson, M. and Jackson, E. (2017), 'Making the Middle Classes on Shifting Ground? Residential Status, Performativity and Middle-Class Subjectivities in Contemporary London', online first, *British Journal of Sociology*.

Birch, J. (2017), 'The Trouble with Leasehold', *Inside Housing*, 13th April.

Blackstone, W. (1765), *The Commentaries on the Laws of England*, London: Dawsons.

Blandy, S. and Robinson, D. (2001), 'Reforming Leasehold: Discursive Events and Outcomes, 1984–2000', 23(3), *Journal of Law and Society*: 384–408.

Blomley, N. (2003), 'Law, Property, and the Geography of Violence: The Frontier, the Survey, and the Grid', 93(1), *Annals of the Association of American Geographers*: 121–41.

Blomley, N. (2014), 'Disentangling Law: The Practice of Bracketing', 10, *Annual Review of Law and Social Science*: 133–48.

Blomley, N. (2016), 'The Boundaries of Property: Complexity, Relationality, and Spatiality', 50(1), *Law and Society Review*: 224–55.

Boehm, T. and Schlottmann, S. (2008), 'Wealth Accumulation and Homeownership: Evidence for Low-Income Households', 10(2), *Journal of Policy Development and Research*: 225–56.

Bowes, A. and Sim, D. (2002), 'Patterns of Residential Settlement among Black and Minority Ethnic Groups', in P. Somerville and A. Steele (eds), *'Race', Housing and Social Exclusion*, London: Jessica Kingsley.

Bright, S. and Hopkins, N. (2011), 'Home, Meaning and Identity: Learning from the English Model of Shared Ownership', 28(3), *Housing, Theory and Society*: 377–96.

Bumiller, K. (1988), *The Civil Rights Society: The Social Construction of Victims*, Baltimore: Johns Hopkins University Press.

Burridge, A. (2010), 'Capital Gains, Homeownership and Economic Inequality', 15(2), *Housing Studies*: 259–80.

Callon, M. (1984), 'Some Elements of a Sociology of Translation: Domestication of the Scallops and Fishermen of St Brieuc Bay', 32(1), *The Sociological Review*: 196–233.

Callon, M. (1986), 'The Sociology of an Actor-Network: The Case of the Electric Vehicle', in M. Callon, J. Law and A. Rip (eds), *Mapping the Dynamics of Science and Technology: Sociology of Science in the Real World*, Basingstoke: Palgrave Macmillan.

Callon, M. and Latour, B. (1981), 'Unscrewing the Big Leviathan: How Actors Macro-Structure Reality and How Sociologists Help Them to Do So', in K. Knorr and A. Cicorel (eds), *Towards and Integration of Macro and Micro Sociology*, London: Routledge.

Carr, H. (2011), 'The Right to Buy, The Leaseholder, and the Impoverishment of Ownership', 38(4), *Journal of Law and Society*: 519–41.

Christie, H., Smith, S. and Munro, M. (2008), 'The Emotional Economy of Housing', 40(1), *Environment and Planning A*: 2296– 312.

Cloatre, E. (2013), *Pills for the Poorest*, London: Palgrave Macmillan.

Cloatre, E. and Cowan, D. (forthcoming), 'Materialities and Legalities: Some Observations', in A. Philippopoulos-Mihalopoulos (ed), *Routledge Handbook of Law and Theory*, London: Routledge.

Cohen, M. (1927), 'Property and Sovereignty', 13(1), *Cornell Law Review*: 8–30.

Cole, I. and Robinson, D. (2000), 'Owners, Yet Tenants: The Position of Leaseholders in Flats in England and Wales', 15(6), *Housing Studies*: 595–612.

Cooper, D. (2007), 'Opening Up Ownership: Community Belonging, Belongings, and the Productive Life of Property', 32(3), *Law and Social Inquiry*: 625–64.

Daily Telegraph (2013), 'John Coward—Obituary', *Daily Telegraph*, 21st November, http://www.telegraph.co.uk/news/obituaries/politics-obituaries/10481998/John-Coward-obituary.html

Davies, M. (1997), *Property: Meanings, Histories, Theories*, London: Glasshouse.

Department for Communities and Local Government (2015), *Proposals to Streamline the Resale of Shared Ownership Properties*, London: DCLG.

Department of Environment (1971), *Fair Deal for Housing*, Cmnd 4728, London: HMSO.

Department of the Environment (DoE) (1977), *Housing Policy—A Consultative Document*, London: HMSO.

Department of the Environment (DoE) (1995), *Our Future Homes: Opportunity, Choice and Responsibility*, Cm 2901, London: DoE.

Dowling, R. (1998), 'Gender, Class and Home Ownership: Placing the Connections', 13(4), *Housing Studies*: 471–86.

Easthope, H. (2004), 'A Place Called Home', 21(3), *Housing, Theory and Society*: 128–38.

Easthope, H. (2014), 'Making a Rental Property Home', 29(5), *Housing Studies*: 579–96.

Elsinga, M., Hoekstra, J. and Dol, K. (2015), 'Financial Implications of Affordable Home Ownership Products: Four Dutch Products in International Perspective', 30(2), *Journal of Housing and the Built Environment*: 237–55.

Engel, D. and Munger, F. (2003), *Rights of Inclusion: Law and Identity in the Life Stories of Americans with Disabilities*, Chicago: University of Chicago Press.

Ewick, P. (2008), 'Consciousness and Ideology', in A. Sarat (ed), *The Blackwell Companion to Law and Society*, Oxford: Blackwell.

Ewick, P. and Silbey, S. (1998), *The Common Place of Law: Stories from Everyday Life*, Chicago: University of Chicago Press.

Flint, J. (2002), 'Social Housing Agencies and the Governance of Anti-social Behaviour', 17(4), *Housing Studies*: 619–37.

Flint, J (2004), 'Reconfiguring Agency and Responsibility in the Governance of Social Housing in Scotland', 41(1), *Urban Studies*: 151–72.

Forrest, R. and Hiroyama, Y. (2015), 'The Financialisation of the Social Project: Embedded Liberalism, Neo-Liberalism and Home Ownership', 52(2), *Urban Studies*: 233–44.

Forrest, R., Lansley, S. and Murie, A. (1984), *A Foot on the Ladder? An Evaluation of Low Cost Home Ownership Initiatives*, Working Paper No 41, Bristol: School for Advanced Urban Studies, University of Bristol.

Forrest, R., Murie, A. and Williams, P. (1990), *Home Ownership: Differentiation and Fragmentation*, London: Unwin Hyman

Fox O'Mahony, L. (2014), 'Property Outsiders and the Hidden Politics of Doctrinalism', 67(1), *Current Legal Problems*: 409–45.

Freeman, R. (2008), 'Learning by Meeting', 2(1), *Critical Policy Analysis*: 1–24.

Freeman, R. and Maybin, J. (2011), 'Documents, Practices and Policy', 7(2), *Evidence and Policy*: 155–70.

Fritsvold, E. (2009), 'Under the Law: Legal Consciousness and Radical Environmental Activism', 34(4), *Law & Social Inquiry*: 799–824.

Giuliani, M. (1991), 'Towards an Analysis of Mental Representations of Attachment to Home', 8(2), *Journal of Architectural and Planning Research*: 133–46.

Grabham, E. (2016), *Brewing Legal Times: Things, Form and the Enactment of Law*, Toronto: University of Toronto Press.

Graham, N. (2011), *Lawscape: Property, Environment, Law*, London: Routledge.

Gurney, C. (1999a), 'Lowering the Drawbridge: A Case Study of Analogy and Metaphor in the Social Construction of Home-Ownership', 36(7), *Urban Studies*: 1705–22.

Gurney, C. (1999b), 'Pride and Prejudice: Discourses of Normalisation in Public and Private Accounts of Home Ownership', 14(2), *Housing Studies*: 163–85.

Halliday, S. and Morgan, B. (2013), 'I Fought the Law and the Law Won? Legal Consciousness and the Critical Imagination', 66(1), *Current Legal Problems*: 1–32.

Hamnett, C. (1999), *Winners and Loser: Homeownership in Modern Britain*, London: Routledge.

Hargreaves, J. (2014), *Mr Messy*, London: Egmont.

Herbert, C., McCue, D. and Sanchez-Moyano, R. (2013), 'Is Homeownership Still an Effective Means of Building Wealth for Low-Income Households? (Was It Ever?)', Joint Centre for Housing Studies, Harvard University, http://www.jchs.harvard.edu/sites/jchs.harvard.edu/files/hbtl-06.pdf

Heywood, A. (2016), *From the Margins to the Mainstream: A Study of the Prospects for Shared Home Ownership in the North West*, London: The Smith Institute.

Hillyard, P. and Watson, S. (1994), 'Postmodern Social Policy: A Contradiction in Terms?', 25(3), *Journal of Social Policy*: 321–46.

Honore, A. (1961), 'Ownership', in A. Guest (ed), *Oxford Essays in Jurisprudence*, Oxford: OUP.

Hull, K. (2016), 'Legal Consciousness in Marginalized Groups: The Case of LGBT People', 41(3), *Law and Social Inquiry*: 551–72.

Hume, D. (1740)[2004], *A Treatise of Human Nature*, London: Penguin.

Hunter, C. (2015), 'Solar Panels, Homeowners and Leases: The Lease as a Socio-Legal Object', in D. Cowan and D. Wincott (eds), *Exploring the 'Legal' in Socio-Legal Studies*, London: Palgrave Macmillan.

Hurdley, R. (2006), 'Dismantling Mantelpieces: Narrating Identities and Materializing Culture in the Home', 40(4), *Sociology*: 717–33.

Jacob, M-A. (2017), 'The Strikethrough: An Approach to Regulatory Writing and Professional Discipline', 37(1), *Legal Studies*: 137–61.

Jacobs, J. and Smith, S. (2008), 'Living Room: Rematerialising Home', 40(3), *Environment and Planning A*: 515–9.

Jacobs, K. and Gabriel, M. (2013), 'Introduction: Homes, Objects and Things', 30(3), *Housing, Theory and Society*: 213–8.

Johnson, J. (1988), 'Mixing Humans and Nonhumans Together: The Sociology of a Door-Closer', 35(3), *Social Problems*: 298–310.

Jorgensen, C. (2016), 'The Space of the Family: Emotions, Economy and Materiality in Homeownership', 33(1), *Housing, Theory and Society*: 98–113

Karn, V., Kemeny, J. and Williams, P. (1985), *Home Ownership in the Inner City: Salvation or Despair?*, Aldershot: Gower.

Keenan, S. (2013), 'Property as Governance: Time, Space and Belonging in Australia's Northern Territory Intervention', 76(3), *Modern Law Review*: 464–93.

Keenan, S. (2015), *Subversive Property: Law and the Production of Spaces of Belonging*, London: Routledge.

Kennett, P., Forrest, R. and Marsh, A. (2013), 'The Global Economic Crisis and the Reshaping of Housing Opportunities', 30(1), *Housing, Theory and Society*: 10–28.

King, P. (2010), *Housing Policy Transformed: The Right to Buy and the Desire to Own*, Bristol: Policy Press.

Latour, B. (1987), *Science in Action: How to Follow Scientists and Engineers Through Society*, Harvard: Harvard UP.

Latour, B. (2000), 'When Things Strike Back: A Possible Contribution of "Science Studies" to the Social Sciences', 51(1), *British Journal of Sociology*: 107–23.

Latour, B. (2005), *Reassembling the Social: An Introduction to Actor-Network-Theory*, Oxford: OUP.

Latour, B. (2010), *The Making of Law: An Ethnography of the Conseil d'Etat*, Oxford: OUP.

Latour, B. and Woolgar, S. (1986), *Laboratory Life: The Construction of Scientific Facts*, Princeton: Princeton UP.

Law, J. (1996), 'Traduction/Trahison: Notes on Actor-Network Theory', TMV Working Paper Number 106, Oslo, Norway: University of Oslo.

Law, J. (1999), 'After ANT: Complexity, Naming and Topology', in J. Law and J. Hassard (eds), *Actor-Network Theory and After*, Sociological Review Monographs, Oxford: Blackwell.

Law, J. (2002), *Aircraft Stories: Decentring the Object in Technoscience*, Durham: Duke UP.

Law, J. (2004), *After Method: Mess in Social Science Research*, London: Routledge.

Law, J. and Mol, A. (1995), 'Notes on Materiality and Sociality', 43(2), *The Sociological Review*: 274–94.

Malpass, P. (2000a), 'The Discontinuous History of Housing Associations in England', 15(2), *Housing Studies*: 195–212.

Malpass, P. (2000b), *Housing Associations and Housing Policy: A Historical Perspective*, Basingstoke: Macmillan.

Manzi, T. and Morrison, N. (2017), 'Risk, Commercialism and Social Purpose: Repositioning the English Housing Association Sector', forthcoming, *Urban Studies*: 1–18.

McDermont, M. (2010), *Governing, Independence, and Expertise: The Business of Housing Associations*, Oxford: Hart Publishing.

McKee, K. (2011), 'Challenging the Norm? The "Ethopolitics" of Low Cost Homeownership in Scotland', 48(16), *Urban Studies*: 3399–413.

McKenzie, D. (2006), *An Engine, Not a Camera: How Financial Models Shape Markets*, Cambridge, Mass: MIT Press.

Mercer, P. (2016), 'Could Shared Ownership Help Sydney's Housing Affordability Crisis?', *BBC Online News*, http://www.bbc.co.uk/news/business-37116439

Merrill, T. and Smith, H. (2001), 'What Happened to Property in Law and Economics?', 111(2), *Yale Law Journal*: 357–98.

Merry, S. (1990), *Getting Justice and Getting Even: Legal Consciousness among Working-Class Americans*, Chicago: University of Chicago Press.

Miller, D. (2010), *Stuff*, Cambridge: Polity.

Morrison, N. (2016), 'Institutional Logics and Organisational Hybridity: English Housing Associations' Diversification into the Private Rented Sector', 31(8), *Housing Studies*: 897–915.

Mullins, D., Czischke, D. and van Bortel, G. (2014), *Hybridizing Housing Organisations: Meanings, Concepts and Processes of Social Enterprise*, London: Routledge.

Murie, A., Niner, P. and Watson, C. (1976), *Housing Policy and the Housing System*, London: Allen & Unwin.

Murie, A. and Williams, P. (2015), 'A Presumption in Favour of Home Ownership? Reconsidering Housing Tenure Strategies', 30(5), *Housing Studies*: 656–76.

Murtha, T. (2015), 'The Housing Association that Will No Longer Build Homes for the Poor', *The Guardian*, 7th August.

National Audit Office (2006), *A Foot on the Ladder: Low Cost Home Ownership Assistance*, HC 1048 Session 2005–2006, London: NAO.

Nedelsky, J. (1990), 'Law, Boundaries, and the Bounded Self', 30(1), *Representations*: 162–89.

Nielson, L.B. (2000), 'Situating Legal Consciousness; Experiences and Attitudes of Ordinary Citizens about Law and Street Harassment', 34(4), *Law and Society Review*: 1055–90.

Osborne, H. (2014), 'Poor Doors: The Segregation of London's Inner-City Flat Dwellers', *The Guardian*, 25th July.

Pawson, H. and Mullins, D. (2010), *After Council Housing: Britain's New Social Landlords*, Basingstoke: Palgrave Macmillan.

Penner, J. (1996), 'The "Bundle of Rights" Picture of Property', 43(3), *UCLA Law Review*: 711–820.

Penner, J. (1997), *The Idea of Property in Law*, Oxford: OUP.

Piketty, T. (2015), 'Property, Inequality, and Taxation: Reflections on *Capital in the Twenty-First Century*', 68(2) *New York University Tax Review*: 631–47.

Radin, M. (2012), *Boilerplate: The Fine Print, Vanishing Rights, and the Rule of Law*, Princeton: Princeton UP.

Riles, A. (2006), 'Introduction: In Response', in A. Riles (ed), *Documents: Artifacts of Modern Knowledge*, Ann Arbor: University of Michigan Press.

Riles, A. (2011), *Collateral Knowledge: Legal Reasoning in the Global Financial Markets*, Chicago: University of Chicago Press.

Robertson, D. (2006), 'Cultural Expectations of Homeownership: Explaining Changing Legal Definitions of Flat "Ownership" Within Britain', 21(1), *Housing Studies*: 35–52.

Rose, C. (1985), 'Possession as the Origin of Property', 52(1), *University of Chicago Law Review*: 73–88.

Rose, C. (1994), *Property & Persuasion: Essays on the History, Theory, and Rhetoric of Ownership*, Boulder, Col: Westview.

Rose, N. (1999), *Powers of Freedom: Reframing Political Thought*, Cambridge: CUP.

Sarat, A. (1990), '"The Law Is All Over …": Power, Resistance and the Legal Consciousness of the Welfare Poor', 2(2), *Yale Journal of Law and the Humanities*: 343–79.

Sassen, S. (2014), *Expulsions: Brutality and Complexity in the Global Economy*, Cambridge, Mass: Belknap Press.

Saunders, P. (1990), *A Nation of Home Owners*, London: Allen and Unwin.

Savage, M., Bagnall, G. and Longhurst, B. (2004), *Globalization and Belonging*, London: Sage.

Savills (2016), *Spotlight Shared Ownership*, London: Savills. http://pdf.euro.savills.co.uk/uk/residential---other/spotlight-shared-ownership-2016.pdf

Silbey, S. (2005), 'After Legal Consciousness', 1(1), *Annual Review of Law and Social Science*: 323–68.

Silbey, S. (2010), 'J. Locke, op. cit.: Invocations of Law on Snowy Streets', 5(2), *Journal of Comparative Law*: 66–91.

Silbey, S. and Cavicchi, A. (2005), 'The Common Place of Law: Transforming Matters of Concern into the Objects of Everyday Life', in B. Latour and P. Weibel (eds), *Making Things Public: Atmospheres of Democracy*, Cambridge, Mass: MIT Press.

Silbey, S. and Ewick, P. (2003), 'Narrating Social Structure: Stories of Resistance to Legal Authority', 108(6), *American Journal of Sociology*: 1328–72.

Smith, S. (2015), 'Owner-Occupation: At Home with a Hybrid of Money and Materials', 40(3), *Environment and Planning A*: 520–35.

Tang, C., Oxley, M. and Mekic, D. (2017), 'Meeting Commercial and Social Goals: Institutional Investment in the Housing Association Sector', 32(4), *Housing Studies*: 411–27.

Teruel, R. (2015), 'The New Intermediate Tenures in Catalonia to Facilitate Access to Housing', 2, *Revue de Droit Bancaire et Financiere*: 115–8.

Underkuffler, L. (2016), 'A Theoretical Approach: The Lens of Progressive Property', in S. Blandy and S. Bright (eds), *Researching Property Law*, London: Palgrave Macmillan

Valverde, M. (2003), *Law's Dream of a Common Knowledge*, Princeton: Princeton UP.

Valverde, M. (2005), 'Authorizing the Production of Urban Moral Order: Appellate Courts and Their Knowledge Games', 39(2), *Law and Society Review*: 419–56.

Van Oorschott, I. and Schinkel, W. (2015), 'The Legal Case File as Border Object: On Self-Reference and Other-Reference in Criminal Law', 42(4), *Journal of Law and Society*: 499–527.

Wallace, A. (2008), 'Knowing the Market? Understanding and Performing York's Housing', 23(2), *Housing Studies*: 253–70.

Walt, A van der (2009), *Property in the Margins*, Oxford: Hart.

Watt, P. (2009), 'Living in an Oasis: Middle-Class Disaffiliation and Selective Belonging in an English Suburb', 41(12), *Environment and Planning A*: 2874–92.

2

Shared Ownership and Housing Policy

Introduction

This chapter presents a study of housing policy from the periphery. As we develop below, it is not its numerical significance as a tenure that makes shared ownership so important; rather, it is its totemic significance in housing policy and its location as a social housing low-cost homeownership "product" which make it an object of study. Our argument is that, in the very way in which it is discussed and represented in policy and by policy-makers,[1] shared ownership appears as a very simple "product", albeit one which has gone through a series of different iterations. And, most of all, shared ownership is constructed as *ownership*. That very simple ownership product, at heart, is how shared ownership came to be represented and translated by a range of others, including buyers—to adopt the metaphor widely used in policy documents, enabling people to "get a foot on the ladder" of "homeownership". And, of course, these are very legal translations.

This then is a story about how a product is made and re-made, and how, almost serendipitously, it became mainstream. It is about what the theorists describe as the production of an "actor-world"; that is, a world imagined and a world in which other actors become enrolled. This world needs to be defined and it needs policy entrepreneurs (which may be human or non-human in our rendering, cf. Kingdon 2011). This is a story (and, mostly, a his-story) about how legality was brought into being, of how the values of ownership overtook and subverted all other initiatives, and how the legal consciousness

---

[1] We are using the term "policy-makers" in this chapter in an inclusive sense.

© The Author(s) 2018
D. Cowan et al., *Ownership, Narrative, Things*, Palgrave Socio-Legal Studies,
https://doi.org/10.1057/978-1-137-59069-5_2

of shared ownership came to be formed out of its absence. Despite accounting for roughly 0.8 per cent of the tenure of all households in England, shared ownership has taken up considerable policy space, and has been the subject of numerous policy evaluations as well as what we might loosely describe as policy talk, all of which "collud[es] to enact it into being" (Law 2002: 7). In short, something as insignificant as shared ownership has drawn a range of resources together and taken on significance.

We begin by telling a story of how shared ownership seems to have come into being in the first place. It is a crucial story about labels and the significance of ownership, and a very legal problem: its absence from legal categories. That construction as ownership led to the already quite well-developed alternatives (at that time) being unceremoniously ditched. We then go on to look at the ways in which shared ownership was promoted, and the ways in which it was re-made to suit. This story is wrapped up in the development of the idea of "social housing", an idea of housing provided beyond state-actors but by independent bodies called housing associations. The story of their rise has been told many times (see, e.g., Malpass 2000b; McDermont 2010), but here we develop that history from the periphery and demonstrate the ways in which private finance became enfolded in social housing. It should be emphasised that the story told in this chapter is particularly partial in the sense that it leaves out of consideration the development of the technology of the lease, which is the subject of the next chapter, but which was a key part of this historical development.

Shared Ownership: Key Moments

Shared ownership emerged in the 1970s from the policy primeval soup (Kingdon 2011: 122). A policy window opened because of the emergence of a particular problem about tenure, and the opening enabled key players to "push their pet solutions" (*id.*, 165). We tell the story here of its emergence and the critical significance of labelling it as "ownership"; that label, which implies a particular version of legality (correct or otherwise—it does not matter), did and does particular work. For the purposes of this chapter, the work it did was in establishing shared ownership in a kind of pole position of the constellation of low-cost homeownership initiatives that begun to be developed at this time. What emerges from our discussion is that shared ownership was actually fraught with complexity, which was at both legal and policy levels, and raised questions about the extent of the power of housing providers, particularly local authorities.

Beginnings

The history of shared ownership presents itself almost as a problematic in its own right. Our key stakeholders with long memories reflected back on the 1970s. Different people "claimed" shared ownership as their own.

Malpass (2000a: 196) has observed, "Writing history requires hard choices, about what to put in and what to leave out, and about what is important and what is not." A range of starting points presented themselves. For example, we found that Birmingham had been advocating a "half:half" scheme from about 21 September 1973 (Birmingham City Council Housing Committee Report). This seemed to be the date at which a version of shared ownership emerged as a distinct policy solution, although we recognised that its genesis might have occurred elsewhere.

One could just as easily have started with the publication of a "little pamphlet" by John Stanley, shortly after he was elected to Parliament in April 1974, and endorsed by Margaret Thatcher, then shadow Minister for the Environment, *Shared Purchase: A New Route to Home-Ownership* (Stanley 1974). The significance of this little-known publication was its translation into national policy by the policy entrepreneur—John Stanley himself—when taking office as the first Housing Minister in the first Thatcher government from 1979.

This rough period from around 1973 to 1983 has been the subject of significant analysis in terms of housing policy, generally, and more specifically in relation to low-cost homeownership initiatives (Forrest et al. 1984; Murie 2016)—in short, rising building costs, interest rates, and inflation, particularly as a result of the breakdown of the Bretton Woods agreement and the OPEC-induced rise in oil prices, combined with significant public expenditure cuts to housing following the IMF bailout (Malpass 2005: Chap. 6). The 1974 election, called to decide "who governs Britain?", produced a coalition government followed by a minority Labour government, which subsequently, following the October election, had a small majority. Stuart Lowe (2004) describes it as a critical juncture in housing policy, an intense moment of political and institutional transformation. Malpass (2005: 104) argues that "despite the intensity of the political debate housing policy was shaped at least as much by economic exigencies as by ideology" (see also Jacobs and Manzi 2017: 2). However, this was also a period when housing associations were becoming "instruments of government" (Malpass 2000b: Chap. 6; see below).

Birmingham

Birmingham City Council appears to have been something of an entrepreneurial authority in the early 1970s, as it developed a package of opportunities for ownership for its tenants and others, from lower-cost mortgages to sales of its homes (Murie 1975). It applied to the Department of the Environment ("DoE") in September 1973 for permission under the Housing Act 1957 to have the site of the former Kings Norton golf course developed by a private contractor and then sold on a "half:half" basis. The DoE's permission had to be sought as a result of the 1957 Housing Act, but it was appreciated by the DoE that it had no power to grant permission for this novel type of arrangement. In fact, a rather obscure provision relating to the payment of subsidy for this type of transaction had to be inserted into Schedule 1 of the 1975 Housing, Rents and Subsidies Act to give it that power.

Permission was then given on 17 April 1975 by Reg Freeson, the Housing Minister, who wrote that he hoped that the creation of this scheme would "fill an important gap between the existing stark choices of renting and owning" (Letter, 17 April 1975, Greater London Council Archive). The first property was sold to John and Denise Eliot in September 1975 (Birmingham Mail 1975), *The Times* newspaper describing it as "the housing scheme Whitehall thought impossible" and a new type of owner-occupier (Osman 1975). Birmingham publicised their scheme as the "Half Half Scheme". This leaflet described the construction of the product in the following terms:

> **WHY** … bother?
> This could be your chance to start on the ladder of home ownership. Don't forget you can buy the "other half" as soon as you are able to afford it. Your lease is for 99 years and in all respects you reap the benefits of an owner-occupier with an asset increasing in value, but also accepting responsibilities such as repairs. Isn't it worth it to have a home of your own?

It is clear that Reg Freeson, the then Housing Minister, took a keen interest in the Birmingham development and tenurial alternatives more generally; first, Jack Straw (then an Islington Councillor and, subsequently, a Labour party grandee) reported that he had met the new half:half owners (presumably including the Elliots), writing a note that "[b]oth couples said that they had no difficulty in understanding the concept of the scheme, and both appeared very grateful that the scheme had given them a chance to become owner-occupiers which they would not otherwise have had" (HLG118/3358, 21 October 1976). Freeson also wanted to invite Stanley to meet with him, following a seminar given by Stanley in 1975 (but his officials suggested that Stanley's desire to involve private finance was unworkable).[2] And, finally, it was said of Freeson that he "has been particularly anxious to encourage equity sharing" (C.R. Durham, H7c, 5 December 1977, HLG118/3059) but, also, perhaps conversely, with a co-operative element.

The Birmingham scheme was noted in the highest echelons of government, added as Option C to Prime Minister Wilson's consideration of alternatives to Thatcher's suggestion of the right to buy, with the advantage that "[p]eople can get a firm foothold in owner occupation" (Prem 16/930). In the "policy primeval soup", alternative forms of tenure were on the government agenda for what appear to have been three reasons. First, Thatcher's development of the right-to-buy policy appeared to be gaining traction, which led to Wilson's discussion of the right to buy at a Chequers policy weekend and consideration of alternatives which would be politically acceptable to local authorities.[3] Secondly, there were entrepreneurial authorities such as Birmingham and the GLC seeking to develop alternatives for their tenants and those on their waiting lists.

Thirdly, there was an understanding of the problem of tenure as a result of contemporary economic "reality". Stanley referred to the "50:50 divide between the half of the nation that owns and the other half that rents [which] is liable to become self-perpetuating". The DoE's unpublished report by Campbell Working Group's "New Forms of Social Ownership and Tenure" set out the problem of tenure starkly:

> We consider that there is an indisputable need for a wider choice in the housing market to meet the serious problems of many people in gaining access to housing and to provide greater flexibility of movement. There is a danger of access being confined to owner-occupation on the one hand and local authority tenancies on the other. The private rented sector which used to provide access for many of those who need housing quickly, or who find it difficult to meet the qualifications imposed by the building societies and local authorities, is rapidly diminishing and, in any circumstances which are likely to obtain in the foreseeable future, will before long become very small indeed. (1976: para 32)

---

[2] Stanley was cited as saying: "[W]hat he feels is most needed, to free this new departure from dependence upon public sector finance, is a 'half-and-half' scheme linked to an agency drawing upon private funds. … Even the building society people present began taking notes at that point" (New Society 1978, p. 257, 2 February 1978; "The Minister has seen the article … He was interested to see Mr Stanley's involvement": HLG118/3059 c).

[3] In fact, this fell away because of concerns about the adverse effect on Labour councillors in the impending local elections.

It gave rather faint praise to the prospect of what were by then known as "equity sharing schemes" (an equally inaccurate title[4]): "Equity sharing would not of course help all those with housing access problems. But some people would benefit, in our view, from alternative tenure arrangements" (para 37). Alternative tenures became a feature of the 1977 Housing Green Paper (DoE 1977: 11.20, 11.25–6).

However, any development of equity sharing schemes was largely stifled by the "chaos" that developed subsequently (AMA representations to DoE: HLG118/3059). In the course of taking legal advice on a different matter (the GLC decision to offer all their tenants a 10-year option to purchase their property), it was noted by the DoE's barrister that the relevant powers in the 1957 Housing Act did not allow for local authorities to provide options to purchase: "I think that the full tactical point is that things are perhaps unlikely to turn nasty but if they do, they could turn very nasty. More important is the need to protect occupiers under these schemes" (C.R. Durham, 19 January 1978, HLG118/3059).

Although the accuracy of this advice was controversial, and different barristers took different views, it was said that a provision in the Housing Act 1957 "seems to have the effect, in a situation of mortgage default, of preventing a mortgagee in possession of the leasehold interest from disposing of it in order to clear the outstanding mortgage debt. The [Building Societies Association ("BSA")] legal department … raised this with the Department (H7)" (M. Clarke, 7 February 1977, minute, HLG118/2968).

The Minister announced this problem in Parliament on 25 May 1978 (to stop Sunderland announcing their decision to enter into a scheme). The BSA wrote to Peter Shore, the Secretary of State, that "[b]uilding societies have for some time been under pressure to lend to lessees of properties under 50/50 schemes of the type pioneered by Birmingham … Clearly, therefore, your statements in the House mean that we cannot currently advise societies to lend on the basis of this lease and that our discussions with Birmingham must be suspended" (20 June 1978, HLG118/2968).

That might have been the end of shared ownership but for the fact—almost extraordinary among the welter of other initiatives at the time—that there was cross-party support for it. Indeed, the Conservative manifesto for the 1979 election clearly highlighted, "We shall encourage shared purchase schemes which will enable people to buy a house or flat on mortgage, on the basis initially of a part-payment which they complete later when their incomes

---

[4] As there was no "equity" being shared in these schemes.

are high enough." The Conservative government took shared ownership in a rather different direction from that proposed by Labour, but, as we develop below, that was a combination of events (the rise of the right to buy, which diminished the shared ownership offer for council tenants; a change in the underlying economy; and the involvement of housing associations, including their trade body, the National Federation, and funder/regulator, the Housing Corporation).

The 1980 Housing Act created the ameliorating power, facilitating the development of local authority schemes, and also enabled housing associations to dispose of land (s. 122), subject to the Corporation's consent and not necessarily for the best price reasonably obtainable, thus facilitating shared ownership (another previous area of doubt).

Labels

The development of the label "shared ownership" is a key part of this story. Birmingham's creation of the scheme demarcated the product as ownership, but the transition from half:half, to shared purchase (as Stanley had described it), to equity sharing, to shared ownership is important in two respects. First, the creation of a label also creates a knowable product in the sense that it becomes legible. Secondly, the label produces something which becomes marketable both to policy-makers and to producing consumers.

At the DoE, labelling the product was a struggle. They had to instruct barristers, they had to talk about it and advise government, they had to engage with other players such as building societies and housing associations. The clearest problems occurred when lawyers got hold of this product following the option chaos. The DoE searched for an ameliorative power that could be given legislative effect, but, in a rather telling intervention, the DoE's lawyer wrote:

> I am up against the difficulty, which I am afraid I have already reiterated rather tiresomely, that I do not know what an "equity sharing" scheme is. … I am afraid all this will seem unhelpful, but it is really impossible to advise on what can safely and accurately be said or implied, in terms of legal concepts such as options and leases, in relation to a concept ("equity sharing") which has not been formulated (R. Cumming, Legal A, 3 May 1978, HLG118/3059)

Similarly, the Parliamentary Counsel wrote, as late as 27 February 1980, when drafting an ameliorative clause in the then Housing Bill:

Here is a speculative draft new clause … The draft is speculative because I have had no precise instructions on which to base it. Helpful as our meeting was, I think that you will agree that it left us all feeling unsure of the precise nature of the target.

We know about a number of schemes and there are one or two labels (eg equity sharing, shared ownership, sheltered housing and community leasehold) which seem to be in use. But there may be other schemes that I am unaware of and in any event none of these labels are capable of being used with any precision. (HLG118/3358)

It was at around this time also that the label "shared ownership" began to stick. Indeed, a few months earlier, in an aside, a DoE civil servant had sent some papers in response to a request for further information: "I attach some papers about equity sharing schemes. The Minister [Mr Stanley] prefers the term 'shared ownership' so we now use the letter [sic]" (Letter, A. Melville, DoE, to N Pittman, Scottish Development Council, 21 August 1979). As KS2 put it, "[Shared ownership] was born – it got its name from John Stanley and rang bells politically – the word ownership was important politically." Stanley, in interview, gave his reasons for this name change:

[W]hat we now come to is shared purchase, which I then decided shared ownership was a better phrase, because shared purchase just suggests a one off. But shared ownership has a greater …, at least I felt it was a stronger phrase and it is, it's ownership. So that's why I rechristened it.

This term "ownership" was not politically or technically neutral. That label gave it undoubted appeal to a Conservative party focused on low-cost home-ownership initiatives. It also had technical consequences. An owner has responsibilities and obligations (which are discussed in the next chapter) and the price of shared *ownership* was an acceptance of those. As shared *ownership*, the justification for those responsibilities and obligations could be more robust. Labels, in other words, allow things to move on rather more quickly.

Thereafter, matters moved rather swiftly. Various shared ownership programmes were set in motion—"shared ownership off the shelf" (SOOTS) in 1981; local authority shared ownership model terms and conditions, 1981; Housing Corporation model leases for shared ownership, 1981 and 1983; followed by the 1983 Housing and Planning Act and the Corporation's "do-it-yourself shared ownership" (DIYSO) scheme, 1983–84. The latter scheme was so successful that it ran out of money quickly and funds were siphoned to this programme. Two other factors helped push shared ownership along.

First, the National Federation of Housing Associations (NFHA) shared ownership working group was set up and met from September 1979; secondly, the DoE, through the Corporation, set generous grant levels (H. Parker-Brown, minute, 5 December 1980, HLG118/3966: "[The Minister] has noted that shared ownership schemes simply will not work if cost equals value.").

Neutralising the Alternatives

The policy problem that there was "an indisputable need for a wider choice in the housing market" having been crisply acknowledged by the Campbell Working Group, there were already a range of alternatives which were much further developed and much less problematic than shared ownership. The shared ownership story, which might otherwise have been presented as inexorably linear, is also the story of how something—which was technically complex and produced doubt over a range of alternatives which, if one were to be naïve, appeared better and more suitable—achieved pre-eminence.

It was by no means a given nor an inevitability that shared ownership would become the chosen alternative; nor, indeed, that there would be a single alternative. A range of schemes were in action other than shared ownership: community leasehold, co-ownership, co-operative, and leasehold schemes for the elderly. Indeed, in December 1978, the Housing Corporation announced a programme of funding for community leasehold and co-ownership. The re-labelling of shared *ownership* provided it with a veneer of value acceptability. In this section, we develop an argument about the neutralisation of the alternatives to shared ownership, essentially as largely not aligning with the incoming 1979 Conservative government's values, although there were also emerging questions about economic feasibility and the desirability of those alternatives.

Furthermore, shared ownership was by no means an accepted or politically acceptable alternative within the housing community. Policy entrepreneurs, such as Freeson and Stanley, were interested but had different ideas for its development. Stanley saw a significant role for private finance from a financial institution such as a building society or pension fund to enable the withdrawal of state subsidy (Stanley 1974: 7–8). Freeson appeared wedded to a local authority or co-operative model. While some housing specialists were actively working on the development—Notting Hill Housing Trust set up a subsidiary, Addison, because of definitional problems around their charitable status—others expressed concerns:

It was about '76 [when I joined X Housing Association] and my first reaction was, "What are [X] doing?" …. My immediate reaction at that time, this is mid-70s don't forget, was this is a travesty. This is taking resources away, scarce subsidy away from the rented housing programmes. We should be here to help the poorest, not those who could go halfway to buying a house. So I was somewhat anti it actually in the first year or so. (KS20)

In this section, we look at the way that two of the three alternatives gradually became neutralised.

Co-ownership

Co-ownership was a co-operative scheme under which members owned the freehold of the property and paid the mortgage. Their optimum size was said to be 40–50 units (Note of DoE/HC meeting: HLG118/3180). As the Campbell Working Group (1976: para 78) put it, the scheme "would not be attractive to people who preferred to think of themselves as owners". Even at that time, though, it was recognised that those schemes formed in the 1970s "have found themselves in difficulties" (para 75), and, by May 1980, "[i]t was agreed that the further development of this model should be reviewed in the light of changes in the economic climate which had made it less attractive" (Note of meeting, DoE and HC, 6 May 1980, HLG118/3865).

For a period, though, it appeared that co-ownership would be preferred. The 1975 Housing Rents and Subsidies Act set up the Co-Operative Housing Agency, a role adopted by the Housing Corporation. The Agency was powerfully supported by Reg Freeson (Hansard, 12 April 1978, cols 1385–6). The Housing Corporation set aside 10 per cent of its budget for co-operatives in 1977–78 and 1978–79, "the only difficulty is finding enough schemes to finance" (Background Note PQ 1511/77/78, HLG118/3356).

What neutralised co-ownership as an alternative were three things. First, the 1979 election took co-operatives largely off the agenda—Stanley and colleagues were not in favour. Secondly, as noted above, the financial environment simply was not favourable. Thirdly, the 1980 Act inserted a power of sale into co-ownership agreements, which was interpreted as meaning that a majority of co-owners could vote for sale over and above the wishes of others (HLG118/4140), and Stanley pressed Sir Hugh Cubitt, the then Chairman of the Housing Corporation, for action on the disposal of the remaining units (21 February 1983 HLG118/4140).

Community Leasehold

Community leasehold schemes bore an almost mimetic resemblance to the Birmingham half:half scheme. They were new-build and rehabilitation developments, under which residents bought a 50 per cent share and received a long leasehold interest (NFHA 1978: 1–2). The scheme appears to have been originally proposed by Richard Best, then Director of the NFHA, in a proposal put to the DoE on 21 February 1975 (HLG118/2703). It was recommended by the Campbell Working Party on Housing Co-Operatives. Originally, the proposal was for a co-operative tenure, tying in with Freeson's government agenda, but it was also proposed by Roger Evans of Barratts Developments, a private construction company, "which I shall be touting around the housing associations in the next few weeks, as part of my marketing drive" (HLG118/2982). He had proposed it as a "conventional solution to [property law difficulties]".

Despite this resemblance to the Birmingham scheme, there were also a number of key differences. First, and most significantly, unlike the Birmingham schemes, the "buyers" were not given an option to purchase the whole, as government grant was only payable in respect of dwellings "let or available for letting". This proved to be a significant reason for the scheme's subsequent neutralisation (although it should be acknowledged that this policy problem could have been altered quite simply). Secondly, the Birmingham schemes had struggled unsuccessfully to obtain the support of local and other building societies, which refused to lend on them. They relied on local authority mortgages. Community leasehold, on the other hand, was worked up by Richard Best and Rosie Boughton for the NFHA, *in conjunction with* the BSA, Housing Corporation, and DoE. Freeson wrote, "I consider this to be another valuable policy initiative which we should back" (Minute, 17 February 1977, HLG118/2982). This meant that "after long and tortuous negotiations", which lasted over a year (NFHA 1978: 2), the BSA approved the NFHA arrangements (W.F. Jackson minute, 14 December 1977: HLG118/2982). The approval extended to the model lease, which was developed by the NFHA. Subject to local building society office approval, buyers were potentially able to access private finance. By 14 December 1978, five schemes of 88 properties had been approved (Letter by J. Peel [Housing Corporation] to R. Mills [DoE], 14 December 1978). Further development, however, stalled because of problems in obtaining grant approvals: "As we predicted the delays in getting any [grant] approvals for [community leasehold] schemes are badly undermining the programme" (Richard Best, letter to B Quilter, DoE, 24 January 1980: HLG118/2703).

After the 1979 election, community leasehold as a product was a victim of a shift in political values. Whereas community leasehold had previously formed part of the government agenda, the 1979 election effectively killed it off. Geoffrey Finsberg, the new Under-Secretary of State at the DoE wrote, on 21 December 1980:

> As you know we have been considering the future of these schemes, and we have now decided that future shared ownership schemes should include staircasing arrangements and an option to buy. Shared ownership schemes provide an invaluable stepping stone to home ownership, and it seems to us very important that people should be able to proceed towards ownership of their existing home, and not have to move to become an owner occupier. (HLG118/2703)

From January 1981, no further schemes were approved (internal manuscript memo, DoE, I. Jordan to R. Warne, January 1981: HLG118/2703; see also Housing Corporation Circular 14/80: para 2).

Community leasehold could be seen as a policy failure. However, that is not the case. As hinted in the memos and minutes, it was that conversion into shared ownership units which was significant. Indeed, the technologies through which community leasehold was delivered—government grant, the lease, construction at below–Parker Morris standards—together with the deliverers—housing associations—and their networks—the BSA, Housing Corporation, and DoE—were a potent mix of participants. And these participants largely formed the key players in the development of shared ownership as well.

Leasehold Schemes for the Elderly

Equally significant, in terms of the understanding of shared ownership, as opposed to numerically, were leasehold schemes for the elderly. Following resolution in the Housing Act 1980, government grant was payable in respect of 30 per cent of the capital cost and the leaseholder paid 70 per cent of the remainder. The scheme was designed for downsizing outright homeowners in later life. There was no option to purchase and the lease was non-assignable—it could not be passed on and was not a mortgageable asset. The leaseholder paid a service charge to cover running costs. What is interesting about this scheme, as opposed to community leasehold, was that it was absolutely ring-fenced in discussions—there was no question about neutralising it, no doubt because the schemes were small in number and, politically, changing them would not have been helpful because of the affected constituency of consumers. Perhaps the most significant reason for low take-up was the recognition that the scheme was not a suitable product for most people.

The Housing Corporation and the Charity Commission took the view that charities could not undertake these schemes (28 October 1980, HLG118/3180). However, following *Joseph Rowntree Foundation v Attorney-General* [1983] 1 Ch 159, 175–6, it was held that such activities could, in law, be charitable. There was no requirement in charity law for benefits to be withdrawn if, for example, a beneficiary ceased to qualify (e.g. by becoming wealthy). This meant that a long lease was a legible method through which charity could be delivered. Secondly, the payment of economic consideration such that the schemes could be "a commercial enterprise capable of producing a profit for the beneficiary" was not a problem because profit was not a primary objective. This was significant because, until that point, housing associations engaging in shared ownership had been forced to set up equity sharing/shared ownership organisations (Notting Hill Housing Trust set up Addison, for example); after that point, these organisations could be charitable. So again, a battle fought regarding an alternative product facilitated the growth of shared ownership.

The Promotion of Shared Ownership

We have argued that shared ownership eventually overtook the alternatives because of the way it was conceptualised as ownership and could be more convincingly expressed as such. The political economy of housing made this transition possible. Yet, there were signals that shared ownership was much more problematic because of its lack of legal form and its hybridity. Use of the word "ownership" clearly had meaning for policy-makers, and implied choices as well as a responsibilisation of the buyer. In this section, we demonstrate how the understanding of ownership implied within shared ownership has become central to its promotion at the level of policy. This simple word, ownership, carries significant meaning in this context.

Since the 1980s, shared ownership has formed and maintained a significant part of the central government "low-cost homeownership" strategy, alongside other offerings. It has been touted as the "fourth tenure" (in addition to ownership, private, and social renting) (Sinn and Davies 2014). At times, it has been a second or third string, such as in the 1980s (when the focus was on enabling local government tenants to buy their homes and the financial environment was less conducive to its development) and the early 2000s (when policy shifted briefly to social rental housing provision and rehabilitation), or in 2010, when the majority of government grant went to its pet project to create what it liked to call "affordable rent" (in which rents were set at 80 per cent of the market rent, which paradoxically made these properties unaffordable to many on low and no income). But, what cannot be doubted is that shared ownership has outlasted many of these other pet projects, and returned to prominence again more recently, as it has become recognised (independently of, but exacerbated by, the 2008 global financial crash) that households are "stuck" in the private rented sector, paying high rents, and priced out of owner-occupation.

Over this period, shared ownership has been zealously promoted by some key players (both organisations and individuals). There was Stanley, of course, who stands out in this early period. Beyond government, housing associations themselves have been key promoters. However, what has developed is an almost unholy coalition of organisations which now advocate in shared ownership's favour. For example, two rather differently oriented organisations concerned with housing issues and the fortune of low-to-moderate income households have proposed an expansion and mainstreaming of shared ownership options (de Santos 2013; Resolution Foundation 2013). This represented something of a *volte face* for the housing charity, Shelter, given their previous concerns about lower-income households' poor access to shared ownership (Shelter 2010). However, their promotion of shared ownership appeared to be a pragmatic response to ever-worsening conditions in the wider market. Both of these reports argued that in the context of structural undersupply of housing, and the constrained access to both social housing and full homeownership, shared ownership provided access to a stable, secure form of occupation that was absent from the private rented sector and does so for a wider range of households than other low-cost homeownership schemes are able to reach.

Nevertheless, despite this quite remarkable policy discussion about shared ownership, what does stand out is that demand has been problematic. Of course, in high-value areas during property market boom periods, demand is strong because it appears to be the only choice for some low-income households "to get on the property ladder". But one of the reasons why shared ownership is re-branded is that, in other areas and at other times, demand can be problematic. Until recently—and it is difficult to put a finger on the timescale—shared ownership was not a part of mainstream property talk. One can see this as a kind of treason in the buyers not responding to the incentives and inducements to enter shared ownership, despite the awareness-raising campaigns and copious marketing.

What we develop in this section is an argument that shared ownership has been designed to meet policy aspirations; it has been taken on and developed by housing associations to meet their own ends; the provision of an expanded notion of social housing beyond purely rented housing, as a result, has been developed and the reasons for that development have been driven by a financial imperative (it is a potentially profitable enterprise for housing associations and allows them to cross-subsidise their other activities) and consumer aspirations for ownership. In order to make it work, the limited risk of shared ownership is promoted to mortgage lenders, as their funds that would also underwrite any expansion in the sector. However, its design has not always been driven by considering outcomes for owners, a point to which we return in the next chapter.

The Early Cabal

The 1979 Thatcher government committed itself to bringing forward a Housing Bill to give council tenants the right to buy their home at the earliest possible opportunity. That Bill clearly pre-occupied Stanley and the DoE. However, despite that commitment, Stanley went out of his way to promote shared ownership publicly and privately. One of his first public commitments was to open an Addison scheme. In his first significant public speech after becoming Housing Minister, he said:

> For more than 5 years I have been among those advocating equity-sharing as one of the most attractive and practical means of bridging the divide between owning and renting. It is a divide that tends to be self-perpetuating. It is generally far easier for the children of homeowners to become homeowners themselves than it is for children of tenants. … Equity sharing … provides a bridge across that divide. (HLG118/2703)

His agenda for shared ownership was clear from the outset. He was a "hands-on" minister—his handwritten notes were all over the files which we considered at the National Archive ("[U]nless you are prepared to get into the detail, all the time you've got to see the wood for the trees, absolutely. But … if you just say oh well you look after the detail, I'll just deal with the main headlines. I'll tell you, you have a very, very serious likelihood of not actually delivering."). As one of our key stakeholders put it, Stanley's approach "was quite an extraordinary approach from a minister actually, it was incredibly, almost anorak. … He was a detail person". Stanley pushed shared ownership in a number of different directions. He was the source of many new policy ideas, some of which were workable, others not.

Shared ownership emerged from the alternatives as a genuine, well-developed policy that leached into a variety of different identities: "SOOTS", a label devised by Stanley ("[H]e will be ditching 'Shared Ownership at Minimum Cost' because it sounds too dreary.": H. Parker-Brown, memo to I. Jordan, 9 March 1981), and "DIYSO", a Housing Corporation–funded programme which overran its funding limit because of excess demand, leading to money being siphoned, at Stanley's suggestion, from other Corporation programmes and extended to properties needing repair (Manuscript memo, n.d., c 1983: HLG118/4148; effectively ended by 1983 election and BSA's withdrawal of support for this extension, letter 2 June 1983).

However, what was particularly significant for shared ownership's development was the relationship which developed between Stanley and the DoE, the NFHA, and the BSA (as well as individual building societies).

The NFHA set up a working group in 1979, at the instigation of Stanley and the DoE, to discuss the development of shared ownership. Chaired by Richard Best, other members included John Coward and others involved in housing association development. However, underpinning that discussion was a recognition that the principal object of that development was Stanley's idea for self-financing provision—in other words, to take social housing provision of this type off the public sector books. Various papers were produced for this working group by its members. Graeme Duncan (a private investment consultant to the NFHA), for example, prepared a document for the third meeting on 13 January 1981, "Shared Ownership and the Quest for Private Finance", which was designed for submission to Stanley. It accompanied a kind of draft prospectus for institutional investors, and began as:

> The attached is an outline proposal to the institutional investment world to create an initial spark of interest and to try to dislodge the entrenched resistance of fund managers to put money into housing on other than a strict mortgage basis.

A principal output from that working group in June 1981 was an unpublished document, "Private Finance for Housing Associations: An NFHA Paper Intended to Stimulate Debate" (HLG118/3969). This document can be seen as the moment at which the involvement of institutional finance in the provision of social housing (often wrongly regarded as being the mid-1980s) became thinkable. As the NFHA put it, "If institutional investment could be attracted to fund the half (or whatever percentage) of the cost of each scheme not covered by the individual's mortgage (or personal cash) then shared ownership schemes would have no impact at all upon public expenditure" (6), and, further, by way of conclusion, "A real breakthrough in the use

of private finance might be possible for schemes of shared ownership if …
institutional money could be attracted into equity investment" (7). Stanley
certainly was pushing the NFHA to develop private finance to dispense with
housing association grants (Letter to Richard Best, Director NFHA, 7
December 1981, HLG118/3969; manuscript note: "Why haven't these proposals [government grant + private finance] come to me – please bring them
to this meeting": Minute, R Brown, 6 August 1981, HLG118/3966).

Shared ownership would not, however, have been possible without building society "buy-in" to the idea. The Birmingham and other local authority
schemes developed in the 1970s had been funded by local authority mortgages, but the 1979 Thatcher government effectively undercut that avenue.
That left shared ownership with a potential development problem—it would
be unaffordable to its potential customers. Building society investment in
shared owners themselves facilitated an accounting trick, therefore, in taking
the portion of shared ownership bought by the shared owner off the public
sector debt.

The enrolment of building societies was, therefore, essential, a *sine qua non*
for the development of shared ownership. The building societies, as we have
seen, had been encouraged to lend in the 1970s, but the option chaos did not
bode well for the next enrolment. It is not surprising, then, that there are
numerous letters signed by Stanley in the files at the National Archive, sent
personally to directors of the large building societies and the BSA, asking both
for their involvement in shared ownership and for them to provide information about any impediments. This is wrapped up in the story of the lease,
discussed in the next chapter, but the key point here is that these organisations
were, and were regarded as, the obligatory passage point.

The Housing Policy Aim

So far, it can be said that the idea of shared ownership produced alliances
around which people and things danced—the idea of promoting low-cost
homeownership other than through the right to buy; the possibility of lever-
ing institutional investment into its development, as opposed to central government grant; and the development of building society, instead of public
sector, loans for shared owners. Policy-makers found themselves having made
something around which they could construct an offer which appealed and
which drew on existing ownership-type legal relationships.

However, there was always an idea that shared ownership should be delivered to people in housing need. This was what animated policy-makers and

housing associations, which are (or, until recently, were) set up to meet that need. Indeed, shared ownership is said to fulfil a number of aims of housing policy: the aspiration of both policy-makers and households (assessed through tenure preference surveys) to facilitate growth in homeownership; it is said to contribute to the development of mixed-tenure estates, regeneration, and sustainability, as well as enabling more people to share in asset wealth (ODPM 2005: paras 1.4 & 2.1; see also Page 1993). In a government evaluation of shared ownership schemes, it was said that shared ownership offers value for money against a number of indicators in regions where house price markets are strong, but a weak case in other regions (Bramley et al. 2002: 82–4). Thus, there are considerable regional variations in where shared ownership properties have been developed (Bramley et al. 2002: 82–4; Pharaoh et al. 2015; NAO 2006).

Shared ownership came to be targeted on those on low incomes, those currently occupying social housing, key workers, regional priorities, armed forces personnel, as well as homeless households and/or those on social housing waiting lists for accommodation, thus plausibly contributing to meeting housing need. The verb "target" is important here because this is the "customer group" expressed through the regulatory body's capital funding guide. As Clarke (2010: 185) put it: "This has been termed the 'double whammy' effect whereby both acute housing need by the poorest households seeking social rented housing, and the aspirations of better-off existing tenants for home ownership can be met simultaneously" by creating social housing re-let opportunities as occupants move on to shared ownership. However, from 2016, the government removed all priority groups for assistance, except for armed forces personnel; it simply now states that shared ownership is aimed at "people that are in housing need who are otherwise unable to purchase a property on the open market" (HCA 2016b: 3.1.1). During 2014–15, 15 per cent of new sales were made to former social housing tenants, compared with 41 per cent who had previously been private renting and 27 per cent who had been living at home with their parents (DCLG CORE Sales Logs); only 143 sales were made to former armed forces personnel.

Despite the government desire for shared ownership to meet housing need, and the previous targeting of certain households, there was always some doubt about whether those were realistic aims. A 1993 evaluation suggested that part of the allocation process was demand led, so that if there was low demand, flexibility would be required, and target groups were not defined. Further, it noted that housing associations engaged in a "fairly rigorous process of financial scrutiny for all shared ownership applicants" (Cousins et al. 1993: 2.39). An evaluation of a particular scheme in the early 1990s, which required at least 60 per cent of buyers to be social housing tenants, noted that housing associations struggled with that target, so they sought to "define the 60% in a more flexible way" (Bramley et al. 1995: 6.14).

The requirement for buyers to have financial security, and because some social housing occupiers may well have left the sector at some point in the future in any event or purchased a property, makes the evaluation of this aspect of shared ownership problematic (see, e.g., National Audit Office 2006: paras 44–7; Clarke 2010). Eligibility criteria are now implemented by "agents", who "have effectively targeted first time buyers but this group is not necessarily the most important local priority group" (see ECOTEC 2008: para 3.5.1.3; see also Battye et al. 2006). In any event, the most recent data suggest that only 5 per cent of shared owners came from social housing rented accommodation, as opposed to 13 per cent in 2003; further increases in prices mean that buyers are generally older, mostly single, and with higher incomes (Pharaoh et al. 2015; cf. Bramley et al. 2002). Pharaoh et al. (2015: 9) make the important point about rising prices meaning rising incomes of buyers:

> As house prices across the country have increased over the past decade (albeit at different rates) so too have the prices of shared ownership properties—and of course any share of them. And this has meant that, unsurprisingly, the incomes of shared ownership buyers (both as couples and singles) have also increased. In London, for example, where prices have risen the most, the average income of a single shared ownership buyer has increased from £26,187 in 2003 to £35,449 in 2014. Given that this comes at a time when, on average, wages have remained fairly static, the higher income profile of shared ownership buyers is likely to indicate a change in the types of people moving in to shared ownership, in terms of, for example, the kinds of employment background they have.

Those average incomes are higher than the median incomes, and have risen at a steeper level over that period. The Annual Survey of Hours and Earnings median full-time annual wage was £21,008 in 2003 and £26,936 in 2014, a 28 per cent rise. Pharaoh et al.'s data suggest rises in occupier incomes by 35 per cent, a seven percentage point higher increase. As Wallace (2008b) suggests, it is unclear whether shared ownership is meeting housing need or housing demand.

(Re-)Branding

We have seen how the creation of the label "shared ownership" was so significant to its progression. However, that label has been overtaken by a number of re-branding exercises. For example, DIYSO and SOOTS were created under Stanley's tenure. There was a further attempt at DIYSO in the early 1990s, when it was offered in concert with what was termed "conventional shared ownership". In the late 1990s, an incipient scheme called "Homebuy" was created (see Bramley et al. 2002). In the mid-2000s, the New Labour government developed the shared ownership profile exponentially (see, e.g., ODPM 2005; DCLG 2007). It had become concerned about the range of available low-cost homeownership initiatives available, and had restricted council tenants' right to buy their homes. Nevertheless, the starting point for its 2006–11 review was that

> [t]he Government supports home ownership. People's homes have become more and more important to their sense of security and well-being. Yet it is becoming harder for people to bridge the gap from renting, or living with parents, to owning a home for the first time. (ODPM 2005: para 4.1)

As such, it proposed a major programme of building for low-cost home-ownership ("over 80 000 first time buyers and key workers [will be helped] to achieve their home ownership aspirations": 39), including a particular re-branded shared ownership programme. New Labour, being a particular brand in its own right, created its own new brand, "HomeBuy", and grouped the various schemes under that brand (ODPM 2005; see also Low Cost Home Ownership Task Force 2003). The intention was to simplify the complex arrangements and different processes underpinning the array of shared ownership schemes. HomeBuy incorporated four different generic schemes—social HomeBuy, new-build HomeBuy, HomeBuy direct, and rent to HomeBuy (which also incorporated a new initiative to assist first-time buyers)—and two specialist schemes—for older people and people with long-term disabilities (see ODPM 2005). The range of schemes then available reflected the ability of housing associations to seek out new areas of demand for shared ownership.

Policy 2010–

The 2010–15 Coalition government's programme for government was equally forthright in its support for shared ownership: "We will promote shared ownership schemes and help social tenants and others to own or part-own their home" (DCLG 2010: para 12). However, as has been noted above, despite that statement (and we were told in the course of our research that policy-makers were unsure how that clear commitment ended up in the programme document), the development programme focused on affordable rented products: "Offers from providers (or consortia) that only include affordable home ownership, with no Affordable Rent within the overall proposal, will not be considered" (HCA 2011: 4.5).

Since that time, shared ownership has returned to prominence, in part because of a recurrence of the same kinds of housing problems which spurred its development. The 2015–16 Cameron government had a mono-tenurial housing policy which focused solely on ownership. This was emphasised in the Conservative manifesto, where the housing policy was headed "Helping you buy a home of your own", and we were told that "everyone who works hard should be able to own a home of their own" (Conservatives 2015: 51). High rents and high property values in many areas, combined with retrenchment within the mortgage industry following the 2008 financial crisis, created the conditions in which shared ownership again provided a particular solution (not *the* solution—others were, of course, available, but many, such as controlling or regulating rents, seemed beyond the limits of government thinking).

In 2016, the UK government allocated £4.7 billion for social housing in the Affordable Homes Programme 2016–21 (HCA 2016a), and in the November 2016 Autumn Statement, it allocated a further £1.4 billion to the programme (HCA 2017a). Rather than allocate the majority of this money to programmes of social and affordable rent, this programme "marks a decisive shift towards support for home ownership" (HCA 2016b: para 3); 88 per cent was destined for shared ownership, with the aim of building 135,000 new shared ownership properties over this period. In his Ministerial Foreword to this programme, Greg Clark, the Secretary of State, wrote that "we are providing the help that aspiring home owners need right now. … For many people, [shared ownership] is a chance they didn't have before to get on to the housing ladder" (HCA 2016a: 3).

This kind of framing of shared ownership reflected Prime Minister Cameron's own framing in a speech delivered in December 2015, where he announced a major expansion to shared ownership, in which he promised "plans to radically re-invent the shared ownership scheme – opening the door to an extra 175,000 aspiring homeowners and helping to deliver [the Conservative manifesto] commitment to create 1 million more homeowners over the next five years":

> For years, we've had Shared Ownership, where you part-buy, part-rent a property. So many people are attracted to this idea, especially those who thought they'd never have a chance of owning a home.
> …
> Yet again, a government that delivers, building a nation of homeowners. (Cameron 2015)

The 2017 housing White Paper made clear that the May government continued the love affair with shared ownership, alongside other so-called affordable rent initiatives: "[W]e have made changes to simplify the [shared ownership] product in response to concerns from lenders, developers and prospective buyers. Alongside funding, this will enable the tenure to expand and help more households get a foot on the ladder where they would otherwise have been unable to" (DCLG 2017: 4.29). Furthermore, spying an opportunity, the White Paper expressed itself to be supportive of institutional investment in shared ownership (whether or not provided by housing associations) (at para 3.19), suggesting its expansion beyond the social housing sector into a more commercial arena.

Financing and Developing Shared Ownership

From the outset, shared ownership took a proportion of central government grant to the housing association sector. In the period between 1980 and 1990, there were 36,047 sales of shared ownership properties, and between 1983 and 1990, shared ownership accounted for £348.8 million of government grant (Cousins et al. 1993: Tables 1.1 and 1.2). In the period from the early 1990s until 2010, many billions of pounds of central government grant and private finance were levered into shared ownership. Although there were funding troughs, in general terms, shared ownership was well served by housing grants from central government funds for social housing development, distributed through its funding agency (the Housing Corporation and then, its successor, the Homes and Communities Agency (HCA)). Between 1990–91 and 1993–94, it captured between 11 and 17.5 per cent of the overall development programme for housing associations in England, rising to 28.5 per cent in 1996–97 (Bramley and Dunmore 1996: 109–10). That proportion rose to 30 per cent in 2004–05, and the Housing Corporation's 2006–08 investment programme devoted £970 million to shared ownership out of £3.9 billion (Hills and Lomax 2007: 15). Other developments were funded without grant by associations (around 12 per cent in 2007: Spenceley 2008: 12). We have seen above how shared ownership has been favoured in government policy more recently and how the 2016–21 grants programme has particularly targeted the development of shared ownership.

Financialisation

In addition to the policy imperatives discussed above, whether or not they have been fulfilled, there is another aspect of shared ownership development which has undoubtedly contributed to its growth: the financialisation of social housing. One of the quite simple reasons for favouring shared ownership in house building grants has been that it represents relatively good value for money, at least in certain areas, compared with social rented accommodation. As the National Audit Office found, conventional shared ownership used up around less than a half of the government grant required for social rented accommodation, and that "every £1 of public grant enabled [housing associations] to invest in £4 worth of shared ownership properties" (NAO 2006: 42 & 49, respectively; see also Bramley and Morgan 1998: 581). Furthermore, the capital grant is repaid at a faster rate than it would be otherwise with that attributed to social rental property development. And since private finance has become de rigueur in the sector, mixed with government grant, in many cases, government grant can be reduced—indeed, a good number of shared ownership developments now occur without government grant at all.

The significant financial incentive also applies to housing associations. This is not just because they were able to game the funding regime by overestimating the amount of grant they required (NAO 2006: 54–6). It was because shared ownership was a surplus-making event. Associations were entitled to keep all surpluses over and above the grant they received. This was to be placed in their recycled capital grant fund (Bramley et al. 2002: 18–9). That fund had to be spent on other housing and related activities by the association, but it gave them considerable leverage in obtaining other grants (because they could bid at a lower-cost level) or they could simply develop further schemes without grant (thus potentially freeing themselves from HCA regulation in relation to those schemes).

Although there are risks of any shared ownership scheme, such as when a new scheme is met with limited demand, the potential financial rewards—surplus—are significant. First, the lag between the award of grant and the sale of the share itself means that the value of the property might have increased. Secondly, if a buyer purchases a further share (a process known as staircasing) in a rising market, this will be at the then current market value and will give rise to further surplus. Thirdly, the association was entitled to retain interest on the recycled grant fund. This prospect of making a surplus created a capital incentive for associations to engage with the shared ownership programme. In 2014–15, for example, sales of extra shares in properties raised £239 million and sales of shared ownership properties made £924 million, "delivering a contribution to surpluses of £250 [million]" (HCA 2016c: 3); there has been annual growth in these contributions to surpluses (HCA 2017b). Further, the association will receive rent in respect of the non-purchased share, and rent rises are built into the lease (at retail price index + 2.75 per cent or thereabouts—the + factor may differ, but is usually between two and three). In other words, assuming that the units sell, the association will make a profit, which can then be used to cross-subsidise its other operations. That is why so many housing associations now operate in this sector (in 2005, it was said that there were over 300 associations engaged in shared ownership, 40 per cent more than a decade before) (Whitehead et al. 2005).

Development

There are broadly two methods by which shared ownership units might be developed. Housing associations might develop a plot of (greenfield or brownfield) land, often provided at below market value (and sometimes free) by a local authority or other public sector organisation, or they might take on units as part of a social housing subsidy from a developer under what are known as "Section 106" agreements (under Section 106, Town and Country Planning Act 1990). Of these two mechanisms, the latter requires further explanation, more particularly as it provides a central structural backdrop to some of the issues in Chap. 4.

In order to get planning permission for a development, a commercial developer will often be required by the planning authority to secure a certain number of social housing units (and/or pay a cash sum for its provision). This will be in the form of a Section 106 agreement. The housing association must pay the developer for the land, which is usually in high-value areas, and development costs—grant is payable and the negotiations between the developer, planning authority, and association bring the price down to HCA levels (Crook and Whitehead 2010). Some of this land is used for social rented housing, but developers tend to favour social ownership tenures "because they regard key workers, and more generally employed households, as good neighbours for market purchasers" and "less stigmatised" (Crook and Whitehead 2010: 111, 113). The benefit of this kind of development in policy terms is that it contributes to the development of estates with mixed tenure, which is a common policy goal, but most significantly, "the core rationale has been to achieve greater value for money from government grants and to increase the quantity of affordable housing that can be achieved" (Crook et al. 2016: 3391). S. 106 became a highly significant route for the development of affordable housing and low-cost homeownership generally, although evidence suggests that buyers of new homes moved from private sector housing or were newly formed households (*id.*, 3400).

As our data demonstrate, there are a number of pinchpoints in relation to this type of shared ownership provision (which can be summed up under the label "poor doors", that is, treating shared owners differently from others; problematic managing agents; frequently, higher specific services leading to higher service charges; and tight eligibility criteria). However, a more general pinchpoint is that this type of planning gain is susceptible to the vicissitudes of economics and, particularly, the downturn—fewer planning permissions are granted and fewer developments completed during recessionary periods. Further, government planning policy now enables developers to renegotiate these agreements on the grounds of "viability" (Section 106BA-BC) (Burgess et al. 2013).

The Geography of Shared Ownership

We have already made the point that most shared ownership is provided by housing associations, and that it is mostly concentrated in the more expensive, high-density areas. It was acknowledged in the late 1990s that government resource allocation should be "regionally skewed and targeted" (Bramley et al. 2002: 24). By 2000–01, that skew was particularly in favour of London, which received the majority of investment (56 per cent), and against the midland and northern regions (which received 15 per cent) (*id.*: para 4.3). At that time, 69 per cent of shared ownership stock was in London and the South (*id.*: Table 4.11). Given the demand in London and the South, these were also areas where there was less developmental risk and greater value for money. However, in higher-priced northern areas, Heywood (2016: 40) describes the shared ownership market as vibrant, with potential for greater development, although anecdotally, some northern providers are unsure whether shared ownership is viable in all locations. The other point—which is significant, as it links with our buyer data—is that many shared ownership properties are on estates next to owner-occupation, private and social rented properties.

Conclusions

In this chapter, we have developed the idea that shared ownership became regarded as ownership over a period of time; not that it *is* ownership, but that it became regarded as ownership through a variety of discursive techniques. This idea was significant because, as a result, it became a chosen vehicle for central government's low-cost homeownership plan (to the extent that it can be described as a plan). Behind the right to buy and help to buy, shared ownership was prominent. This was as much because shared ownership "fit" more than other schemes.

In a sense, this was quite remarkable and anything but inevitable. Shared ownership was a problematic product from the outset. It might have been killed off by the chaos it caused at different moments. True, there were key proponents, but that was also because shared ownership fit with the world to be created, a financialised world with a non-local authority, off-the-books, method of meeting housing need through ownership (and, thereby, getting people off the books, in the sense that they were owners from social housing providers, and not social renters). Organisations whose mission was to meet housing need—housing associations—bought into this vision of the future financialised world, for which shared ownership can be seen to have been the prototype. It might be said that they went with the wind, in the sense that it was clear in which direction the first Thatcher government blew. The Chair of the Notting Hill Housing Trust, Sir Roger Ormrod (a Lord Justice of Appeal), began his March 1981 report with the pessimistic note that "[g]overnment pronouncement and action in the last 18 months have confirmed that that optimistic period [following 1974] is now all but at any end" (Holmes 2005: 107). It is no surprise that associations, such as Notting Hill, with their eye on development, were following the wind; Notting Hill's subsidiary, Addison Housing Association, was formed in 1980 "to develop an expanding programme of low cost home ownership" (*id.*).

One can see this idea of shared ownership as ownership being followed through in the various re-branding exercises. From SOOTS to DIYSO, which also created "conventional" shared ownership, to the consolidation of the low-cost homeownership "programme" as HomeBuy, shared ownership has become a product marketed as ownership. We develop this marketisation of shared ownership further in Chap. 4, but the key point here is the idea, or, as Callon puts it, the actor-world.

Bibliography

Birmingham Mail (1975), 'Half and Half Homes Plan Is Launched', *Birmingham Mail*, 17th September 1975.

Battye, F., Bishop, B., Harris, P., Murie, A., Rowlands, R. and Tice, A. (2006), *Evaluation of Key Worker Living: Final Report*, London: DCLG.

Bramley, G., Dunmore, K., Durrant, C. and Smart, G. (1995), *Do-It-Yourself Shared Ownership: An Evaluation*, London: Housing Corporation.

Bramley, G. and Dunmore, K. (1996), 'Shared Ownership: Short-Term Expedient or Long-Term Major Tenure?', 11(1), *Housing Studies*: 105–31.

Bramley, G. and Morgan, J. (1998), 'Low Cost Home Ownership Initiatives in the UK', 13(4), *Housing Studies*: 567–86.

Bramley, G., Morgan, J., Cousins, L., Dunmore, K., Three Dragons Consultancy and MORI Social Research (2002), *Evaluation of the Low Cost Home Ownership Programme*, London: ODPM.

Burgess, G., Crook, T. and Monk, S. (2013), *The Changing Delivery of Planning Gain through Section 106 and the Community Infrastructure Levy*, Cambridge: Cambridge Centre for Housing and Planning Research.

Cameron, D. (2015), 'This Is a Government that Delivers', 7th December, https://www.gov.uk/government/news/prime-minister-this-is-a-government-that-delivers

Campbell Working Group (1976), *New Forms of Social Ownership and Tenure*, Unpublished.

Clarke, A. (2010), 'Shared Ownership: Does It Satisfy Government and Household Objectives?', in S. Monk and C. Whitehead (eds), *Making Housing More Affordable: The Role of Intermediate Tenures*, Oxford: Wiley Blackwell.

Conservatives (2015), *The Conservative Party Manifesto*, London: The Conservative Party.

Cousins, L., Ledward, C., Howe, K., Rock, G. and Taylor, G. (1993), *An Appraisal of Shared Ownership*, London: HMSO.

Crook, T. and Whitehead, C. (2010), 'Intermediate Housing and the Planning System', in S. Monk and C. Whitehead (eds), *Making Housing More Affordable: The Role of Intermediate Tenures*, Oxford: Blackwell.

Crook, T., Bibby, P., Ferrari, E., Monk, S., Tang, C. and Whitehead, C. (2016), 'New Housing Association Development and Its Potential to Reduce Concentrations of Deprivation: An English Case Study', 53(16), *Urban Studies*: 3388–404.

De Santos, R. (2013), *Homes for Forgotten Families: Towards a Mainstream Shared Ownership Market*, London: Shelter.

Department for Communities and Local Government (DCLG) (2007), *Homes for the Future: More Affordable, More Sustainable*, Cm 7191, London: DCLG.

Department for Communities and Local Government (DCLG) (2010), *The Coalition: Our Programme for Government on Communities and Local Government*, London: DCLG.

Department for Communities and Local Government (CLG) (2017), *Fixing Our Broken Housing Market*, London: DCLG.

Department of the Environment (DoE) (1977), *Housing Policy—A Consultative Document*, London: HMSO.

ECOTEC (2008), *Evaluation of the HomeBuy Agents in the Delivery of the National Affordable Housing Programme 2006/08*, London: ECOTEC.

Forrest, R., Lansley, S. and Murie, A. (1984), *A Foot on the Ladder? An Evaluation of Low Cost Home Ownership Initiatives*, Working Paper No 41, Bristol: School for Advanced Urban Studies, University of Bristol.

Heywood, A. (2016), *From the Margins to the Mainstream: A Study of the Prospects for Shared Home Ownership in the North West*, London: The Smith Institute.

Hills, S. and Lomax, A. (2007), *Whose House Is It Anyway? Housing Associations and Home Ownership*, London: Housing Corporation/Coventry: CIH.

Holmes, C. (2005), *The Other Notting Hill*, Studley: Brewin Books.

Homes and Communities Agency (HCA) (2011), *Affordable Homes Programme 2011 to 2015: Guidance and Allocations*, London: HCA.

Homes and Communities Agency (HCA) (2016a), *Shared Ownership and Affordable Homes Programme 2016–21: Prospectus*, London: HCA.

Homes and Communities Agency (HCA) (2016b), *Capital Funding Guide*, London: HCA.

Homes and Communities Agency (HCA) (2016c), *2015 Global Accounts of Housing Providers*, London: HCA.

Homes and Communities Agency (HCA) (2017a), *Shared Ownership and Affordable Homes Programme 2016–21: Addendum to the Prospectus*, London: HCA.

Homes and Communities Agency (HCA) (2017b), *2016 Global Accounts of Housing Providers*, London: HCA.

Jacobs, K. and Manzi, T. (2017), '"The Party's Over": Critical Junctures, Crises and the Politics of Housing Policy', 32(1), *Housing Studies*: 17–34.

Kingdon, J. (2011), *Agendas, Alternatives and Public Policies*, Boston: Longman.

Law, J. (2002), *Aircraft Stories: Decentring the Object in Technoscience*, Durham: Duke UP.

Low Cost Home Ownership Task Force (2003), *A Home of My Own*, The Report of the Government's Low Cost Home Ownership Task Force, London: Housing Corporation.

Lowe, S. (2004), *Housing Policy Analysis: British Housing in Comparative and Cultural Context*, Basingstoke: Macmillan.

Malpass, P. (2000a), 'The Discontinuous History of Housing Associations in England', 15(2), *Housing Studies*: 195–212.

Malpass, P. (2000b), *Housing Associations and Housing Policy: A Historical Perspective*, Basingstoke: Macmillan.

Malpass, P. (2005), *Housing and the Welfare State: The Development of Housing Policy in Britain*, Basingstoke: Palgrave Macmillan.

McDermont, M. (2010), *Governing, Independence, and Expertise: The Business of Housing Associations*, Oxford: Hart Publishing.

Murie, A. (1975), *The Sale of Council Houses: A Study in Social Policy*, CURS Occasional Paper No 35, Birmingham: University of Birmingham.

Murie, A. (2016), *The Right to Buy: Selling off Public and Social Housing*, Bristol: Policy Press.

National Audit Office (2006), *A Foot on the Ladder: Low Cost Home Ownership Assistance*, HC 1048 Session 2005–2006, London: NAO.

National Federation of Housing Associations (NFHA) (1978), *A Handbook for Community Leasehold*, London: NFHA.

Office of the Deputy Prime Minister (2005), *HomeBuy—Expanding the Opportunity to Own*, Consultation Paper, London: ODPM.

Osman, A. (1975), 'A New Kind of Owner-Occupier', *The Times*, 18th September.

Page, D. (1993), *Building for Communities*, York: Joseph Rowntree Foundation.

Pharaoh, R., Holland, J. and Wooton, J. (2015), *A Fair Share? Understanding Residents' Experiences of Shared Ownership*, London: Viridian Housing.

Resolution Foundation (2013), *One Foot on the Ladder: How Shared Ownership Can Bring Owning a Home into Reach*, London: Resolution Foundation.

Shelter (2010), *The Forgotten Households—Is Intermediate Housing Meeting Affordable Housing Needs?*, London: Shelter.

Sinn, C. and Davies, S. (2014), *Shared Ownership 2.0: Towards a Fourth Mainstream Tenure*, London: Orbit Group; Coventry: Chartered Institute of Housing.

Spenceley, J. (2008), *Trends in Housing Association Stock in 2007*, A Dataspring Briefing Paper on Behalf of the Housing Corporation, Cambridge: Dataspring.

Stanley, J. (1974), *Shared Purchase: A New Route to Home-Ownership*, London: Conservative Political Centre.

Wallace, A. (2008b), *Achieving Mobility in the Intermediate Housing Market: Moving Up and Moving On?*, York: Joseph Rowntree Foundation.

Whitehead, C., Spenceley, J. and Kiddle, C. (2005), *The Role of Housing Associations in the Intermediate Market*, London: Housing Corporation.

3

The Lease

Introduction

In the previous chapter, we developed a history in which some fairly complex ideas became enjoined into one simple, financialised product, and which became known as shared ownership. Despite the complexity inherent in the idea of ownership, shared ownership had a fit with housing policy. We noted how the label led to a legal puzzle, for there was no such thing as shared ownership. This chapter is concerned with how shared ownership became legible. It is a story of the way a long-used and well-known technique, the lease, was manipulated so that it became the device through which shared ownership was and is delivered. It is another remarkable story. It enabled KS3 to say, in one breath, that shared ownership is not complicated, and, later on in our interview, recognise that it was rather more complicated than that. It was the lease which produced the option chaos and, as we develop in this chapter, other problematics. Nevertheless, despite its well-known failings (see, e.g., Karn et al. 1985; Stewart 1981), the lease was adopted as the legal technique for the delivery of this complex idea.

If the key to shared ownership is the idea of ownership, then the use of the lease emphasised its in-betweenness. The shared owner's property interest is defined through the medium of a lease. The lease is used both for other flat-owners, as a long lease (e.g. for 99 or 125 years), and for renters, usually as a periodic lease (e.g. as a monthly tenancy[1]) or a lease for a shorter fixed term. For property lawyers, whether they are short or long, the two are exactly the

---

[1] The "lease" and the "tenancy" are, in law, the same device.

© The Author(s) 2018
D. Cowan et al., *Ownership, Narrative, Things*, Palgrave Socio-Legal Studies,
https://doi.org/10.1057/978-1-137-59069-5_3

same device—the leasehold estate in land. In housing policy terms, however, an awkward distinction is drawn so that the leaseholder "fits" with its own coding as owner or renter. In the usual run of events, that coding may well represent the on-the-ground reality. However, as we noted in the introduction, the long leaseholder/owner must also recognise that they do not have the control over the property that is implied by the ownership label. In shared ownership, this lack of control is particularly emphasised through the lease.

In this chapter, we analyse why the lease was selected over and above other legal techniques as the medium through which the complex idea of shared ownership was carried. We look at the further problems (beyond the option chaos) that this caused initially. Then, we drill down into particular terms of the lease to demonstrate two points: first, how the lease was designed to simulate the idea of ownership, or at least how ownership as a comparator was used to justify what might be regarded as penal clauses; and secondly, how the audience for the lease was not the buyer—their interest was largely secondary— but the building societies. Just as in the previous chapter, our understandings are rooted in history, but we also demonstrate how some translations have produced awkward moments in the lifetime of shared ownership.

This chapter marks a significant point in this book. Our discussion about the lease symbolises a turn towards a mixture of people and things. It is here that our argument, outlined in Chap. 1, that things can have a legal consciousness takes life. We make good on our assertion that although the lease itself has no consciousness, it becomes invested with the hopes, fears, anxieties, and consciousness of the entities by and through which it is selected as the appropriate technique, drawn, re-drawn, and interpreted.

This chapter has itself been made possible by two interventions that challenge conventional understandings of the lease as a neutral, technical legal artefact, or, as Hunter puts it, a "dry and dusty document full of clauses" which is "blackboxed" so that its inner working are taken for granted and unexamined. Instead, in a case study of a conflict between a freeholder and leaseholders about the installation of solar panels, Hunter prompts us to think of the lease as a socio-legal object with potentially profound abilities to shape the social world, which has tangible effects upon the social networks of which it is a component (Hunter 2015). Secondly, on a different scale, Keenan (2013) analyses the use of compulsory leases of aboriginal land by Australia's federal government. Noting that the signature right granted by a lease—exclusive possession—was not taken up by the government, she suggests that the use of leases in these circumstances should lead to an analysis not only of what belongs to whom, but also "the space that property produces, the space that governs who and what belongs and who and what are out of place" (Keenan 2013: 492). Taking this suggestion out of its setting, that is also the purpose of this chapter. Our analysis in this chapter demonstrates how an apparently neutral legal document produces its own actor-world and gives life to a peculiar form of government.

The Lease: An Original Narrative

It was by no means apparent that the lease would be the selected legal technique for delivering shared ownership. There were other options available, although in the mid-to-late 1970s, each of these other options had flaws. It was noted that "it is for consideration whether there are ways and less cumbersome to achieve equity sharing than the present schemes [sic] for leases and options – but nothing worthwhile has yet been suggested" (Minute, J. Golding, "Equity Sharing Arrangements", July 1979, HLG118/3772).

Alternative mechanisms had been canvassed at different times. For example, in 1976, there was discussion over whether the local authority might sell the freehold of the property subject to a rentcharge[2]: "I do not wish to flog a dead horse, but the idea of equity sharing schemes on the basis of occupier as freeholder and the local authority as rentcharge owner continues to have potentially substantial attractions compared with the basis of occupier as lessee and local authority as lessor adopted in the Birmingham scheme" (C. Durham, minute, 19 October 1976 to R. Cumming, HLG118/2968). However, by that time, the Law Commission had published a report recommending the "severe curtailment of the rentcharge system ... [which] has been accepted and will be put into legislation" (H7b, handwritten memo, 20 October 1976 [HLG118/2968]). The one option which does not appear to have been considered was the trust for sale, which would have enabled the property to be held in trust for the benefit of the housing association and the buyer in their respective shares, but this may be explained by its problematic status in land law at that time.

In any event, and rather more mundanely, the DoE's resources were stretched at the key moment in time, as the Department was working on reviews of housing finance and the Rent Acts (Internal DoE paper, "Alternative forms of tenure: Submission to the Minister", n.d., c 1976). The lease had been used by Birmingham, and apparently copied by the GLC, which had

---

[2] A periodical payment in respect of land that is not related to a landlord and tenant relationship—so, the buyer could take the freehold of the property subject to a rentcharge in favour of the housing association.

received details of Birmingham's scheme and lease. The local authorities appear to have simply adopted that lease. A mimetic process is apparent. The real genius of the use of the lease for local authorities lay in its creative use of the funding scheme. The local authority obtained Exchequer subsidy on the rented part *and* was entitled to receive subsidy on the portion of loan charges remaining in its housing revenue account (Letter, Birmingham City Council to Sir Idwald Pugh, DoE, 13 March 1975). Following that letter, there was a meeting at the DoE, which resulted in a formal response from the DoE:

> As regards subsidy, I am glad to be able to confirm the Department's agreement in principle that when a half interest in a housing revenue account dwelling is disposed of under the scheme, the Secretary of State's discretion under paragraph 8 of Schedule 1 to the Housing Rents and Subsidies Act 1975 will be exercised so as to reduce the housing subsidy payable in respect of that dwelling to 50% of the amount that would otherwise be payable. (Letter, 10 June 1975, GLC archive)

The Birmingham lease gave the council the right of first refusal—known as a right of pre-emption—if the owner wished to sell their interest in the property (either by way of assignment or by way of underlease) within five years of the date of sale (Clause 16(A)). The DoE's letter confirmed their view that "it would be reasonable in principle in those circumstances simply to restore subsidy to its 100% level", although settlement would have to be on a case-by-case basis.

In other words, Birmingham's transactions were protected whatever they decided to do, and this was dependent on the legal technique adopted, that is, the lease. In fact, within the DoE, this hedging of subsidy caused some consternation:

> [W]ith local authority schemes, subsidy continues to be paid after the initial leasehold disposal of the house to the occupier, in proportion to the local authority's remaining interest. In the case of the housing association schemes, there is capital grant on the houses! – can such capital grant be too easily represented as an unacceptable subvention to the occupier of the house, perhaps to the extent of a scandal? (Minute, J. Golding, "Equity Sharing Arrangements", July 1979, HLG118/3772)

This choice of the lease caused further technical problems and uncertainties. There was the option chaos, of course. But, in addition, there were issues around stamp duty and enfranchisement. As regards stamp duty, the problem was when this tax should be paid. Ordinarily, stamp duty is paid as a percentage of the purchase price of a property. However, a key question was whether the entire stamp duty should be paid upfront or whether it could be paid only on the percentage purchased. The legislation suggested the former, and the matter had to be settled by further legislation (s. 96, Finance Act 1980) to enable the buyer to choose when to pay the stamp duty (either upfront or when the freehold was bought).

Enfranchisement was a rather more significant problem. Legislation had been introduced in 1967 to enable long leaseholders to force the freeholder to sell them the freehold interest at a low price. This would be a problem for the shared ownership lease. The resolution by Birmingham and others was to keep the rent above the level at which the right to enfranchise became available. However, that meant that the rent level was actually higher than it might have been. It also meant that local authorities could not sell at intermediate values between 50 per cent and 100 per cent. As was accepted by the DoE, the problem was "a serious obstacle to the Minister's intention to make shared ownership more flexible" (H9a, minute 23rd April 1980, HLG 118/3358). Birmingham and the other early local authority providers complained to Stanley, who committed himself to ameliorating the problem. The simple outcome was to remove shared ownership leases from the general law on enfranchisement in the Housing Act 1980 (s. 140).

Developing the Lease

That the lease was used as the legal technique for delivering local authority shared ownership in the 1970s does not necessarily explain why it was used by housing associations subsequently. The historical record suggests that rather different reasons emerged, and its subsequent development into a *model* lease and required clauses by the Housing Corporation for use by housing associations was equally significant. Three particular features of the lease made it the appropriate vehicle for the translation of the policy aspirations: precedent, adaptability, and universality. It is important to this narrative that there were positive choices for using the lease. Not only did the lease bound what was possible, it also produced the conditions that made the product possible in the long term. While the characteristics of a lease were well known, there was still the ability to tinker at the margins. And it was this particular characteristic that proved the saving of the scheme.

Precedent

Precedent is second nature to the law; the scope for invention is limited, particularly as regards land—as was said in 1834, "[I]t must not be supposed that incidents of a novel kind can be devised and attached to property" (Lord Brougham,

Keppell v Bailey (1834) 2 Myl & K 517, 535). That is the lawyer's problem with housing tenures (see Blandy and Goodchild 1999), which effectively limited the legal technologies available to the pioneers of shared ownership.

The lease is a historical artefact, having been formed in the twelfth century, and is a curious mixture in its own right of contract and property law. It is both a personal contract, with rights and obligations, as well as giving rights and obligations in property law. As a subject area, the lease had been through successive translations in its lengthy history until it had reached a kind of stability by the time of the Conveyancing and Law of Property Act 1881. There were learned treatises (the best known practitioner text, *Woodfall's Landlord and Tenant* was first published in 1890). The law was developing case by case, but, by and large, its terms had crystallised. That stability was reached by a process of interpretation, translation, and further interpretation until meanings of terms such as "rent", "repair", and "forfeiture" had become more fixed and understood, at least within a certain milieu. Even outside that milieu, as Stanley put it, "I know full well the legal complexities of equity sharing. But the technical complexities of a modern aircraft do not debar ordinary people from flying. Nor should the technicalities of equity sharing come in the way of people enjoying its benefits" (Speech to Shelter, July 1979, HLG118/3168).

The other significant aspect of precedent lay in the format of the shared ownership lease to be developed. There was the Birmingham lease, but, as it developed, that was less significant because building societies tended to refuse to lend on that lease as security—the original shared owners received local authority mortgages. However, there were other live precedents. Recall from Chap. 2 that shared ownership effectively replaced community leasehold, and the leasehold schemes for the elderly were accepted. Both were dependent on leases. Both had standardised precedents (NFHA 1978), the former of which was acceptable to the BSA because it had been negotiated alongside the BSA. Both were adaptable to shared ownership.

The community leasehold lease had formed the basis for the draft Housing Corporation model, which then formed the basis for the Notting Hill Housing Trust (Addison) lease (Ralph Raby, Director, Addison Housing Association, paper prepared for NFHA Shared Ownership Working Party, 18 September 1981, HLG118/3966). Furthermore, "[t]he NHHT lease seems to be well received by [Building] Societies which have seen it. We are now sending it out to five leading Societies, asking if they will give one mortgage each on five flats to be completed shortly as a test working of the new system. So far this has had a good reception". And as was said of the leasehold schemes for the elderly lease, "After considering various forms of tenure, a long lease was selected as the best means of safeguarding the interests of the leaseholder, the association and the government grant. It is acceptable by lawyers, familiar to the layman and the conveyancing procedures are similar to those for freehold property" (NFHA 1978).

Adaptability and Universality

Precedent, however, does not imply ossification. The real creativity was the manipulation of this mundane document to meet the requirements of something rather new. It was this document and the ideas it contained that did the rounds between barristers, solicitors, the NFHA, the BSA, the DoE and its Ministers. More than this, it was this document which structured the discussions and negotiations. To be sure, policy-makers drove it forward, but the lease made their positions simultaneously both possible and impossible. Crucially, the NFHA Working Group and the BSA were able to devise significant protections for lenders *on the terms of the lease itself.* We detail these adaptations below.

Despite their evident complexity as a tool for lay persons, they were a generally understood technology by the "key" players (in the policy community). Such a document could be negotiated; model clauses could be produced. Indeed, the fact that *model* leases could be negotiated, agreed, and produced was hugely significant. As John Stanley put it in our interview, "Thank Heavens for the lease. It made uniform nationwide coverage possible." It was the model lease which made replication on a large scale possible.

However, that is slightly reductive. In the late 1970s, housing associations and local authorities were developing shared ownership. By the mid-1980s, however, the mantle had fallen to housing associations. By that time, there was statutory provision enabling local authorities to grant shared ownership instead of the right to buy, but the market and the discount meant that few shared ownership properties were sold by local authorities. In any event, it is plausible to suggest that the die had already been cast. The great move was the promulgation by the Housing Corporation of a model lease in 1981.

The DoE—against Stanley's judgement—had set its face against a model lease, producing model clauses and a Circular. There had been "[a] series of discussions, aimed at producing a shared ownership lease acceptable to the building societies, ... between Birmingham City Council (the pioneer authority in shared ownership sales) and several leading building societies. These talks were held with the approval and assistance of the Building Societies Association. Some progress was made but there were still two major legal obstacles" (HLG118/2968). The two problems—questions over the validity of the option clause and concerns that a prohibition on assignment meant that the lender's security might not be safe—were largely resolved by the Housing Act 1980. Nevertheless, these tentative discussions came to an end.

And with their coming to an end, the BSA approval, which the Minister jealously sought, was not forthcoming. True, the BSA had agreed the model clauses produced by the DoE, which were circulated on 6 February 1981. However, as the BSA put it, in Circular 2457 on 10 February 1981, "The [DoE] told the [BSA] in August 1980 … that it had decided against a recommended standard lease. The [BSA] replied that this would mean much more work for societies and that Shared Ownership would be less likely to succeed with local authorities." And further, their agreement with the clauses was, at best, lukewarm: "The [BSA's] working group has completed its discussions with the [DoE] … and it is believed that they are now in a form which should make them more acceptable to building societies."

Following a letter from Stanley to the managers of the leading building societies inquiring what the issues were with the local authority scheme, and whether their society had issued guidance to its branches endorsing lending on shared ownership (22 September 1981, HLG118/3966), the responses were clear:

> [W]hile I dislike the inflexible imposition of model leases, they do in fact save a lot of time. Some of the leases produced by Local Authorities while beyond reproach as comprehensible and protective documents, are too clumsy and too long. (Letter, J. Spalding, Deputy General manager, Halifax Building Society to J. Stanley, 18 November 1981)

> The extent of the variations sought by these local authorities is such that consideration and approval of the documents is a time-consuming task. … [], no local authority shared ownership scheme has been approved by the society since 1st October last. There is no doubt whatever that it is the absence of standard documentation which brings this situation about. (C. Thonton, General Manager, Abbey National, letter to J. Stanley, 13 January 1982)

This point was reinforced at a seminar by the BSA: "I grabbed the opportunity to find out what points were causing difficulty and why the BSA wanted a model lease. He agreed to send me a bit of the variety of provisions being inserted in the many different leases used by local authorities. However, the desire for consistency was clearly uppermost in their minds" (R. Mance, handwritten memo to Mr Corner following meeting with Mr Armstrong [BSA], 11 May 1982, HLG118/4123).

The groundwork for the 1981 model housing association shared ownership lease was done by the NFHA Working Group and the Housing Corporation. It was recognised at the first meeting of the Working Group on 25 November 1980 that this was a priority because "any changes would affect other matters relating to shared ownership schemes". In other words, the model lease wagged the shared ownership tail. The reasoning behind the drafting of a model lease will, by now, be familiar: "The [Housing Corporation] argue that [a model lease] will encourage building societies to provide mortgages and prevent associations needlessly repeating one another's work. Small associations in particular may accept shared ownership more readily if they can use a model lease. In the face of these arguments we are not seeking to dissuade the Corporation from preparing the model" (J. Bradley, submission to the Minister, 18 August 1980, HLG118/2259).

Acceptability

What emerged from these discussions was the model lease promulgated by the Housing Corporation in February 1981 (Housing Corporation Circular 14/80, Annex A). The draft was much discussed and negotiated. For example, an issue arose over nomination rights, which are akin to the right of first refusal. Housing associations wished to retain the ability to nominate a new buyer for the property when a shared owner wished to sell. The BSA's concerns about those rights were assuaged because of their "ultimate security over the freehold and full value of the property ... their objections to restrictions on re-sale and on nominations are only concerned with the freedom of the owner occupier and they were reassured that, although this did limit freedom, it ensured that shared ownership was not open to abuse and gave benefit .... to the occupier, who would not have to pay estate agents to find a purchaser" (Richard Best, NFHA Memo to Working Party, 8 October 1981). As Hugh Cubitt, the Housing Corporation Chairman, put it to Stanley, following representations made by the Bradford and Bingley Building Societies, these nomination rights were exactly the same as existed in the community leasehold lease (18 December 1981, HLG 118/3969).

Ultimately, the lease met with the BSA's approval. The degree to which attention was given to the BSA's interest, and subsequently, is explained in the following extract from a letter from the Corporation's solicitors, which had drafted the lease in which they explained their purpose in so doing:

The shared ownership lease that we drafted for the Housing Corporation was drafted amongst other things to be readily saleable upon the open market. With this objective in mind we consulted the Building Societies Association and attended numerous meetings with a panel of Building Society Solicitors which was set up to consider the scheme and the draft lease. Ultimately the BSA – insofar as they are able – gave their seal of approval to the Model House and Flat lease produced. ... Since the original BSA approval we have kept continuously in touch with the BSA and various minor amendments have with their agreement been made to the Model form. (Hamlins, Grammer & Hamlin, Letter re South Shropshire DC controversy, 16 January 1983: HLG118/3358)

The BSA publicised its acceptability in its quarterly letter to its members, in rather more glowing terms than it had done regarding the local authority model clauses:

The Housing Corporation is about to promulgate to housing associations in England and Wales a new model lease for shared ownership. The draft of this model has been discussed with the Association and seven major societies over recent months and many amendments and alterations had been made at the request of the Association and those societies. ... It is hoped that in the modified form ... it ought not to cause too many problems. (BSA information letter, October 1981, para 53: HLG118/3969)

Even that approval in itself was negotiated. Richard Best, the Housing Corporation, and its solicitors negotiated with the BSA so that they "omitted the off-putting remarks of an earlier draft concerning the model clauses for nominations/restrictions on sales" (NFHA Working Group minutes, 16 November 1981, HLG 118/3865).

Clauses

The model lease which took shape was, in one sense, in conventional form. It looked like a long lease (for 99 years) and was in the form of what is commonly described as a "full repairing lease", which underpins most flat ownership in England and Wales. That is, the buyer was responsible for the payment of all repairs and all service charges, expressed as a proportion attributable to their property. Various other non-standard clauses were also inserted, however. There was the nominations clause, there were provisions regarding the calculation of the rent and increases (Sch. 4), and there were provisions regarding staircasing and the calculation of the premium (Sch. 5).

In this section, we address the reasons behind two clauses: the buyer's repairing obligations, and what is known as the "mortgagee protection clause". As regards the former, there is a singular question which is troubling: an occupier buys a share but, on the terms of the model lease, is responsible for the *entire* cost of repairs and service charges apportioned to their unit of accommodation. So, for example, if you buy a 25 per cent share, you will still be responsible for 100 per cent of the repairs and service charge. How can this be fair? As regards the latter, this clause guarantees lenders the return of their capital, interest, and costs in the event of a repossession; the outstanding point is that it does so over and above any state subsidy paid to the housing association, so that, in certain circumstances, the association can make a loss on a lender's sale of the property.

Our point in this section is that these clauses involve the translation of two rather different sets of ideas into the one document.

Repairing Obligations

3.4.3 To pay to the Landlord on demand a fair and proper proportion (to be conclusively determined by the Landlord (who shall act reasonably)) of:
(a) the expense of cleaning, lighting, repairing, renewing, decorating, maintaining and rebuilding any Communal Facilities; and
(b) the reasonable costs, charges and expenses incurred by the Landlord in connection with the provision, maintenance and management of the Communal Facilities.
(HCA 2013: Clause 3.4.3)

On Stanley's idea for the scheme, the buyer was responsible for 100 per cent of the repairs, essentially because of the administrative work involved in apportioning the costs. Although he struggled with this element, his rationale was that responsibility for upkeep "represents a fair *quid pro quo* for the small element of subsidy in the scheme. It also provides the occupier with an incentive to buy out the institutional interest in the house; this is desirable as far as the Exchequer is concerned as it reduces the risk of a cash shortfall in the agency" (Stanley 1974: 16). There is something significant about Stanley's struggle here, because it is the incentive to buy the whole that provides the significant rationale. Indeed, this clause can be regarded as a totem for other clauses which appear to be weighted against the consumer.

The other central reason that was provided for this clause gives an indication of the train of thought encapsulated in it. Consumers were *buyers* and *owners*, not renters.[3] In an early draft of ministerial guidance, the following (with original gendered language) demonstrates civil servants' expression of this rationality:

> A share owner secures his property by means of a lease. He is an <u>owner</u> and no longer a <u>secure tenant</u> .... He should be regarded as far as possible as an owner occupier – he has taken on his house with a view to full home ownership at a later stage – and enjoy those rights and responsibilities. ... He would be responsible for maintenance costs and keeping his property in a reasonable state of repair. (Dated 1979, annexed to note of meeting: Shared Ownership Model Scheme, 6 May 1980, HLG 118/3865; original emphasis)

This assumption of staircasing out to full ownership at a later stage is one which underpins the idea of shared ownership—it only works financially for the buyer if that is what they do—but frequently buyers are unable to do so because of affordability problems. Similarly, in a draft commentary on a draft local authority scheme, the point was starkly made:

> Although a shared owner is often referred to as part tenant and part owner, he is, in fact and in law, a lessee who has paid a substantial premium for his lease and entitled to be regarded as an owner occupier. Therefore, insofar as his lease contains covenants concerning his rights and responsibilities, these should not differ from the covenants that would be contained in a more conventional long lease. (N.H. Perry, Shared Ownership: Model Scheme, 28 July 1980, para 21: HLG 118/2259)

The apparently neutral but also apparently inexplicable clause by which the consumer who buys a quarter share but is nevertheless responsible for the whole of the apportioned repairs now becomes explicable. By a sleight of hand, the relationship between the lease and the shared ownership label (a product of John Stanley himself), combined with the political priority to produce "low-cost homeownership", produced a way of thinking about the consumer as owner, and which produced the apparent inequity of this clause.

---

[3] There was a similar discussion about exempting shared owners from the registration of their rents under the Rent Act 1977: "The justification for the proposal would be that shared ownership is perceived as a form of owner-occupation, not of renting, *whatever the legal position may be*, and ought to be treated as such": *Promotion of Privately Financed Shared Ownership*, 1986, HLG 118/4195; our emphasis.

The Mortgagee Protection Clause

If a mortgagee of the leaseholder … exercises the right to purchase the Lease of the Premises … and directs the Landlord … to grant the Lease to another and the purchase price obtainable from that other person in the grant of the Lease is insufficient to meet:

a. |the mortgagees reasonable and proper expenses incurred in exercising its power of sale under the mortgage deed and in exercising the right to purchase the Lease of the Premises (as aforesaid).

b. The premium payable for the said Lease …

c. The amount of the principal and not exceeding 12 months unpaid interest due to the mortgagee under the terms of the mortgage. (Model Shared Ownership Flat Lease, October 1981, Clause 8)

Mortgagees are given additional protection under the shared ownership lease than is offered in conventional mortgages. This gives Mortgagees the right to be able to recover a certain amount of loss from providers as Landlords. In accordance with our instructions we have altered the operation of the Mortgagee Protection Clause. The amount of the claim is now defined as the "Mortgagee Protection Claim". (HCA 2010: para 2.1.2)

Inscription is rarely without purpose or meaning. The production of legibility of shared ownership was tied up with a question which provided focus and purpose: the generation of private finance. The rolling out of shared ownership as a product would have been impossible without the lending institutions. What we demonstrate here is how the audience was engaged (and intended to be engaged) by the terms of the lease, both in its drafting and in the selection of format.

The "mortgagee protection clause" was modelled on the provision in the community leasehold lease (J. Hill, Shared Ownership with Staircasing: Draft Model Lease, 9 July 1980, para 8: HLG 118/2259). The BSA requested the same protection in the shared ownership lease, as in that lease. Given that the principle/precedent had been previously agreed, that protection was never in doubt. It was used as leverage by the NFHA Working Party's legal representation to obtain the nominations clause. However, it was still recognised that the mortgagee has "exceptional security" (Hamlins, Grammar & Hamlin, Letter 16 January 1984). In papers to the NFHA Working Party meeting on 16 November 1981, a worked example of the mortgagee protection clause was provided by Ralph Raby, who noted:

I should like to point out how well the Mortgagee is protected by the new lease … [worked example] This shows that the Mortgagee cannot lose even if the value of the property falls by 25%, the Mortgagor has no equity (ie 100% mortgage), interest arrears are a year at top rates and expenses are over 8% of value. The Mortgagee is so well secured that he could hardly object to any terms in the lease, but how did the DoE make such a concession. (Letter, R. Raby, Director, Addison Housing Association to C. Adams, Housing Corporation, 5 November 1981)

The lenders to whom we spoke in the course of our research similarly regarded it as "better than you will get in any other market. It is a pretty golden comfort blanket" (KS10).

The only question was whether the BSA should be given that protection, which caused a risk to government subsidy, or should be given an indemnity from the Housing Corporation (under s. 111, Housing Act 1980), which would come from public money. The latter would have to be scored against their guarantee limit and would have resulted in less public money for housing association development. There were also concerns about the use of s. 111 powers being the thin end of the wedge:

Our board has agreed in principle to the use of s.111 powers in this context but we wonder whether it is necessary to set in train a process which will be hard to stop. We prefer the [mortgagee protection clause] leaving any shortfall to be funded by the association, which would usually mean through a less than 100% repayment of [government grant]. Such a solution has a number of attractions, not the least being that in contrast to a claim under s.111, for which the Corporation has not specific funds available, settlement via [grant] has no effect on current financing. (John Gatward, letter to I. Jordan, 12 May 1981, HLG118/3966)

Having been granted the former, a problem emerged at a seminar run by the Chartered Building Societies Institute on 23rd September 1981:

I was taken to task by representatives of a number of different societies, including the Halifax, about the reluctance of the Housing Corporation to provide guarantees to building societies under s.111. …

If the Corporation's views have been accurately represented, it does appear unreasonable that they should set aside sufficient funds to meet the unlikely contingency that all guarantees would be called, and all in the same year. Nor do I believe that the provision in the model lease for shared ownership whereby a building society lender would have first charge on the whole of the equity is an adequate substitute for s.111. It does not give the society the assurance that it will be saved the delay, expense and opprobrium of having to take action for possession. (P. Fletcher, Housing Corporation, and s. 111 Indemnities, 24 September 1981)

Individual building societies advocated for this guarantee in correspondence with the Minister—indeed, the Abbey wrote that it was standard practice to require such a guarantee (C. Thornton, Chief General Manager, Letter to Stanley, 16 November 1981: HLG 118/4123), and the Halifax, that its absence was a difficulty (J. Spalding, Deputy Chief General Manager, to Stanley, 18 November 1981: HLG 118/3865). The DoE and Corporation stayed firm, however; the principal concern appears to have been that, in fact, building societies were willing to lend on shared ownership leases, and once an indemnity had been offered, "they would become a general building society requirement, for no good reason" (I. Jordan, memo, "Shared-ownership and mortgage indemnities", 24 November 1981: HLG 118/3865). The lenders, in other words, did not get their own way all the time, but this was a minor skirmish that was lost.

The Lease Translated

Over the succeeding years, the model lease has been tinkered with and slightly amended, but it has remained constant and consistent. Its clauses have become settled and apparently accepted as standard. In short, they have become blackboxed. However, that box has only ever been loosely shut. Indeed, the courts have had their say in its interpretation, producing a paradoxical result. We discuss this result in the second part of this section. In the first part, we look at a significant modification which occurred in 2009. This was the first time that the lid had been opened on the box marked "shared ownership lease". What binds the two parts together is that both suggest that the lease has been unsuccessful in its aims. Lenders generally have not engaged with shared ownership, and although the lease creates ownership from one point of view, it creates a rental relationship from another.

The 2009 Redraft

Consistency in the lease was regarded as a crucial device in its own right. While shared ownership was being re-branded and recreated, the lease remained pretty much in its original form. As we were told by one agency:

"The earliest version [of the model lease] that we have on record dating from 1989 shows that the fundamental clauses remain intact and thus the operation of the lease remains largely unaltered over time." That consistency and standardisation was said to be significant for lenders: "And you know from my dealings with lenders, you know they like to deal in standard processes, they like to understand … and the more straightforward you can make it for them, the more likely they are going to be willing to lend on a product which is to them still a sort of bit player in the sort of big general scheme of things" (KS12).

However, in 2009, the various agencies involved in the promotion of shared ownership (housing association, regulator, and lender agencies) decided to make changes to the lease. Part of the programme was to make the lease more user-friendly. All the participants in this redrafting to whom we spoke recognised that this part of the programme was unsuccessful. As KS3 put it, "It still is a mind-boggling [document]. I run over this with my own staff and sometimes it is difficult for them to understand." This is a significant point to which we return in Chap. 4 because the complexity of the lease produces its own set of problems; a kind of treason in the buyer who is said not to understand its terms—if they did understand its terms, then their demands, we were told, would be different.

The key change in the 2009 redraft was, in fact, to the mortgagee protection clause. Despite the "golden comfort blanket" and the lack of risk in shared ownership, lenders had generally not engaged with shared ownership. For example, Cousins et al. (1993: 4.16–7) found that a bank had "refrained from entering this market" and a building society regarded it as a "high-risk" activity. The building society, in particular, regarded the quality of the loan as poor where the buyer acquired a share that was less than 50 per cent "in terms of the individual's recognition of home ownership responsibilities (maintenance, repair, sense of ownership)". Bramley et al. (2002: 115) commented that mortgages were "reasonably available", but that buyers were "unlikely to have available the full range of mortgage products which an outright purchaser could expect". The extent to which this may change is uncertain, but, more recently, Clarke et al. (2016) found no evidence to suggest that shared ownership was any more risky than the wider market, and since then, the industry has worked to get some additional small lenders on board.

There were concerns about the lack of mortgage products available, and the refusal of lenders to engage with shared ownership, at a time when the mortgage industry was being engulfed by the global financial crisis. The primary audience, then, for the new lease was the mortgage industry:

I mean it's primarily about just helping to shore up lending on shared ownership. I mean I think we recognise that you know in its form at that time the
[mortgagee protection clause] wasn't doing enough to you know encourage
lenders to lend, or it wasn't giving them enough security for them to you know
get them through their sort of audit and risk committees or whatever. So, we
obviously recognise that you know there were things that we could do. (KS14)

The changes in 2009 came about because there were a lot of myths and misun-
derstandings – I don't know if they were deliberate – there was always a perception that the [mortgagee protection clause] wasn't effective and hadn't been
tested in court, and wasn't clear as to what you could claim against. In an effort
to open up the market, we did some work to burst those myths and make things
more straightforward; the Labour government wanted commitments to get
more lenders into the market. (KS6)

So, like the original version of the lease, the 2009 redraft was simply an
attempt to stoke up interest among mortgage lenders and diversify both lenders and products. It might be said, however, that it was rather unsuccessful in
so doing. There is no up-to-date list of lenders involved in the sector, and
available products, but it remains the case that fewer lenders are involved than
in other ownership areas. This was a result of a combination of the following
factors: regulation, systems, complexity, and knowledge.

For building societies, their regulator, the Prudential Regulation Authority,
classes shared ownership as higher risk, despite the mortgagee protection
clause. This regulation means that if a lender is to lend on a shared ownership
product, the loan-to-value ratio is based solely on the share purchased (see
Clarke et al. 2016: 17). Smaller societies' regulation tends to prescribe them
as having a "traditional lending approach which restricts their lending activities mainly to prime quality residential mortgages for owner-occupiers" (FSA
2013: 1.12). This restricts their involvement to less than 15 per cent of their
total loan book. This was not an internal regulatory matter, but something
which was imposed on them by European directives (KS15; KS4). Shared
ownership is an out-of-the-ordinary type of product and, as a result, that creates systemic difficulty. That is, as KS4 (a large lender's officer) put it,

Because of our sausage factory size, we are constrained in terms of what we can
do. Wherever we can, we automate processes, and teams of people; … we have
got [millions of] accounts and very few Shared Ownership accounts. We have
500 collections and recovery agents. What are the chances of them seeing one of
those cases in a year? Slim. How do we maintain the competence and knowledge
and to maintain individual contact with the housing association? If we could
encourage smaller lenders, that would be better; it isn't cost-effective for us to
have a small team dealing with shared ownership cases. If you have less than half
a dozen people, you have resourcing issues.

Complexity and ignorance are the same sides of an oddly shaped coin. Our key stakeholder lenders told us that a product that is regarded as complex tended to breed ignorance because it would simply not be considered. There was a nervousness, for example, about the mortgagee protection clause "because it hasn't been tested in case law. The [clause] is not entirely clear – these things are all very well but until they are tested in case law, there is a massive reluctance to rely on it" (KS5). Complexity is also engendered because shared ownership is different from a "normal" lending relationship in that it involves the provider. The regulator recognises this: "[A]dministering such lending is likely to be more resource-intensive than conventional lending, since the mortgage agreement is three-way and relationships with both the borrower and social landlord need to be maintained" (FSA 2013: 2.2.20). This was combined with a certain prejudice: "My Knowledge is atypical. I'm quite a fan of shared ownership. If you were to have this conversation with our risk director, all the prejudices and negativity which arise over this target market [would come out]" (KS4); "Some of it is lack of understanding and knowledge. There is a perception that this is a high risk of lending; it is a different risk but not as high as standard. … But basically, the amount of ignorance of the product is quite vast. In the last few years, lenders aren't going into new initiatives if it's a product they don't understand or the regulator thinks its high risk" (KS15).

The Lease and the Courts: A Paradoxical Translation

The interaction between the lease and the courts has been on two rather different planes. In the first plane, the lease has been translated as a long lease, which gives the shared owner certain rights. On the other hand, in the second plane, the lease has been interpreted as being similar to an ordinary rental agreement, an "assured shorthold tenancy", with quite devastating consequences.

The Lease as Ownership

A reading of the leasehold reform provisions has rendered the shared ownership lease as a "long lease" for the purposes of Secs. 75 and 76, Commonhold and Leasehold Reform Act 2002: Corscombe *Close Block 8 RTM Co. Ltd v Roseleb Ltd* [2013] UKUT 81 (LC).[4] This means that shared owners have the

---

[4] The reading was controversial because it meant that another sub-section, which specifically referred to shared ownership leases where the shared owner had a 100 per cent share, was rendered otiose.

same rights as long leaseholders, for example, to be consulted about external works contracts and over a right to manage application (i.e. if the leaseholders in a block decide to take over the management of the block themselves). This equates the shared owner with other long leaseholders, and ties in neatly with the narrative about shared ownership as ownership. Nothing more needs to be said about this legal finding for that reason, except by way of contrast with what follows.

The Lease as Rental Contract

In the early days, particular issues had emerged about the lease and its relationship with the Rent Acts. It was certainly assumed that the lease created a Rent Act tenancy and "as a result fair rents are now registered for housing association shared ownership leases as a matter of course" (*Promotion of Privately Financed Shared Ownership*, 1986, para 4: HLG 118/4195). Indeed, there is evidence that the rent officers themselves were in conflict about this process because of valuation difficulties (letter received 21 May 1981 from Institute of Rent Officers, HLG 118/2259). Over time, as the rent officer role became disconnected from rents and more engaged with housing benefit valuations, this knowledge appears to have been lost. The changes to security of tenure in the Housing Act 1988 passed by, and it seems to have become assumed that, as a long leaseholder, shared owners were outside security of tenure legislation. That would make sense because they were *owners*, not *renters*.

However, in *Midland Heart v Richardson* [2008] L & TR 31, Jonathan Gaunt QC, sitting as a Deputy High Court Judge, found that the lease produced an assured shorthold tenancy. This was significant because Ms Richardson, who owned a 50 per cent stake in the property, had run up arrears of the rental element, which gave Midland Heart a mandatory possession claim against her. Indeed, this achieved the same result as a forfeiture in that Ms Richardson lost her capital stake in the property. Ms Richardson's arrears had arisen following her husband's imprisonment; his criminal associates threatened her and she had to leave the property. She lived for a while in a refuge, but housing benefit would only pay for two properties for a certain period, after which the arrears arose. In her absence, it is recorded that the property had been vandalised. Ms Richardson asked Midland Heart to market the property, but it did not sell. On the date of hearing, the arrears were £3009 and a possession order was made. The Judge dismissed the appeal against that order. He went on:

That all said, I have found this case troubling. Miss Richardson has had a rough ride in life and has now lost what is probably her only capital asset. Moreover, she lost it in proceedings brought at a time when, to the knowledge of the housing association, she was actively seeking to sell the house to pay off her debts and the housing association was itself involved in that process. I must say that I find the stance taken by the housing association strange in the circumstances and I have not received any adequate explanation. There may, of course, be many facts and matters in the background that I know not of and so I do not intend to be unduly critical. I simply comment on the timing. [23]

He then was "pleased to record" that Midland Heart had offered *ex gratia* to repay the original capital stake, less rent arrears, costs, and the cost of repairs, noting, "But that still means that Miss Richardson will have lost any capital appreciation between 1995 and now, worth about £45,000, which will represent, in turn, a windfall for the housing association" [24].

There has been plenty of writing about this case by academics and in the blogosphere (see, e.g., Peaker 2013). Much of this writing questions the ideals of shared ownership as a result of the *Richardson* case, and, as Susan Bright and Nick Hopkins have put it, the product is akin to the Emperor's new clothes (Bright and Hopkins 2011). One might be forgiven for thinking that the whole idea is shot. After 30 years, policy-makers would appreciate the error of their ways, and ditch it. Yet, quite the reverse has occurred; never has shared ownership been more highly promoted (and financed) than it has been since that decision, and more particularly under the Coalition and May governments. The purpose of the 2009 redraft, we were told, had absolutely nothing to do with *Richardson*.

This was business as usual. How can this be? There has been no change in the law as a result of *Richardson*; to our knowledge, nobody has said that the decision itself is wrong (alternative propositions have been advanced that might have assisted Ms Richardson: Bright and Hopkins 2009). One answer to this question is that *Richardson* has become law that is not law, in the sense that it has been written off as irrelevant (if it was known about). It is an anomaly that does not require a fix.

Richardson,[5] in its immediate aftermath, might have been a mediator in its text and effects, but its effects were ignored. It still sits there (on our computer), as a file, waiting to be opened. It was opened, for the purposes of an article in 2017, but it was noticeable that it hadn't been opened for 18 months previously. It is a passive actor; one around which a certain mystique has

---

[5] The italics are, of course, important, because that is part of law's alchemy—it turns a human into text.

developed amongst a certain group of people. What is particularly telling about it is that even among many groups advocating shared ownership at the time of our fieldwork, knowledge about *Richardson* was sketchy at best. Where there was some knowledge, the case was written off as being anomalous, the occupier was problematic, or an unnecessary fuss had been made about it by a particular person.

We were told that Ms Richardson's circumstances were unusual:

> I think it's just her circumstances were very unusual in that she had no mortgage and also she was living elsewhere so didn't claim housing benefit. It would be quite unusual for that to be a common occurrence for people. (KS11)

> My understanding of that particular case is that it was a set of circumstances that if you dreamt up you could never replicate – it just wouldn't happen, I mean I feel sorry for the woman in question, but you know clearly you know there was a very peculiar set of circumstances were at play there. ... you couldn't contrive the circumstances a second time, it just wouldn't happen. (KS14)

In this rendering, which was common, *Richardson* was factually anomalous and could not be repeated—"a unique set of circumstances" (KS8). It could not be repeated because there is nearly always a mortgage lender (who will generally pay off the rent arrears and capitalise them against the mortgage). It is hard to discern from the data the extent to which this remains the case, especially among shared owners who have held their interest for a longer period and those who have brought equity from a former property into their shared ownership property. Nevertheless, that is not the point. The point is that this kind of discursive rendering leaves the outcome of this case anomalous.

The mortgage lender has a right, under the 2009 redraft, to at least 28 days' written notice of the housing association's intention to commence possession proceedings. Further associations were "encouraged to adopt the standard undertaking and to work closely with lenders on this issue to maintain the favourable operating environment that has existed in the shared ownership sector. The undertaking is aimed simply at giving the lender time to remedy the breach. ... The potential for the housing association to take legal action that removes the lender's security is a key risk and one which is taken into account by many lenders when considering whether to lend on the shared ownership product in the first instance" (HCA et al. 2010: para 89; see now, HCA 2016: 32–3). That guidance was backed up by a further, rather odd, guidance, the body of which provides contact details for various people, but which also provides the following by way of guidance on the use of the mandatory possession ground for rent arrears:

The key rule when considering taking action over arrears is not to seek possession where there is a reasonable alternative. If this is not possible, [housing associations] are legally entitled to use Ground 8 ....

However, the use of Ground 8 is an extreme step in the context of shared ownership housing, the effect of which is similar to forfeiture. It should not be necessary where the HA and lender work jointly to resolve the problem, if possible with the shared owner. (CML et al. 2014: 2)

Again, this translation of *Richardson* seeks to downplay its significance.

Ms Richardson, on another popular representation, had made her property unsafe:

Given that we have 137,000 [shared owners], there are very few cases when these issues ever arise. And I think that's for two reasons, one because the landlords as registered providers see themselves as having a core focus of protecting people, and therefore they will not try and put people out on the streets. I mean this person, I was reading the papers, had sort of redesigned walls … knocked down walls, built a shed on the balcony and you know had basically made the building almost unstable. So, she had broken the terms in her lease and as a landlord you have responsibility for others who live in the building. So, by making the building unsafe I think there was an issue about. (KS12)

In this rendering, Ms Richardson was the subject of stigma. The housing association was absolved from any blame; it was acting rationally and as a good landlord. On the other hand, *she* deserved to be evicted because she was causing a hazard to the other residents.[6]

A third rendering related it to "that NL guy" (a reference to a prolific and high-profile legal blogger, Nearly Legal). He had written an article in *The Guardian*, entitled The Hidden Dangers of Shared Ownership" (Peaker 2013). He expressed concern that the significance of the *Richardson* case was not more widely known; he wrote that shared ownership would require legislative change to make it work, and that although it "may well be the most promising route into home ownership for many, there are substantial risks for those taking that route". We were told that he had made much more of the case than was necessary, because it was anomalous. And our discussion was brought back to the familiar trope about the "good" association and the "bad" consumer: "[W]hat that article missed was that Ms Richardson was offered a capital sum and had wrecked the property" (KS6).

---

[6] There is no mention of such matters in the case report, which refers only to vandalism at the property as a result of her absence. It is, for example, unlikely (given the size of balconies in modern properties) that Ms Richardson was able to construct a shed on it.

Conclusions

The lease is a curious object. It has an in-betweenness quality, as the housing studies scholars tell us. There is a sense of surprise among those scholars at the discovery that the lease as legal technique appears to undermine the nature and value of the ownership interest that is assumed to have been conveyed to the buyer. The buyer is an owner and a renter, and the lease produces this hybrid. From this perspective, the lease might have been a perfect device to convey the bifurcated idea of shared ownership. That it was used, however, appears to have been the result of a serendipitous combination; furthermore, that bifurcation, although a practical, everyday outcome of the legal device, was relegated because what its progenitors wanted to be established was the idea of ownership.

Other devices were discarded for different reasons, and the lease was the last device left standing, so to speak. But the real genius of the lease was that in formatting shared ownership, it was both a constraining device and a device which can be manipulated. For the trailblazing local authorities, one could see that the lease had value in the sense that they were financially insulated. The lease also created a series of other headaches for them and other providers, and, as we see in the next chapters, a series of practical, everyday problems for the buyers. There needed to be statutory intervention to ameliorate the original problems, which demonstrates that this private device also had a public domain. But the lease made shared ownership knowable. Recall from Chap. 2 the comments about not knowing what shared equity and so on were. The lease answered that question, and there was genius in its balance of the different interests involved.

There were positive reasons for the selection of the lease. Most obviously, as this chapter has demonstrated, it is an everyday legal device, and one which was particularly appropriate as an interessement device, through which others could be enrolled. As we demonstrate in the next chapter, shared ownership could be sold to buyers as ownership; however, the audience for shared ownership at this stage was not the buyer, but the organisations, without which this novel idea would not have been possible. It was the enrolment of the BSA and building societies through negotiating the terms of the model lease which made it possible. And the lease was the device which was manipulated to make that enrolment possible. This is not to deny that other elements—such as government grants, legislative support, and a "home ownership" ideology—were important, but the lease bound everything together in its concept and design.

The mortgagee protection clause—this golden comfort blanket—took the risk out of the product. Lenders to buyers are essentially guaranteed to recover their outlay because they effectively have a charge against the housing association's share of the property. When it appeared to fail to enrol lenders, there was a simple solution which did no violence at all to the lease, which was to enhance the level of comfort for lenders. Even so, this attempt at bracketing the lenders' interest has ended up largely unsuccessful for external reasons.

The lease was so much more than that, though. In its drafting, it was a translation of the ownership narrative. As we demonstrated in our discussion of the repairing covenant—an innocuous and normal clause in a long lease—it conveyed the idea of ownership in shared ownership. How else could one explain to a buyer of (say) a 25 per cent share in a property that they were responsible for 100 per cent of the maintenance and repairs for their building? The apparently inexplicable unfairness inherent in such a clause is counterbalanced by the ownership narrative (or the incentive to own, which is almost the same thing). In its drafting, entirely new clauses appeared, specifically designed for this product and to enrol private lenders. Yet, this careful drafting and thought was susceptible to alternative, treasonous interpretations, as was demonstrated by the *Richardson* case.

Finally, in all these different ways, it can be seen that the lease is imbued with, and co-constitutes, the identity of the shared owner. We have seen how the lease was drawn to reflect the very idea of ownership and how it made the concept of shared ownership possible. The lease came to act as mediator because it was replicable and interpreted by those in the know, although those interpretations took it off in dramatic directions. Without the lease, shared ownership might not have been possible, but with the lease, shared ownership could be translated as ownership and meaningfully so. And this legal consciousness tied in with a certain liberal rationality about progress, making the assumption that buyers would wish to staircase out of shared ownership.

Bibliography

Blandy, S. and Goodchild, B. (1999), 'From Tenure to Rights: Conceptualising the Changing Focus of Housing Law in England', 16(1), *Housing Theory and Society*: 31–42.

Bramley, G., Morgan, J., Cousins, L., Dunmore, K., Three Dragons Consultancy and MORI Social Research (2002), *Evaluation of the Low Cost Home Ownership Programme*, London: ODPM.

Bright, S. and Hopkins, N. (2009), 'Low Cost Home Ownership: Legal Issues of the Shared Ownership Lease', 73(4), *Conveyancer and Property Lawyer*: 337–49.

Bright, S. and Hopkins, N. (2011), 'Home, Meaning and Identity: Learning from the English Model of Shared Ownership', 28(3), *Housing, Theory and Society*: 377–96.

Clarke, A., Heywood, A. and Williams, P. (2016), *Shared Ownership: Ugly Sister or Cinderella? The Role of Mortgage Lenders in Growing the Shared Ownership Market*, London: CML.

Council of Mortgage Lenders (CML), Homes and Communities Agency (HCA) and National Housing Federation (NHF) (2014), *Guidance for Handling Arrears and Possession Sales of Shared Ownership Properties*, London: CML.

Cousins, L., Ledward, C., Howe, K., Rock, G. and Taylor, G. (1993), *An Appraisal of Shared Ownership*, London: HMSO.

Financial Services Authority (FSA) (2013), *Building Societies' Sourcebook*, London: FSA.

Homes and Communities Agency (HCA) (2010), *Updated Consultation Note for Stakeholders Following Informal Consultation Process*, 29th January 2010, available at https://www.gov.uk/guidance/capital-funding-guide/1-help-to-buy-shared-ownership

Homes and Communities Agency (HCA) (2013), *Shared Ownership Model House Lease*, available at https://www.gov.uk/guidance/capital-funding-guide/1-help-to-buy-shared-ownership#section-11

Homes and Communities Agency (HCA) (2016), *Shared Ownership: Joint Guidance for England*, London: HCA.

Homes and Communities Agency (HCA), Council of Mortgage Lenders (CML) and National Housing Federation (NHF) (2010), *Shared Ownership: Joint Guidance for England*, London: CML.

Hunter, C. (2015), 'Solar Panels, Homeowners and Leases: The Lease as a Socio-Legal Object', in D. Cowan and D. Wincott (eds), *Exploring the 'Legal' in Socio-Legal Studies*, London: Palgrave Macmillan.

Karn, V., Kemeny, J. and Williams, P. (1985), *Home Ownership in the Inner City: Salvation or Despair?*, Aldershot: Gower.

Keenan, S. (2013), 'Property as Governance: Time, Space and Belonging in Australia's Northern Territory Intervention', 76(3), *Modern Law Review*: 464–93.

National Federation of Housing Associations (NFHA) (1978), *A Handbook for Community Leasehold*, London: NFHA.

Peaker, G. (2013), 'The Hidden Dangers of Shared Ownership', *The Guardian*, 3rd September.

Stanley, J. (1974), *Shared Purchase: A New Route to Home-Ownership*, London: Conservative Political Centre.

Stewart, A. (1981), *Housing Action in an Industrial Suburb*, London: Academic Press.

4

Managing Shared Ownership

Introduction

A key question to be addressed by a housing organisation with a continuing
interest (including central government grant) in a property is how to manage
that property in the future. There are well-defined techniques for managing
social rented housing, which have developed over the last century. Some social
housing providers also had a stock of (non-shared ownership) long leasehold
properties, the management of which they might have taken on, for example,
following the transfer from local authorities after the sitting tenant had exercised their right to buy. However, shared ownership is a rather different phe-
nomenon from social rented housing and other long leaseholds because of its
in-betweenness, adding a further level of complexity. A key question for providers of shared ownership housing is how they should treat shared owners—
are they akin to long leaseholders or social renters?

Answering this question gives us the opportunity to introduce our case
study housing associations. This is because this apparently mundane, perhaps
overly technical question actually has a different plane as well because it raises
a further question about organisational values. As we have emphasised in this
book, housing associations are complex amalgams of social and commercial
values. As McDermont (2010) identified, the housing association sector's
desire for independence from central government was the wrong target,
because "associations are now so intricately tied up within the controlling
influence of private finance (a world that drives, amongst other things, the
need for larger and larger organisations) that it is not state but economic power
that should be the target of independence campaigns". Those commercial

© The Author(s) 2018
D. Cowan et al., *Ownership, Narrative, Things*, Palgrave Socio-Legal Studies,
https://doi.org/10.1057/978-1-137-59069-5_4

influences now have begun to dominate as government has emphasised its funding limits, controlled rents to lower them, and attacked supposed organisational performance failures (Manzi and Morrison 2017). The need to cross-subsidise between surplus-making and other activities has created greater pressures by way of increased exposure to risk (*id.*; Morrison 2016).

This social/private problematic, which also underpins the idea of shared ownership, provides the backdrop to this chapter. In the first part, we introduce our case study housing associations, "Fixham" and "Greendale", describing their structures and organisations. Both constructed themselves as "social businesses", a kind of leitmotif expression to describe the transactional lash-up and hybrid identity (Boeger 2017; Blessing 2012), and we spend time in this chapter subjecting that conjunction to analysis in the context of the management of shared ownership. As noted, there is a lengthy history of social housing management, and in the second section, we discuss this literature briefly. In the third section, we discuss how Fixham and Greendale made clear choices to treat shared owners as owners, and as a result, sought to produce the conditions under which ownership values provided the basis for their management of these accommodation units. We discuss how our buyer interviewees responded to that treatment. In the final section, we discuss two particular types of problem which were controversial within the associations and which raised questions about the social/private and owner/renting spectra: major repair works and third-party managing agents.

Even though both Fixham and Greendale managed shared ownership as ownership, they recognised that this approach was unstable and required discussion, negotiation, and thought. As we discuss in this chapter, contestations over the production of ownership by our case study housing associations and their buyers suggest that ownership is constantly in action and negotiated—that is, ownership is an interactive, iterative process, which is ongoing, much like an idea which is re-shaped over time. Ownership is produced inductively, according to how one set of organisations, housing associations, create "ownership" and how individual shared owners themselves experience it. It is the way that those organisations' own values infiltrate into their conception of ownership which reflect back on the malleability of ownership. In other words, through our data, we see ownership as a social construction, rather than as a set of norms or values, and thus challenge the existing scholarship about ownership. In this way, we are able to demonstrate how legal consciousness—of property and ownership—is developed within organisations and buyers, through their interactions, as well as in things themselves.

Introducing Fixham and Greendale

Our research method incorporated a 6-week period of observation in summer and autumn of 2014, conducted by Alison, with two housing associations, which we call "Fixham" and "Greendale". During this observation period, informal interviews were conducted with officers and managers so that we could appreciate the kinds of operations and ethos which underpinned their working practices. We hypothesised that the kinds of operating practices of our case study associations and their interactions between buyers formed part of the everyday experience of shared ownership, and that this would be a constituent element in the production of shared owner identity. Therefore, the organisations themselves and how they managed their shared ownership properties form key constituent elements in that production. In this section, we move from a description of the central offices of each association to a discussion of the more general description of their housing stock, management practices, and problems experienced (or, rather, that were observed by the research team).

Fixham and Greendale: Offices

There are many commonalities between Fixham and Greendale, but also some areas where they did things differently. Both were housing associations registered with the regulator (the Homes and Communities Agency at the date of our research). In law, they are "social housing" providers. They operated in London, the East, and the South-East regions of England. They both had a significant general housing needs stock and some leasehold property. They had both been in the business of providing shared ownership properties for some time, mostly funded by a mix of government grant and private finance, although both were moving to a private finance model. They both managed about 4000 shared ownership properties each.

Both organisations self-described as a "social business". Unwrapping this term's meanings is key to appreciating their corporate and individual messages to shared owners. We suggest that one way into this term is through the everyday experience of walking into their offices or, as an employee, switching on the computer. The offices are bright and clean, in the style of corporate offices. In Greendale, for example, the central office location is housed in an open office space, with motivational messages, such as "did you change something for the better today?", or reiterating the group's mission statement. It was recognised that although such statements can become like wallpaper, staff were clearly aware of these organisational values. In Fixham, motivational messages were part of the decoration of the main offices, and values were promoted both to staff and to contractors.

Greendale

Following a string of mergers and takeovers over the years, Greendale has a group structure with offices in different locations. The organisation manages its shared ownership portfolio through a subsidiary that dealt with all its commercial undertakings, from local offices, but with certain specialist functions (lease extensions, enfranchisement, and staircasing) situated in one central team. Each regional office had its own income collection team, service charge team, and property managers. Although the organisational structure of the group is clear, its actual on-the-ground organisation seemed a little opaque and distributed.

Greendale's shared ownership stock was mixed in the sense that it managed dispersed DIYSO properties, mono-tenure blocks, s. 106 units, and mixed tenure estates. We were told that issues tended to arise on mixed tenure estates because it was said that social tenants are less inclined to make sure the property and area are well kept. As the housing management costs were apportioned across the estate, effectively, the shared owners were subsidising the management costs of the general needs stock. As one officer put it, "[T]hey see 10% of [the housing management] but pay for the other 90% too."

Greendale's shared ownership properties were located across the South of England, with concentrations of stock in certain areas. There were noticeably different markets in these areas. As a result, we selected two areas in which shared ownership stock was particularly concentrated. One area (Area 1) was predominantly urban, with much new-build accommodation, and generally the stock was flats. Although this area was at the more expensive end of the shared ownership market, it was understood that this market would be different to others because of the significant employment opportunities available there. The other area (Area 2) comprised counties in which property prices and local earnings were lower, although there had been house price inflation, but comparatively limited employment opportunities. The stock in this area was predominantly houses. We interviewed 13 buyers in Area 2 and 19 in Area 1.

The management approach was to treat and regard shared owners in the same way as long leaseholders were treated and regarded. Alison was regularly told that the onus was on the buyer and for them to be properly advised by their solicitor, but that it was apparent from the inquiries received that any such advice seemed to be lacking. This was particularly the case about buyers' repairing obligations. As a result, Greendale—as did Fixham—provided prospective buyers with a list of recommended conveyancers.

Although not necessarily articulated as such, Greendale recognised that it operated at the interface of the commercial and the social. So, for example, it regularly "soaks up" costs which it did not feel appropriate to pass on to the shared owners, although that was also partly due to a software glitch. However, a subsequent improvement in software meant that more (but by no means all) costs were being passed on to shared owners. Also, if a shared owner could not afford to pay a service charge or cyclical repairs bill within the required period (30 days), they were routinely allowed a longer period to do so, and in the case of repairs, provided with a low-interest loan to do so. Greendale had a downward staircasing policy, although this was usually restricted in Area 1 and more available in Area 2. It routinely signposted shared owners in arrears to money advice agencies. In practice, it went beyond what might ordinarily be expected from a commercial provider.

However, we were also told that the organisation needed to act commercially regarding sales and ongoing building maintenance. The decision to buy s. 106 leases was described as a commercial decision: "[T]here is little scope to subsidise [shared owners] should agent fees go up and there is a bit of a conflict with being a social landlord." Although the organisation sought to work holistically—so that, for example, sales staff were involved at an early stage in developments—there were concerns expressed that the drive for sales might mean that sales staff were less inclined to provide full information and/or point out the pitfalls to prospective buyers.

Officers were well aware of the problems with s. 106 developments (which are considered below) and the creation of "poor doors". The following example was used a number of times to explain the issue to the researcher:

> It can be a difficult relationship. We had a recent case where a shared ownership block, which was managed by a third party, had a gym on site. Greendale opted out of the gym as otherwise it would have made the service charges too expensive. … The managing agents would not even let shared owners use the services of the gym if they paid separately and had a separate individual account. When a shared owner staircased to 100% he expected to be free of [Greendale] but he is a 100% leaseholder of [Greendale] not of the freeholder, and still can't access the gym which is what he wanted. They don't understand why they cannot pay service charges etc direct to managing agent now, so the legal relationship was not made clear to him ever, until he staircased and did not get the result for which he hoped.

This example also demonstrated the issue with some leases in some blocks. That is, when the shared owner staircased up to 100 per cent, they remained in a leaseholder relationship with Greendale. Not all such leasehold relationships are constructed in this way, but that did happen where the Greendale shared ownership leases were held en bloc, that is, in a single head lease. It was recognised that decisions made in the development pipeline about the configurations of head leases and management companies resonated down the chain into the everyday management and experiences within multi-owned apartment blocks.

Greendale had been at the forefront of innovation in design in its new-build properties. It had tended to balance innovation and energy efficiency, on the one hand, with practicality, including ongoing costs, on the other hand. The organisation has experienced particular issues with solar panels because these require annual maintenance (their shelf-life is limited otherwise) and can be expensive; many householders switch them off.

Fixham

Fixham similarly had a group structure, although its organisation and management tended to be both centrally located and easier to appreciate. It operated mostly in one region in England, although some of its shared ownership stock was dispersed as a result of individual DIYSO purchases. Fixham's stock was mostly pepperpotted on estates they managed, DIYSO properties, and in other developments with third-party managing agents.

Shared ownership properties could be purchased through new-build first sales, re-sales of previously purchased property, and purchase of repossessed re-sale property. All sales were handled by different staff with different degrees of "handholding" through the process, and different documentation issued to prospective buyers. There was concern that all staff members had to be confident that buyers were given all the necessary information at the outset, but there was a recognised potential for inconsistencies in the quality of information imparted during the sale.

Fixham organised its housing management generically, so response teams dealt with all tenures—general needs rented housing, shared ownership, and leasehold. We were told that one rationale for this was that the business is about people, not tenure; as one person put it, "Tenure doesn't really matter but what is important is how you deal with the problem." Further, and relatedly, it was said that separate teams produced duplications and, thus, inefficiencies. Fixham officers moved between teams and, therefore, were aware of the systems, processes, and procedures across the whole organisation.

Teams were arranged over three floors of open-plan space in a central building that was both large and modern; the exception was that the neighbourhood management teams were organised and had offices on an area basis. Neighbourhood management officers dealt with approximately 650–750 properties. Staff were focused on the asset, the estate or block.

Fixham was concerned about its shared ownership satisfaction rate, which, we were told, was high when specific teams dealt with it, but was now at a mid-level. Different explanations were given to us by staff for this, but the most common was that the complexity of the different types of tenure meant that neighbourhood officers "don't have the ability to manage shared owners' expectations" because of their "social work" role and the different sort of complaints made by shared owners. The more specific, but related, explanation given was that, as neighbourhood officers were often unavailable because they were out of office, the expectations of shared owners were not always able to be met. Further, we were told that the current computer system tended to prioritise process—that is, dealing with an issue swiftly—over substantive resolution of issues.

Fixham had sought to manage shared owner expectations through a new customer care team, which was responsible for explaining various matters—such as defects periods, repairing obligations, use of white goods, and so on—to new shared owners. Fixham's staff also perceived shared owners to have higher expectations than general needs tenants. So, for example, in a more flippant moment, shared owners were described as "seeing themselves as superior", "forget they rent themselves", "snobbishness among some people", and that managing mixed tenure could be difficult. The customer service and communication skills were said to be different depending on the occupier's tenure. We were regularly told that Fixham will not hold the hands of shared owners, but they operate a kind of social work role with general needs tenants:

> We always aim to offer outstanding service to all regardless of tenure but you communicate differently. Neighbourhood officers are dealing with domestic violence and anti-social behaviour and rightly so, but if someone in a £300K house is complaining about a bush, it's hard to offer them the same level of service as it requires different skills. One person has almost social work skills and the other requires outstanding customer service as a private letting.

Fixham's management recognised the tensions inherent in the idea of a "social business but suggested that those tensions could also be productive as it navigated between the poles". As one officer put it, "We have to be in the commercial world to achieve our social goals. We have a commercial head and a social heart but it is a real balancing act." In general, the social mission was satisfied by recognising that Fixham's shared ownership "sits in the middle ground" between social and private markets. The social mission was also recognised to have a particular impact on individual cases, in which it might be said to be an "orientation" when dealing with "hard cases". Thus, staff justified more lenient, discretionary decisions by reference to the social value. Tangible examples were apparent of decorating re-sales homes to effect a quick sale and remedy crisis circumstances for the previous shared owner, or intervening in terms of financial inclusion work to support owners experiencing debt problems.

More generally, certain practices might be said to be less commercial—so, for example, once a reservation fee was paid on a new shared ownership plot by a buyer, Fixham honoured the originally quoted purchase price even where there were substantial delays and the housing market value of that property had increased; or service charge payments may be made monthly with no interest payable to make them affordable as opposed to six monthly in advance; or Fixham's income maximisation approach, where they assisted with post-application issues with housing benefit, spanning both general needs and shared ownership. Fixham also could do downward staircasing, although the funding criteria were strict due to concerns about moral hazard.

Fixham had a rent arrears management system for shared ownership which was prized. In particular, it had worked to support shared owners in terms of informing them about the availability of benefits, which could also cover service charge payments. If the shared owner was in arrears after service of a notice-seeking possession, Fixham would often inform the lender, which could capitalise those arrears by advancing the shortfall to Fixham. Fixham's assistance to occupiers tended to be enhanced where its officer had some kind of relationship with the lender's officer, so that co-ordinated action could be taken. This was particularly apparent when the mortgagee protection clause was invoked and the association's staff mitigated the debt impacts for the former owner as well as for the association.

"Managing" Shared Ownership

In this section, we discuss how both organisations sought to mimic the experience of ownership in managing their shared ownership properties. In the first part, we summarise the literature on housing management. This part acts as a counterpoint to the subsequent discussion. The business of housing associations was to provide social rented housing, and so the management styles and approaches in relation to that type of property need to be set against the management styles and approaches in respect of shared ownership. In the second part, we consider what is known about the management of shared ownership and then discuss how Greendale and Fixham managed their shared ownership properties.

Managing Social Rented Housing

The concept of "management" in social housing has been the subject of a considerable literature (see, e.g., Cairncross et al. 1997; Haworth and Manzi 1999; Pawson and Mullins 2010). One particular strand of this literature suggests that social housing management strategies and techniques are a response to perceptions about occupiers. Octavia Hill, in her evidence to the 1885 Royal Commission on the Housing of the Working Classes; suggested that housing management was "a tremendous despotism, but it is exercised with a view to bringing out the powers of the people, and treating them as responsible for themselves within certain limits" (Royal Commission 1885: 297). As Cowan and McDermont (2006: 39) argue, the management of council housing became a particular predilection following the re-housing of slum dwellers in the interwar period, who were regarded as requiring a form of training to bring them up to the proper standards:

> We find that the purpose of social housing was ambiguous at the outset but that it germinated into a particular set of questions that coalesced around the potentially problematic character of certain future occupiers in the context of economic crisis in the early 1930s.

An understanding of the nature of the occupier constructed the domain. By 1938, the Central Housing Advisory Committee (CHAC), which had been set up to advise on housing issues, provided a list of the tasks of housing management as follows:

> Advice at the planning stage on estate layout and house design
> Administration of the waiting list
> Letting the houses
> Transfers and exchanges
> Rent collection and advice on rent schemes
> Maintenance and repairs …
> General care of estates and their amenities
> Housing welfare and liaison with the statutory and voluntary social services
> (CHAC 1938: para 134)

Its range today, as Franklin (2000: 914–5) expresses it, is enormous:

The message conveyed [by the social, political and institutional context] seems to be that those working in housing are expected to be all things to all people: policy implementers, performance monitors, rational bureaucrats, caring professionals, job providers, anti-poverty strategists, community developers, agents of social control, promoters of well-being, immigration controllers, custodians of public health and morality, and proponents of better education.

If the CHAC specification provides a version of housing management that was rooted in the everyday role, the specification provided by Franklin conveys a sense of distance of planning and strategising. However, one can still see the Octavia Hill kinds of despotism internalised in both, albeit *sub silentio* in the CHAC list. Other aspects have also come to play a role in this specification of housing management. For example, as McDermont (2007: 81; original emphasis) noted, "[G]iven the expectation of many [housing associations] that they should be expanding to become more competent social *businesses*, it is unsurprising that the sector's perspective on governance has been coloured by events and developments in the business sector." Various committees of inquiry have firmly established the corporate model and financial aspects of governance on housing association practice. Private sector practices, such as call centres and "gold standard" rewards for tenants, are now almost de rigueur in the housing association sector (Walker 2000; Lupton et al. 2003; Flint 2004). These represent a kind of new-century rendering of Hill's despotic housing management, but one which uses the disciplining techniques of rewarding good conduct (e.g. by giving preferential treatment with repairs), and centralises some services (e.g. through repairs "hotlines").

Scholars have also drawn attention to the effects of the governance of anti-social behaviour on housing management practices (Cowan et al. 2001; Brown 2004). There is an explicitly moral dimension to housing management today, which increasingly encourages self-regulation and responsibility amongst its occupants "as governing bodies presume to know what constitutes good, appropriate and responsible conduct" (Flint 2002: 622, 2004) and is increasingly focusing on their propagation (Flint 2002: 625). Housing management and its organisation is a moral enterprise and reflects the—or more accurately a perception of the—target group that requires "managing".

Managing Shared Ownership: The Association Perspective

The Existing Literature

Perhaps one of the most surprising aspects of the existing literature on shared ownership lies in the absence of discussion of the ongoing housing management of properties. This absence is across the board, from associations' own research to most government evaluations and academic research. This is surprising because the housing association retains a stake in the properties through its ownership (in a loose sense) of the unsold part, the use of government grant, and the ongoing need for cross-subsidy. There are satisfaction surveys that have been conducted; some of these have not particularly touched on housing management, but on more general matters, such as the nature of the agreement (see, e.g., Allen 1982: 17). Where they have done, however, it is clear that there are concerns about housing management, including around communal repairs and maintenance, participation in decision-making, and financial obligations (TSA 2009: 35).

The recurrent concerns in the literature, however, have been about the way grant has been used, marketing, shared ownership's value for money, whether it is achieving its role, problems of mobility, and the potential for staircasing. In two evaluations, the question of housing management was raised. In an evaluation of DIYSO in the 1990s, a section on operating procedures and management is largely concerned with the business of selling shared ownership. Where ongoing management has been discussed, the following comment was made:

> So far the costs of management of DIYSO properties once acquired are not seen as either excessive or a problem. The amount of interaction typically needed with buyers is limited. Exceptions would be when arrears happen, which is so far fairly infrequently, and when staircasing occurs. (Bramley et al. 1995: 6.43)

In their 2002 evaluation of the low-cost homeownership programme, Bramley et al. discussed managing low-cost homeownership briefly, saying that housing associations "do not find the bulk of any day to day management of LCHO causes particular difficulty, although service charges, particularly for large or complex developments, were mentioned as an issue by some London based associations" (2002: 117); they go on to say that "[t]he main issue in managing the stock is that of arrears and repossessions" (118). Certain specific management issues have been raised, for example, over re-sale procedures (see Wallace 2008b).

Greendale and Fixham

Greendale's and Fixham's managing techniques and strategies for shared owners were characterised by the _absence_ of management. That is to say, the logic followed by both organisations was that long leaseholders and owners were not to be managed; shared owners were their equivalent; they should not be managed either. In organisations with a mixed tenure profile, this approach of absence reflected a strong statement about the values of ownership as opposed to renting. Renters are managed; owners aren't—although they are all "customers" of the organisation. It was a moral statement about ownership and owners themselves, by way of contrast with social tenants. The absence of housing management was, therefore, a translation of ownership into the everyday practices of the organisation regarding its shared ownership estate.

In Greendale, this moral statement was translated into the way they organise their housing management. There were teams of managers for social rented housing. Shared owners, however, were treated like long leaseholders. Not only was this part of the corporate structure of the organisation—shared ownership was managed by a commercial subsidiary of the main organisation, which was also responsible for leaseholders—the predominant value of this organisation was *caveat emptor*. Thus, when problems arose for shared owners, it was commonly regarded as the product of inadequate advice and conveyancing at the outset. They had various strategies to remedy these advice defects, but our fieldwork notes record that this strategy of absence produced tensions. Alison recorded the following conversation with a property manager in her notes:

> [We] try to treat [shared owners] as leaseholders and not to wait on them hand and foot. In discussion, sometimes people want to be owners and not be bothered, sometimes they want a higher level of service as they're owners and sometimes want [the association] to do everything. People vary between these positions over different issues. Key is that people need to know more about what they're signing up to, they should really know if they're buying they're responsible for everything.

This sense that the problem of managing shared ownership was a question of expectations—which depended on the issue, and which, in and of itself, should have been managed by the legal process underpinning the transaction—was a common theme in our research. It was clear that much was expected of the buyer's lawyer in this transaction, in terms of explaining the deal into which the buyer was entering, but this was a failed translation. There appeared to be two reasons for this failure. First, the nature of modern conveyancing practice is to produce a cheap service through mass supply. The lawyer (or legal executive) responsible for the transaction simply does not have time to provide detailed advice on the nature of the transaction. Secondly, and related, the role of the lawyer is to convey the property, not to advise on the nature of the obligations.

So, for example, Emma, a civil servant and one of our first interviewees produced her conveyancing "file" to us. She had kept it neatly, in part because she had ongoing problems with water dripping through her ceiling and into the flat below hers. The file was thin and had a couple of post-it notes in it. There was a customer care letter from her lawyer which explained about the service she could expect, her lease, and the land registration certificate. Emma explained:

> I've got all the paperwork; I've got all that stuff, yes, so I've got a copy of the lease and I've got the Land Registry stuff for buying the new chunk so I've got all of that … Sorry, excuse all my junk over here. Now I know why I've got it because I've put all these things safely because this is a huge thing for me; home ownership is a huge thing for everybody. I keep hold of everything but I had to get it out because I was trying to find evidence of whether I had a new build guarantee, so hang on … Okay, so that's my Land Registry thing. Well, that's my lease there. Oh, hang on a sec, just one sec.
> I: WHAT, SO YOU'VE GOT POST-ITS?
> Yes. I just had it out the other day because I just – hang on.
> I: I SEE YOU'VE HIGHLIGHTED THE CAR PARKING SPACE.
> Yes, well, she highlighted it to tell me that I'm not supposed to rent it out so …
> I: WHAT, YOU'RE NOT SUPPOSED TO RENT OUT YOUR CAR PARKING SPACE?
> No, although I do, but don't tell anybody! I do rent it out because I don't use it.
> I: SO THESE ARE HER POST-IT NOTES, ARE THEY?
> I think so.
> I: WHEN YOU SAY HER, THE HOUSING ASSOCIATION PERSON OR …
> No, the solicitor. I was given a list of suggested solicitors. We didn't have to go with them but I went with them, with these.

It was a result of this apparent failure of legal advice that led both Greendale and Fixham to provide their own handbooks of the obligations and responsibilities of shared owners.

As we have noted above, Fixham organised its housing management generically, so response teams dealt with all tenures—general needs rented housing, shared ownership, and leasehold. However, this generic organisation approach produced tensions as well. Alison recorded the following interactions with officers:

There is a hierarchy on mixed tenure estates, not all estates. Rented do have more vulnerabilities and issues relating to that but shared owners have invested in their home, paid a lot of money to live next door to vulnerable person with [anti-social behaviour] and the estate is untidy because of the tenant, but then if anyone was doing that other rented tenants would also be annoyed too. Also it's difficult for shared owners to see tenants getting new windows and doors and they have to do it all themselves. We get the odd comment, those people rented and getting all that stuff. The shared owners are investing in property in home-ownership and not getting the perks of the rented tenants.

Shared owners did not always appreciate that they had traded for a lower standard of service in favour of the value/s of ownership. And, more specifically, Alison's notes record the following observation about emergency repairs:

A big problem is that shared owners use [the] out of hours emergency service for repairs and each morning they get the log of actions overnight that the out-of-hours contractor dealt with and there are always some shared owners. They have to call the shared owner and explain that the recommended follow-up work will not be undertaken but that they will not be charged for the "make safe" work undertaken overnight. There is currently no way the contractor on overnight can tell if the tenancy is actually a shared ownership property or not. Most accept it and think they've been lucky in getting something done, occasionally get complainers but people panic in an emergency and call the emergency number; but some do think as we own the majority of their home we should do some repairs for them.

A further way in which shared owners were constructed as different occurred in Fixham. Fixham had a tenant reward scheme used to incentivise good behaviour or penalise poor behaviour, by enhancing or reducing the level of service to its rented tenants, respectively. For example, where a tenant engaged with Fixham's activities and met rent payments, the tenant would receive an enhanced repairs or improvements service, while breaking agreements to repay rent arrears or being responsible for anti-social behaviour would mean improvements were delayed. Fixham staff found this scheme highly effective and were considering how a similar system could work for shared owners, but acknowledged that the incentives were problematic because they provided few services. What this exposed was the tension between renting and owning, and where shared ownership sat on this continuum. After all, if shared owners were owners, such a question would not have arisen—for traditional owners, community engagement was not sought or rewarded, and non-payment of service charges was penalised by the legal action available to them and as stipulated in the lease. This discussion in Fixham reflected its less binary approach to shared ownership expressed through its organisation of housing management. That is, although Fixham's approach to housing management of shared ownership lay in its absence, its generic organisation meant that it was always experienced by way of comparison with other housing tenures. We see both organisations adopting this less binary perspective in the final section in this chapter.

Managing Shared Ownership: The Buyer Experience

We noted above that satisfaction surveys suggested a level of dissatisfaction among buyers with housing association management. We also noted that Fixham was particularly concerned about satisfaction among its shared owners. We asked a rather different question, however. Our question was whether shared owners themselves wanted housing management or not. Our expectation was that if shared owners constructed themselves as owners, then they would not want to feel that they were being managed. That would be consistent with the ethos of ownership, and consistent with the way in which ownership was translated into housing association management as an absence of management.

Buyers expressed a strong rejection of the housing association's newsletter. It is accepted housing management practice for social housing organisations to provide information to their residents through newsletters, for example, about the services they provided or about key dates (such as for meetings). Buyers raised the newsletter issue commonly when we discussed with them whether they felt like an owner. They were reluctant to be associated with general needs tenants, but secondly, highlighting the services offered to general needs tenants also served to reinforce negative perceptions that some shared owners held in respect of the lack of services or commitment from the providers in exchange for their rental payments.

For example, Paula wondered, "[W]hat they're trying to achieve, saying stuff like, 'Do you need help getting back in to work?' I'm like no, I don't. I don't need help with that, I'd like you to help with – they've got a problem with pests in the building, they had mice. … I haven't reported it to them because I just don't really know if they'd do anything or not." Joanne was upset by the newsletter "because they have a Decent Homes – it was spun over, they had one of their magazines with the Decent Homes. 'This is what we've changed for one of our residents.' Well, the crappy old kitchen was the one that I've got". And Alicia assumed that Fixham was "quite a bloated organisation because they've got a lot of time and money to be sending letters all the time, so I think well, is it my rent and is it my service charge that are all going to an efficient organisation?"

Julie, whom we interviewed with her husband, Albert (who had been housing association tenants around 10 years previously), admitted:

> *Julie*: The other thing is, okay, I'm probably a snob, I admit, but I do feel, personally, I have always at the back of my mind I'm being treated a bit like a council tenant.
> *I*: IN WHAT WAY? HOW MIGHT THAT MANIFEST ITSELF, IN WHAT WAY?
> *Julie*: For example, we get things around newsletters from time to time. They're very definitely aimed at the more, the council tenants' side of things, aren't they, than the home ownership?

Joshua, who worked in a regulator's office as an economist, remarked during a discussion of the costs and benefits of shared ownership:

> I got a spreadsheet out and worked it out and then thought this actually financially to me gives me an option in future but also immediately constrains how much my rent can increase and it gives me a quality of property far higher than any other possible scenario. So, I'm coming at it as a kind of individual person just trying to maximise my own benefit but you find that, at the end of the day, the person you're doing this from is through a housing association who, other than the shared ownership stuff, will do a lot of more traditional social housing type stuff. They do send us newsletters and things on a kind of I think quarterly or something basis which is a lot of stuff that feels more geared to a traditional social housing demographic. So, it feels a bit patronising to someone that's – it's all about how to get into work and come to our CV workshop and it's like, well, I have a job and all that. So, I understand why they do that, if they're just sending stuff out and that's most of their customer base but it is a social enterprise getting shared ownership and all this kind of stuff but coming at it from a different angle, you feel a bit different to the traditional. So, I don't know what I'm trying to get at but there is a bit of a kind of disconnect I guess to the traditional base maybe, I don't know.

The confusion expressed by Joshua at the end of this monologue reflected the conflict between, on the one hand, understanding the social/private and ownership/renting as binaries or as a spectrum, on the other.

While our shared owner participants generally welcomed the "hands-off" approach to management, some particularly long-standing shared owners expressed some resentment about the lack of provider involvement, however minimal. While the absence of the providers in their daily lives helped foster the feelings of ownership and might have been welcomed, after some time, shared owners complained that their provider had not shown any interest in them or the property since the purchase. These contradictory sentiments were fuelled by the housing associations identity as *social* landlords, which attracted some expectations that there would be some element of a social safety net, in providing advice or support in later life (which was not borne out from older shared owners' experiences), even though few research participants regarded themselves as being part of *social* housing; but also because they were "shared" owners, and therefore expected the association to be interested in the bricks and mortar because they retained a large share in it:

> I thought that Fixham would have a bit more involvement, been a bit more nosey, but no, they've been spot on really, just stayed out the way. (Carl)

> *Jeanette*: We've never had any inquiry on the state of the property either written or verbal or telephone, or email, any such kind of how we are doing as tenants, how's the state of the building, if they wanted to view the building to see how we have looked after it. I am absolutely astonished in 12 years as tenants they've never, ever sent a representative in person or sent documentation.
> *I*: WOULD YOU WANT PEOPLE TO COME?
> *Zack*: Frankly no, but as it is their investment as well I'm astounded that they've not sent a representative to look, just to see how we're actually living at the property, you know primarily what state the property is in, but how we're actually doing as a family in this community. I find it ironic. (Jeanette and Zack)

This last comment reflects precisely that sense of contradiction around the experience of the absence of housing management.

Indeed, that feeling about being managed was associated by buyers with negative feelings about being looked down upon. So, for example, Donna explained to us that she had not had a good experience with Fixham from the very beginning. She lived on a mixed tenure estate. She went on and described a visit from a Fixham housing officer:

> *Donna*: I never realised there would be a stigma to having shared ownership until I dealt with the Fixham Housing and the individual people that look down their nose at you, look down their nose at the client.
> *I*: REALLY? TELL ME ABOUT THAT.
> *Donna*: It's different things. The first time someone – I don't know who he was – didn't announce himself. We get letters about them doing estate walks and they never turn up or they cancel it. There are things there, I've not really been invested in it and I work as well so I was never here to do it. You get to

a point where you just leave them to do it. But one day I remember I had a day off work and I was in my gym clothes, not especially glam but I was going to the gym because I had a day off midweek. This man knocked on the door and he looked me up and down and went, "Not another one in bed." I said, "I beg your pardon?" "Yes, just" … "I've just been next door; I got him up." I was like, "The gentleman next door works nights." I was like, "Excuse me but who are you?" He changed his tactic and I was like, "Oh, so you're looking at" – and I don't feel like I'm any different to the people who are housing association who aren't shared ownership. But where we are from that side, the house next door onwards was council.

I: SO THEY'RE RENTED?

Donna: So yes, the people working for Fixham were just, I don't know whether it was some sort of stigma about council house scroungers or something just laying in bed. Clearly, to make a comment about how many people they got out of bed and then.

Two Management Issues

In two cases, we observed and discussed with buyers particular problematics of housing management. These represented moments when the question whether shared ownership was a binary or a spectrum between social/private and owner/renter became sharpest. These cases concerned third-party managing agents and excessive service charge payments.

Third-Party Managing Agents

For some of our properties we are not the freeholder, but we have a head lease and will have given a sub-lease to our own leaseholders. For these properties we are often not responsible for providing services to the block. The detailed arrangements are set out in the head lease agreement between us and the third-party landlord. If you live in a block with a third-party landlord, we will provide information about who is responsible for providing services to the block. (Greendale, *Owners' Handbook*)

The story above of the exclusion of shared owners from the on-site gym, even when the shared owner staircased to 100 per cent, due to the way the various levels of leases had been organised, shows how these legal structures are configured resonated down the years and across the various teams of the housing association. A number of quite complex issues arose where blocks were managed by third-party managing agents, most commonly as a result of s. 106 agreements. This appeared to be the sharp end of where the tension between the commercial arm of Greendale was in tension with the social ethos. We have already mentioned the "universal truth" about the issues that arose in these properties, and that more complaints arose from shared owners with external managing agents than other shared owners. The same was the case in Fixham. One of the problems here was that the association could only deal with the managing agent and not the freeholder; the shared owner could only deal with the association, and neither the managing agent nor the freeholder would engage with them. The managing agent and the freeholder were distant from issues that affected the shared owner's home, although directly responsible for them. Not surprisingly, Alison was told that shared owners "certainly don't" understand the relationships.

Both Greendale and Fixham tried to intervene in these relationships. For example, we were told that Fixham sought to ameliorate the issues in relation to third-party agents through actively seeking relationships with them, by "being strong and championing" shared owners, negotiating with the agents on behalf of the shared owners, removing and replacing an ineffective or inefficient agent, and trying to develop relationships with the agent in advance of a new development. Greendale also intervened with third-party managing agents if its shared owners were concerned that they were being overcharged, but frequently experienced delays in managing agents providing accounts, which led to uncertainties about the charges being made. At one time, Greendale would subsidise the third-party agents' costs and was not seeking to recharge shared owners in some properties at the full rate, as otherwise it would be unaffordable.

In this tripartite relationship of buyer–association–managing agent, some of our buyer participants felt that *they* were treated like *they* were the "third party". This feeling was experienced in different ways and, here, the participants' narratives were themselves significant. Paula, whom we met briefly above, when describing her response to the newsletter, complained over the management of car parking. Alison asked who managed her estate and car parking. Her response was revealing in the sense of an absence of knowledge— that the relationship transcended her everyday experiences; she grounded her response by reference to the organisation with which she had a financial relationship (Fixham), but also there was a sense in which that legal nexus was intangible:

There's a managing agent, but I don't know who the managing agent is, because I pay my service charge to Fixham, I don't pay it to anyone else, but they'll

[make] the link between them, I'm the third party and then they just step aside when there's problems and say it's between you and whoever. ... [T]his is where it's quite legal isn't it, and I don't know all about how that works.

The resort to "it's quite legal" was a recognition of the limits of her knowledge, both of the specifics of the situation and the more general comment that she did not know how that worked.

In particular, the problems with this kind of third-party arrangement were that the management charges were often high, the governance arrangements opaque, and shared owners' involvement or opportunity to participate in the structures of management of their home often limited. As one buyer put it, when discussing their service charge, emphasising the kind of "poor doors" feeling: "I pay mine and the house that's private next door pays theirs. They made a Residents' Association and didn't invite us. The managing agents didn't think to invite any of us." Staff members from both Fixham and Greendale struggled to obtain relevant accounts and information from some third-party management companies, and often had little power themselves to intervene to secure adequate billing information to pass on to shared owners. Third-party management companies were reported to use loopholes in the law regularly, if not routinely, to withhold the production of annual accounts repeatedly. But the issue was also reflected in other ways.

Buyers often, perhaps understandably but unfairly, blamed the provider for many of the problems. They tended to feel that the association should exercise greater power because of its size and influence. As Donna put it, expressing her own feeling of powerlessness:

> If you want to get out of your managing agent, you have to have some sort of committee and have the whole estate put together and have a majority vote and everything, meet in the village hall and take over – which isn't going to happen. Whereas I feel that we've got Fixham; they should be on our side and they should be advocating. They should say, "I'm not handing over a portion of your rent to a company that does nothing or that charges what they like when it's disproportionate to the work they do."

Aisha and Joe bought their flat in 2007. The flat was in a block developed by a large building company, which sub-contracted its management. The block was made up mainly of owners, but about a third was shared ownership. The block had a concierge, who was responsible only for the owners and not the shared owners. Aisha and Joe read the lease in detail together—as Aisha said, "[W]e read through stuff and make sure we know what we're getting into." However, what they were unaware of at that time ("because we haven't bought a house before") was "who was responsible for this, who was responsible for that". As Aisha put it, "[T]he actual well we don't do this they do it, oh they own it, they do this, they do this, we own this, we've employed these people, it was very, very confusing." The agents had been many and poor over the years, and the service charge fees had ramped up from around £80 per month to £200–230 per month:

> *I:* SO THEY PUT THE SERVICE CHARGE UP ON WHAT BASIS, THE
>   CHANGE OF CONTRACT?
> *Joe:* Basically that they'd made mistakes. The contract does say something about
>   if there's any extra or you've paid too much then they right it at the end of the
>   year. But the service charge accounts for a start were being delayed year on
>   year on year and we were never getting them and we kept getting these notices
>   saying it's been delayed blah blah and then eventually they said oh we've
>   made a horrible mess of this, we're going to have to charge you all this extra
>   money basically.

Apparently, there had been many mistakes in the past, which led to undercharging and, consequently, increases. Clearly, neither Aisha nor Joe had envisaged the service charge increasing at such a rate over that short period. As Aisha said:

> I do think the issue as well that we've got to, when you sort of think about it you
> think, "well no one is really going to say this, are they"; but of course we had a
> lease, and we read through it; but what wasn't in the lease was you may be asked
> to pay above the rate of inflation for no reason. Obviously no one is going to put
> that in writing because no one wants to admit it but that should've been a con-
> dition of us moving in.

Aisha went on,

> I work as self-employed on a very, very low income so it's very, very difficult as
> you see just getting further and further financially screwed. It made me quite
> angry and upset that not only was this happening but that I from my personal
> financial point of view and we as a couple there's nothing we could do about it.
> I felt particularly that because we'd been accepted onto the scheme which at the
> time with the shared ownership it made it look as if it was helping us in our
> financially difficult position, had actually said actually no, we're just going to
> screw you over later. So I felt quite sort of deceived and let down.

Service Charges

A service charge is a payment in addition to rent which recompenses a landlord or managing agent for their costs of repair and maintenance. There are complex legal rules about the recovery of service charges, which are thankfully unnecessary to deal with here (see Davey and Bates 2014). Both Fixham and Greendale had particular problems with significant service charges on the shared ownership properties they managed. In dealing with these charges, both recognised their obligations to their occupiers.

The "social" in the "business" was emphasised when it came to matters such as spreading the financial cost of external repairs to the fabric of the building. For example, Greendale would take a view about whether it was affordable to marginal home owners to pass on all such costs. In some cases, it would soak up such costs itself. Our fieldwork notes include the following observation of a meeting where such repair costs were in issue, which illustrates the kinds of dynamic underpinning this issue:

> When preparing the [repair] notices [officers] were acutely aware of the very high charges and feel "ouch" for the people they're sending them to: "We know it will be painful for the person on the other side." Staff all agreed that the costs were excessive: "We can't bill them that." The notices ask for full payment within 30 days of receipt. … The manager then called the boss in [Greendale Group] and tells them of the high costs that have come out, and asks for approval before they're sent out. He says: "I'm not kidding you … we can issue them Friday and turn the emails and phones off!" … The Director is then called … Discussion about whether they'll decide to cap costs, but this may set a precedent.

Service charges represented a perennial "bugbear" of practically all of our shared owner participants, who expressed considerable frustration about them. Most buyers did not appreciate how they were calculated, and complained about the level of information they were given, the quality of service, or the fact that the service was apparently not provided. Staff from both associations noted that shared owners were more financially challenged than other leaseholders, and so had a greater tendency to query any bills and charges they received. While issues around service charges are a feature of all leasehold properties, the often-limited control over, and sensitivity to, increased costs means that service charges are an issue particularly keenly felt by our shared owners. Moreover, shared owners pay the entire proportion of their proportion of the estate or building upkeep regardless of the amount of equity share they hold.

Working out whether there was a miscalculation required a great deal of tenacity, it seems:

> There's one of my neighbours is insidious in looking at the, he persuades them to give him a breakdown of what the bill is for. If he didn't do that and didn't say, "Why are we being charged £4.20 every time a light bulb goes in the hall?" They used to charge us for weeding a communal garden; we don't have a communal garden. It's lots of things like that. If he didn't go through that list and, we're very lucky in the fact that there is somebody who works in a bank who's bothered about columns because I would probably look at it and go, "I'll do that when I've got some energy." (Bob, Greendale)

Janine was concerned that she and her husband were paying a service charge to Fixham for gardening services to a small area in their communal car park, which they knew were not being done. They conducted an experiment:

> *Janine*: Now, the thing is, from then on, we noticed that, like, before, they used to drive their van in, sit in their van in the car park for two minutes, then drive back out. I understand there's not a large area to maintain. I get that. But me and my husband put some rubbish in the … thorny bushes and everything, beside the car park. And we thought, "We'll see how long that stays there."
> *I*: OH, I SEE. YOU TESTED IT, SORT OF THING.
> *Janine*: Yes. I think it was nine months. And then until someone from Fixham came out, and then the weed was – no word of a lie, I'm five foot three, and it was a little bit taller than me. That's how long they didn't maintain it. And we were paying £11 a month for this. So that's been going on for a couple of years. Eventually, after – basically, you call through to Fixham, go through the first point, which is their customer care team, then obviously they're just taking notes: "Someone will call you back." Never, ever get a call back, ever. So of course, it's an 0845 number, so that's a nice charge for you on the phone.

Bethany's issue arose over the calculation of service charges in her block. She told us that the association increased the management fee in the block by 89 per cent, to which she objected "quite strongly". For her, the calculation of her service charges and her treatment by Greendale produced her own sense of identity and positionality. One of Alison's conversations with Bethany proceeded as follows, with Bethany accepting, possibly, that she was in social housing, but equally defining herself out:

Bethany: This is the really annoying thing, because I think sometimes when you're on social housing people assume you're ill-educated and ill-informed, and I'm actually very well-educated.

I: DO YOU SEE YOURSELF AS IN SOCIAL HOUSING?

Bethany: I suppose – I don't know, I suppose it is kind of social housing, isn't it? I don't know what – but, you know, that kind of … I think the assumption is if you're in shared ownership, you're probably, I don't know, … my feeling was, first of all, I got brushed off which I find most people just brush you off, which just annoys me, because I refuse to be fobbed off. It went from, I don't know, £40-odd something, 50 quid, or something, it was £50-odd to £150. Anyway, it was 89 per cent; I remember calculating it, and I got told the reason they were doing that was because they'd benchmarked it.

I: WHAT DOES THAT MEAN?

Bethany: They were comparing it with other buildings. So unless you compare it with a one-bedroom flat in [the area], it's not actually benchmarking, is it? I could benchmark it with housing in [ ] and I'm guessing I'm paying too much. They wouldn't show me the benchmarking figures, and they sent me a big letter explaining what benchmarking was. It's like I speak five languages, I've got a degree and masters, I know what benchmarking means. I said, "Well, just show me where in my lease, what things in my lease are you refer-ring to?" [where] it lets you say you can benchmark it and increase my charges.

Bethany struggled with whether she was in social housing, but was able to avoid that question by distancing herself from a type of person in social housing—as Goffman (45) puts it, within parentheses, "The natural history of a category of persons with a stigma must be clearly distinguished from the natural history of the stigma itself."

Bethany's struggle about "social housing" and differentiation (to which we return in the next chapter) was told in a different way by Emma. Emma's main narrative was about the leak. However, in the middle of that story, she broke off and told a different story, which, for her, was about a similar issue to do with her service charge but which also was used by her to illustrate her own positionality:

Another issue with shared ownership which, I understand why it happens – well, I don't really understand why, it's annoying – is that we're obviously in a so-called affordable housing, although it's not really very much. We pay a service charge and this block is a mixture of privately-owned tenants, shared ownership and social housing. I completely agree with that principle; it means you don't always get the greatest neighbours and a big mix of neighbours but I understand the importance behind it. But I presume the social housing side of it doesn't pay any service charge. I don't know how that works exactly.

We've had a couple of incidents with people in the social housing side that have been fly-tipping and causing a lot of rubbish. There was a Roma family over there but there were others as well that they have since been kicked out. But during that time – and I complained about this a few years back to the housing association – shared ownership people and I presume the private, our service charge goes up because it's the general maintenance. Our proportion goes up and it went up by something like £100 each a year for an issue that is nothing to do with us. I remember going to – we had a residents' forum and I was saying, "Why is our service charge coming up because we're not doing anything wrong, but other people are?" Everyone else was there; it was only me from the shared ownership side. Everyone else was saying, "Oh, we're really happy that our rent has gone down."

Although I'm shared ownership and affordable housing, I know it's probably unavoidable but we do feel that we're subsidising other parts when actually we can't really afford to do that. We're trying to be good tenants and maintain things and report things if things are fixed so they get it all done. Other people aren't playing their side of it. I know that's probably unavoidable but I just think that's unfair for people that are on only 25, 30, 40 per cent ownership that it really went up a lot. Then when this particular family moved, you saw how much it went down because they itemise the amount. So you know that rubbish clearance – and it was obvious because there were rats and we had a lot of problems, luckily on that side. But it was down to that particular family so.

Emma's differentiation was caused by the calculation of the service charge and her understanding—correct or not—that her service charge increased because of the deviant behaviours of her social rented housing neighbours.

Conclusions

In approaching the management of shared ownership, our case study housing associations understood that it should be regarded as closely aligned with ownership. This meant an absence of housing management, which also reflected, as a general rule, the kind of ethos of the buyer themselves. However, that clearly was not uniform, and there were moments when buyers wondered whether the association really cared about the property, in which they both held a stake. One might say, with Keenan (2010), that the absence of management was "holding up" ownership in this context. This ceding of control was not necessarily based on legal values. It was the case that, for Greendale, the basis of its strategy was founded in an idea about *caveat emptor*, but this was rather an *ex post* rationale because of the way in which shared owners were said to be more demanding renters.

We considered two particular housing management issues in which the identity of shared ownership was particularly formed: third-party managing agents and service charges. In both of these, these ideas of ownership/renting and social/private were particularly at the fore as association officers and buyers negotiated these apparent binaries with each other, others, and themselves. We have argued that rather than operating on a binary, each of these operates along a flexible spectrum. In particular, for example, the buyer's identity on this spectrum is understood by reference to the stigmatised *other*, a point to which we return in the next chapter.

Whether in being absent from managing shared ownership or in buyers' active engagement in the problematic costs and management of their properties, law–property–society was being performed and legal consciousness produced. One might say that buyers' responses were to seek to work with the system, while simultaneously challenging it, for example, through experimentation (whether the services were actually provided by the housing association) and audit (requiring explanation of charges). The nature of the bargain into which the occupiers had entered was continually in action, as was the production of their identity as owners, by reference to the *other*, the social rented tenant. In this situated context, in which legal consciousness is wrapped up with tenure, this kind of selective belonging is particularly critical, and in shared owners' narratives, it was expressed through things, such as rubbish and benchmarking.

Bibliography

Allen, P. (1982), *Shared Ownership: A Stepping Stone to Home Ownership*, London: HMSO.

Blessing, A. (2012), 'Magical or Monstrous? Hybridity in Social Housing Governance', 27(2), *Housing Studies*: 189–207.

Boeger, N. (2017), 'The New Corporate Movement', in N. Boeger and C. Villiers (eds), *Shaping the Corporate Landscape: Towards Corporate Reform and Enterprise Diversity*, Oxford: Hart.

Bramley, G., Dunmore, K., Durrant, C. and Smart, G. (1995), *Do-It-Yourself Shared Ownership: An Evaluation*, London: Housing Corporation.

Bramley, G., Morgan, J., Cousins, L., Dunmore, K., Three Dragons Consultancy and MORI Social Research (2002), *Evaluation of the Low Cost Home Ownership Programme*, London: ODPM.

Brown, A. (2004), 'Anti-social Behaviour, Crime Control and Social Control', 43(2), *Howard Journal of Criminal Justice*: 203–11.

Cairncross, L., Clapham, D. and Goodlad, R. (1997), *Housing Management, Consumers and Citizens*, London: Routledge.

Central Housing Advisory Committee (CHAC) (1938), *The Management of Municipal Housing Estates*, London: HMSO.

Cowan, D. and McDermont, M. (2006), *Regulating Social Housing: Governing Decline*, London: Routledge.

Cowan, D., Pantazis, C. and Gilroy, R. (2001), 'Social Housing as Crime Control: An Examination of the Role of Housing Management in Policing Sex Offenders', 10(4), *Social and Legal Studies*: 435–57.

Davey, F. and Bates, J. (2014), *Leasehold Disputes*, 3rd ed, London: Legal Action Group.

Flint, J. (2002), 'Social Housing Agencies and the Governance of Anti-social Behaviour', 17(4), *Housing Studies*: 619–37.

Flint, J (2004), 'Reconfiguring Agency and Responsibility in the Governance of Social Housing in Scotland', 41(1), *Urban Studies*: 151–72.

Franklin, B. (2000), 'Demands, Expectations and Responses: The Shaping of Housing Management', 15(6), *Housing Studies*: 907–28.

Haworth, A. and Manzi, T. (1999), 'Managing the "Underclass": Interpreting the Moral Discourse of Housing Management', 36(1), *Urban Studies*: 153–165.

Keenan, S. (2010), 'Subversive Property: Reshaping Malleable Spaces of Belonging', 19(4), *Social and Legal Studies*: 423–39.

Lupton, M., Hale, J., Sprigings, N., and Chartered Institute of Housing (2003), *Incentives and Beyond? The Transferability of the Irwell Valley Gold Service to Other Social Landlords*, London: ODPM.

Manzi, T. and Morrison, N. (2017), 'Risk, Commercialism and Social Purpose: Repositioning the English Housing Association Sector', forthcoming, *Urban Studies*: 1–18.

McDermont, M. (2007), 'Mixed Messages: Housing Associations and Corporate Governance', 16(1), *Social and Legal Studies*: 71–94.

McDermont, M. (2010), *Governing, Independence, and Expertise: The Business of Housing Associations*, Oxford: Hart Publishing.

Morrison, N. (2016), 'Institutional Logics and Organisational Hybridity: English Housing Associations' Diversification into the Private Rented Sector', 31(8), *Housing Studies*: 897–915.

Pawson, H. and Mullins, D. (2010), *After Council Housing: Britain's New Social Landlords*, Basingstoke: Palgrave Macmillan.

Royal Commission (1885), *Royal Commission on the Housing of the Working Classes*, vol II: Minutes of Evidence, London: HMSO.

Tenant Services Authority (TSA) (2009), *Existing Tenants Survey 2008: Shared Owners*, London: TSA.

Walker, R. (2000), 'The Changing Management of Social Housing: The Impact of Externalisation and Managerialisation', 15(2), *Housing Studies*: 281–99.

Wallace, A. (2008b), *Achieving Mobility in the Intermediate Housing Market: Moving Up and Moving On?*, York: Joseph Rowntree Foundation.

5

Selling and Buying Shared Ownership

Introduction

In the previous two chapters, we have discussed how and why shared ownership became knowable. In this chapter, we move on to consider how shared
ownership is sold and why it is bought. One of the issues confronting housing
associations wishing to sell shared ownership is the general lack of knowledge
about it, even after 40 years or so. That lack of knowledge may be less since
the advent of the internet's search ability and since some Web-based property
sale platforms have introduced a shared ownership filter. However, there is
still a need to "sell" shared ownership, both in terms of the concept and in
terms of marketing properties.

This is the translation of the complexity inherent in the idea of shared ownership into something singular that draws things together, like the model
lease. Recall Stanley's metaphor that "the technical complexities of a modern
aircraft do not debar ordinary people from flying", but the idea of flying still
had to be sold, people's fears had to be addressed, and the important thing was
not to let the technicalities of shared ownership come in the way of selling it.
Without demand, there would be no shared ownership. In order to produce
that demand, the world of shared ownership needed and needs to be constructed, and key questions need to be answered in order to be able to make
it knowable beyond the policy board, "to construct a world, their world, to
define its constituent elements, and to provide for it a time, a space, and a
history" (Callon 1986: 21). Callon puts it best (*id.*: 25–6):

© The Author(s) 2018
D. Cowan et al., *Ownership, Narrative, Things*, Palgrave Socio-Legal Studies,
https://doi.org/10.1057/978-1-137-59069-5_5

Translation builds an actor-world from entities. It attaches characteristics to them and establishes more or less stable relationships between them. Translation is a definition of roles and the delineation of a scenario. It speaks for others but in its own language. It is an initial definition.

This assemblage of entities animates the first part of this chapter. In this part, we draw on a messy range of sources, all of which emphasise the mutuality inherent in what we have described as the law–property–society triptych. We are particularly interested in marketing materials and handbooks, as well as our case study associations' processes for selling their shared ownership units. In particular, we draw on two brochures which market shared ownership estates "off plan" (i.e. before they have been constructed). These brochures were for estates that we have anonymised to "Spirit" and "Hartford Meadow".[1] We picked these brochures up randomly during our research, and they are unrelated to Fixham and Greendale, our case study associations. We use them to demonstrate how shared ownership is translated.

This is from where a kind of legal property consciousness emerges. Our argument is that socio-legal studies can develop a range of ideas from a neglected resource—the leaflet, or, as many housing associations involved in shared ownership now produce, the glossy brochure and micro-website. This kind of thing does not only offer a representation of legal ideas (consider the mortgage leaflet), but also provides a translation of those ideas and imbues it with its own consciousness. In other words, this kind of thing is a legal technique for enrolling people and things. It is a purposeful translation, and one in which the world of shared ownership must be reduced to its core. Key problematics about social/private, ownership/renting, need to be reduced. The ideal buyer needs to be constructed, understood, and targeted. Marketing is a key socio-legal process, and one which is often ignored. We take our inspiration here from John Law's reading of sales brochures for fighter aircraft, in which he argues for naïve readings which produce different objects from the same thing—"objects which carry the same name … but which are quite unlike one another in character" (Law 2002: 15).

In the second part of the chapter, we draw on what we were told by our buyers as to why they purchased that particular property. The question is not whether they were persuaded by the marketing. Rather, it is how they construct themselves in this new world. As the Appendix demonstrates, few of our buyer participants had any experience of ownership, and most had rented previously. What narrative did they offer as regards their engagement with

---

[1] These names have been selected by us to convey a similar ethos to the names of the estates.

shared ownership? There are a number of themes here, which come from their stories—about luck, joy, desperation, the value/s of ownership, comparative affordability between tenures, future intentions. These were stories told in the past, and often to contrast the buyers' current feelings, but they were vividly told as our buyers reminisced about their pathways. They were stories through which they distinguished their positionality from others, commonly using metaphors to describe their status, enacting the law–property–society triptych in their narrative. A further theme is our buyer participants' amazement that they could access shared ownership, believing that they were not suitable candidates. We argue that our participants were often *abstracting their identities from "the social"*, a sense in which they were external to the social relationship. Commonly, this reflected a difference about tenurial perceptions between the social clientele and their aspirations to ownership. Thus, tenure speaks at this point through an abstraction of self, and in so doing an expression of their legal consciousness of tenure and its division.

Selling Shared Ownership

We start with an excerpt from a publication entitled *Shared Ownership 2.0: Towards a Fourth Mainstream Tenure*, which was published in 2014. It bears the imprint of the Chartered Institute of Housing (CIH; the professional body for housing) and Orbit (a housing association provider of shared ownership). The title suggests a re-launch, but also suggests something grander as an objective—that shared ownership should be the fourth tenure, presumably after owner-occupation, social and private renting, and that its ambition is to be mainstream. It sets shared ownership *apart* from the rest, as different, as neither social nor private, but something else. It contains the following, under the heading "Product":

Understanding the brand

Shared ownership has huge strengths as a product. It is a real and affordable alternative to private renting, offering people more choice, the chance to gain some equity and, for some, the opportunity to move into mainstream/full home ownership, should they wish to. It also offers the security of tenure that private renting rarely provides. Shared ownership supports community stability as well; evidence suggests that having a stake in their home makes people more likely to invest in their neighbourhood.

However, shared ownership as a brand suffers from a lack of awareness, and limited understanding of exactly what it is, how it works, who it is for and how to get it – 89 per cent of CIH election panel members surveyed identified tackling this as a key way to grow the tenure.

The current lack of awareness is not helped by variations in the product names used by different providers, and the range of additional eligibility requirements across different localities.

… Fundamentally, the shared ownership concept is easy to grasp, but the brand and product are being inadvertently undermined by well-intentioned but unhelpful inconsistencies in use.

There is also a wider challenge about how the tenure is viewed and used by government, providers and consumers. Historically, shared ownership has been regarded as a "social" product, and this has shaped how people access it. (Sinn and Davies 2014: 14)

This passage beautifully sets out the problematic of shared ownership. Despite all of the support, money, its evident attraction, various evaluations, publicity, and awareness-raising events, ignorance remains and is made worse by inconsistency between its proponents and users. This kind of fractal coherence (Law 2002) suggests natural responses—simplification, cutting bureaucracy, removing the social, increasing satisfaction. The report offers both a vision of the problems and their solution, to achieve an ambition. A shared ownership charter is now promoted by the CIH to support these ideas.

This story has been told many times in fact, as we saw in the previous chapters. This is not shared ownership *2.0* (or, as a subsequent follow-up put it, shared ownership 2.1: Davies and Sinn 2016); we are well beyond that. This, then, is the problem—ignorance is not bliss; or, put another way, the major question is how to get people to interact with, and understand, the product. This is the problem for which marketing is seen as the solution.

Mirroring the Private

The overall impression around the marketing of shared ownership is that it mirrors the private sector. Many personnel involved in the sale in our case study housing associations had backgrounds as private sector lettings or estate agents or involvement in the lending industry. One key point of distinction in both Greendale and Fixham and some other associations was that their marketing and sales staff did not receive commission on sold properties—other associations, we were told, had done this; it was a point of pride because one key aspect of the job was to explain shared ownership to buyers, which was felt to be achieved better, more neutrally, when the agent had no stake in the outcome. There was a sense of achievement in selling a property: "[Sales officer] described how people are happy and cry and she cries with them as they're so moved at being allocated a home. 'It's a lovely feeling, helping someone'" (Observation notes, Greendale). Indeed, the sales process melds market transactions with elements of social housing allocation in that national and/or local eligibility criteria are applied.

The brochures they produce for their estates (in hard copy and electronic copy, often publicised on a scheme's "micro-site" and uploaded as YouTube videos) mirrored those found marketing new developments in the private sector. This was how they were imagining their customers. Nowhere in the brochure was social, or social housing, mentioned at all, although the housing association might be named (often without prominence in the material, such as on the back cover). Indeed, it may be that shared ownership was marketed harder as private than owner-occupation. Alison's observation notes from the marketing of a mixed tenure estate by Greendale note: "On reflection, looking at the private marketing brochure and the shared ownership marketing brochure it is apparent the shared owners is the harder sell. The private brochure is more factual and dry about the flats and provides a series of floor plans where the shared ownership brochure for [X] focuses on the lifestyle of [the area]." In Greendale, Alison was told that "[t]he micro [web]sites [advertising schemes] downplay housing association involvement as people want it to be like the private sector. They used to brand it with [their association] name but no longer, as producing an independent identity gave them a competitive edge over others. Staff believe shared owners buy into being private owners."

Sales teams for a development might have a sales office, with brochures, a touch screen with floor plans and marketing that could be called up onto the screen. There were "launches" of new schemes, and viewing "open days". The common questions at open days from potential buyers included ones about "parking, trains, tenure split, commonly ask about social rented". Considerable thought was put into a new shared ownership scheme's finishings: "They also consider neutral schemes when considering the specification and choices of the new schemes, so they go for more traditional for houses and more funky for flats, but as kitchens in flats they blend floor coverings and don't have high tiles so the colour of walls can be consistent throughout" (Greendale, Observation notes). There are "dressed" show flats, and a sales office may well be a flat in the development. Alison's observation notes of the marketing of one Greendale development are as follows:

> The brochures, marketing material and show flats are designed by third party companies in conjunction with the marketing and sales team. The manager says she likes that part of it and enjoys directing the show flats. They say they don't

want show flats to be bold but neutral colours, they appeal to the target market and also show you can fit normal furniture in. [A]pparently people like the modern look but they can assert themselves on it too. There was a concern in this development that in the open plan kitchens and living rooms the kitchen space in the one and two bedrooms were too dominant and, especially for the one bedroom properties, smaller kitchen areas and larger living space were required. They do a satisfaction survey about sales and marketing process and also property managers' feedback to them what things arise from properties after some time. An example of this was video entryphones that people like but there are lots of problems with them and to limit call outs and repairs these have been changed to normal entryphones.

Photographs from the brochure were screen printed on canvases hung around the corridors. Marketing personnel were involved at an early stage in the potential development, and advised on likely demand for the properties. There was felt to be considerable competition with other housing associations, which meant that they started their marketing earlier than competitors so that their name was more prominent in the scheme. However, although there was pride in working for the particular association, Fixham's own survey evidence indicated that "shared owners don't choose Fixham, they choose location, price and number of bedrooms as the most important factors. Fixham and the involvement of a housing association is not important, only a means to an end" (Observation notes). Shared owners reportedly fed back to Fixham that, as there were local connection requirements to obtain the properties, selling "place" to locals was not necessary, and shared owners reported that they did not always recognise their local area in the marketing material.

Shared ownership marketing material more broadly emphasises the opportunity to become a homeowner and reflects normative values, and experiences, of owning. They used "vox pops" on micro-sites and in their literature such as the following:

Owning my own home is one of my greatest achievements so far.
Owning my own home feels fantastic, it's a real feeling of independence and confidence.
Without the opportunity we'd all still be in rented place which none of us liked, none of us were happy.
We can make it a home rather than a house. That was crucial to us, we wanted to make it a home for the children to grow up in and you can't do that unless you own your own home or you can rent long term without the risk of that changing. It's the circumstances you don't have control over. I can't actually relay how happy and elated we were when we were told we'd been accepted to be honest.

And housing provider staff captured in this marketing reflect the material and cultural attitudes that affords ownership its significance:

> Renting is killing people, raising deposits is out of reach of a lot of people. (Staff member at property fair)
> People are crying, really emotional at having achieved something. (YouTube promotional video)

Selling the Lifestyle

One of the most noticeable things about the marketing brochures that we put together between 2013 and 2015 was that they were not selling a unit of accommodation. They were selling an aspirational lifestyle. The lifestyle is far removed from what one might imagine social housing to be. Photographs and text enhance this focus on the lifestyle. Hartford Meadow's front cover is a picture which, presumably, imagines the market, or what it was assumed the consumer aspired to be. There is a large household of very English people photographed in neo-Edwardian dress, a kind of "English Country" wear, and posed in front of a wood. This household is a traditional family, and the brochure creates the aspirational feel further through reference to local restaurants and shopping malls: "[Y]ou'll find designer name boutiques, beauty salons and spas alongside the usual convenience stores." Similarly, Spirit sells the lifestyle of the area over and above the accommodation, citing the area's vibrance, coolness, and desirability:

> [AREA]. It's as though they took all the best bits of modern urban living and brought them naturally together in one cool place. With a vibrant street culture, fascinating markets, trendy arty types, intriguing restaurants and great shops all vying for your attention. Now [SPIRIT] adds the finishing touch, with a collection of beautiful apartments designed around your lifestyle.

Selling the Grid

Most developments are sold "off plan". Both Spirit and Hartford Meadow's brochure had photographs which were "3D CGI renderings" indicative of a block or particular plots "for illustrative purposes". They also contained grids which map out the estate and particular apartments or houses. The map of the Hartford Meadow estate Fig. 5.1—indicated the different tenures of property by colour.

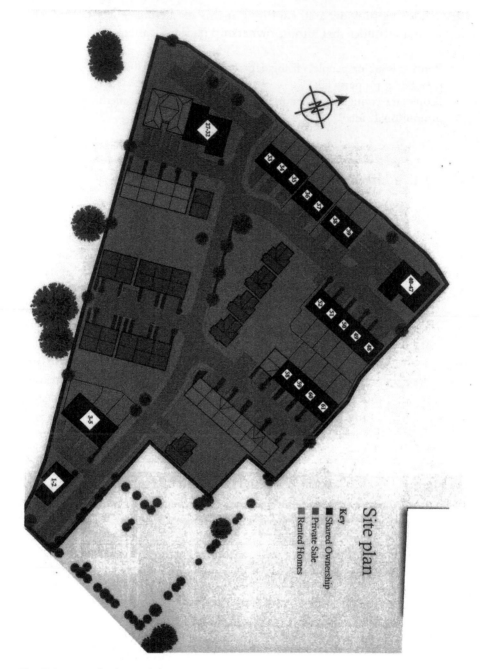

Fig. 5.1 Hartford Meadow Estate Map

Some properties are shared ownership, some are described as "private sale", and the rest are "rented homes". There was no hint as to whether the rented homes were social rent, or for private rent; and the expression "private sale" is equally meaningless, although it is clearly differentiated from shared ownership. Perhaps this expression was used to denote a certain freedom—a recognition that the buyer might not actually live in the property but might buy it to rent out. In this cartographic rendering of the estate, we have a hierarchical list of tenures; as this was selling shared ownership, that is on top.

Although Hartford Meadow's grid did not imagine a separation between the tenures, other developments clearly did and do so. For example, the shared ownership brochure for Spirit did not have the grid, the private ownership brochure (Fig. 5.2) has a grid which clearly demarcated "Block B".

During our fieldwork, there was some media attention to what came to be called "poor doors" (Osborne 2014); mixed tenure blocks of flats, which have separate entrance doors for different tenures. Observation notes in Greendale suggested that they sort blocks of flats "by core (stairwell in one part of block) and by floor". Social rented housing, shared ownership, and ownership properties were separated out. Occasionally, there were pepper-potted properties and sales staff believed that senior managers favoured such developments, "but, on the ground, prospective buyers of shared ownership properties say 'where's the social?'. Shared owners like to be away from social rented. And also, it is preferable to have separation, from the point of view of housing management and service charges. The new homes team asked for separation fences, barriers; they began to joke about the level of separation they ask for, but it is clear they like clear demarcation to support purchases and also operational matters after sales, as they say the housing management approach is different."

The physical segregation of different tenures was brought home to us by Dave's notes of his interview with Pat and Reena:

> I met Pat and Reena on a hot day in their London flat. It was about 7.30pm, and Reena was bathing their son. Pat had just got home from his day job as a housing worker in another area. …
>
> I was late for our interview because I couldn't find the building. First, I could not find the street, because my A-Z was out of date – these were newbuilds. Then, as I walked down the street, I realised that the blocks on either side of the road were given names in alphabetical order. I was looking for block S. But I couldn't find it. The road went from R to U. After five minutes of panicking, I realised that the entrance point for block S was off the main drag, down a flight of steps. It had been designed so that the shared ownership block had been

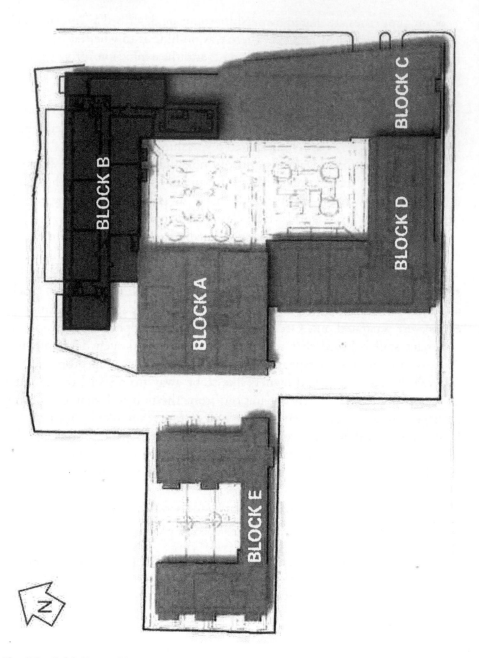

Fig. 5.2 Spirit Estate Map

spatially separated from the owned blocks. The Guardian had recently run a "poor doors" story just before we met, and Pat remarked, "It's no real surprise to me, … I feel, I suppose, I'm a bit of a realist, you know, you get what you pay for." Reena, who joined us towards the end of the discussion, remarked:

> well obviously the other buildings have got the concierge and the gym and stuff, but we're still in a nice area. There's some things where it's a bit kind of – like our entrance is like really hidden away and you feel a bit like, "Oh, okay." Everyone else has got kind of like these open entrances and we're all like – everyone that comes to visit us for the first time is like, "We can't find you, where are you?"

What happened to block T? That, Pat told me, was further down the stairs, and the block next to them. It was the social rented block.

Selling Things

Things, such as kitchen fittings, sell. Photographs and show homes are presented in neutral colours with modern furniture; things represent the lifestyle. Sometimes, these are required to "sweeten the deal" (Greendale, Marketing Representative, Observation notes). In an internal document "Sales Appraisal" for Fixham of a property that they were going to develop for shared ownership in the future, the recommendations were as follows:

1. Offer our standard shared ownership specification but look to enhance the kitchen with integrated appliances
2. Bathrooms to include bespoke mirrors and four recess lights
3. Assuming internal hallways we would recommend recessed down lights
4. Negotiate with the developer to be able to use their branding to include CGIs, fly through, access to their sales suite if possible to launch our units
5. At least one signage board to be located in a prime/central location (approximately 5 ft x 10 ft)

The significance of materials and marketing is clear; the process was about selling things.

So, for example, the Hartford Meadow brochure had a photograph of beautiful kitchen units (from a similar show home), and readers were told that the accommodation unit "is beautifully and thoughtfully designed. The specification has everything you need to make your new home comfortable and easy to live in." Spirit sold "the perfect home to create in your own image. Everything is in place – the well appointed kitchen with its clever proportions, the stylish bathroom with contemporary finishes. Now all it needs is for you to come in and establish your own personal touch." As KS13, who had been particularly involved in marketing at a housing association, suggested,

> People buy it for location, affordability and the fact that white goods and carpets are included in the spec. Those were the three main drivers for people buying with us. When somebody buys one of our homes, they are ready to move in with minimal cost. In most cases, we try to provide branded known white goods so they have more confidence in their brands – not high end, and they all come with a guarantee. We are selling more and more off plan so we can maximise those advantages. ... Turf in the back garden is always important and we do that as a spend item; it costs us little and the whole place looks really nice.

It is the case that this stuff is differentiated in quality from the social rented housing and that sold for owner-occupation. In Fixham, Alison was told that

> [s]ocial rented homes have a lower specification as the housing association is responsible for its maintenance, but shared owners are responsible for higher quality kitchens etc so they put them in (and presumably get the money back?). Hard to sell homes may also get an enhanced specification ... They want to realise the value of the scheme as it means more homes on the ground, by which [was] meant that more [sales] meant more of any homes being built, but especially social housing homes or refurbishment of the social rented stock as "that's the impetus behind us achieving value"

Explaining Shared Ownership

A choice has to be made in materials between seeking to explain shared ownership or not. It is here that the association must decide whether to translate this complex product into its materials, and, if so, how it is to be done. For socio-legal scholars, this is the "crunch" moment; the moment when a complicated legal transaction is translated in a way in which the buyer is expected to understand; when the spectra of owning/renting and social/private is made binary. And the materials did not disappoint in this respect.

Reading across the range of marketing material provided by housing associations, the content was designed to promote shared ownership as a home-ownership option to the Generation Rent cohort, explicitly so in some cases, but occasionally to families and other people who have experienced relationship breakdown. Powerful case studies were frequently deployed, emphasising the delight of buyers moving on from insecure private rented accommodation to what was *clearly* experienced as homeownership. Associations used often identical phrases and online content to affirm that the lease "is a legal document that proves you own part of your home" and "makes you an owner-occupier not a part tenant". Associations judiciously used words to qualify their statements "essentially", implying usually but perhaps not always. So, for example, this statement contained in a brochure explained shared ownership: "The scheme is sometimes referred to as a 'part own-part rent' because you literally own part of the property …"; it reflected the contemporary (over-)use of the word "literally", when what was meant was "figuratively".

Spirit did not describe shared ownership—it merely stated "shared ownership" on the front cover, presumably to distinguish the brochure from that for "Block B—Private Sale". In this way, silence about meaning was rendered powerful. Hartford Meadow did seek to explain shared ownership and did so in a rather fuller way:

Shared Ownership
   Also known as "part buy/part rent", the government-supported initiative helps you to get a foot on the property ladder and work your way up to 100% ownership. You buy a percentage share in a brand new home and pay a subsidised rent on the remaining share.
   At a later stage, you can increase the share that you own in your home. This is called "staircasing". It is a good idea to make plans for staircasing when you first buy your shared ownership home. … The more shares you buy, the less rent you pay.

This way of marketing shared ownership might be regarded as more honest than the "literal" translation as ownership. Nevertheless, one can see in its terms an emphasis on ownership—"a foot on the property ladder"—and a kind of responsiblised ownership at that because you can "work your way up" to 100 per cent. The "ladder" metaphor is one we have seen before and dominates this kind of literature and policy material. This metaphor is used to explain shared ownership because it implies that a state of progression through the housing market will naturally follow the initial purchase. And it others alternative forms of tenure, which represent the antithesis of progress up the ladder.

The incentive to buy 100 per cent was also emphasised by the explanation of staircasing, which emphasised that the bigger share you have, the less rent you pay. It effectively explained the nature of the bargain—that staircasing is the normal, and best, way of approaching shared ownership (even though staircasing is often not achieved in practice: Wallace 2008b). The potential buyer was told that this is a "government-supported" initiative—perhaps underselling that the government itself had a stake through grant and that this was social housing—and that a "subsidised" rent is paid—although the nature of that subsidy is left hanging in the air.

Our two case study providers did presentations on shared ownership and individual explanations of the product to potential customers, as well as provided an explanatory brochure. The promotion of shared ownership and the promotion of a development were rarely combined. Explanatory brochures were forced into explaining what shared ownership actually is. The explanatory brochure has the same descriptive tools and metaphors, for example, "first step on the ladder". But they also have to go beyond this. One explanatory brochure contained this description: "Shared ownership lets people realise their home ownership dreams by offering the chance to purchase a share of a property, while paying a subsidised rent on the remainder of the property." Further, "if you buy through shared ownership", you will "own part of your home, rather than paying rent with no return"; "your monthly mortgage and rent can work out cheaper than buying outright."

Eligibility

So far, we have seen how selling shared ownership is about selling a dream, an aspiration, and, as near as possible, ownership. Although shared ownership is never described as "private", there is a deafening silence about its status on the social/private spectrum. Nevertheless, everything about the marketing emphasises how close it is to the private sector, from its similarity to private development brochures and newspaper advertisements to the idealised occupiers. Nevertheless, there is a bureaucratic process, which must be completed to determine eligibility for a property which is being sold for the first time. That eligibility was constrained, first, by the grant-making body. The regulator's rules constrained eligibility for shared ownership to households with an income below £60,000 (£66,000 in London, and £80,000 if the property had more than three bedrooms)[2] who were unable to buy a property on the open market without assistance. Priority was given to existing social housing tenants and military personnel, as well as to key workers. Where a property was developed through a s. 106 agreement, the local authority might impose extra criteria on a scheme, for example, through reserving properties for local persons or placing a lower-income cap (although housing associations and lenders tend to resist overly tight criteria which diminish the market for the

---

[2] These income thresholds were increased in 2016, after our fieldwork took place.

properties). In any event, in certain areas such as London, shared ownership properties were often unaffordable.

The bureaucracy involved can be demonstrated by Alison's fieldwork notes observing a Fixham officer considering applications for shared ownership:

> She has a long checklist for each person who has reserved a flat that she must go through and action each part, such as getting the wage slips, ID, letter of support from local authority if already a homeowner (so they have to show there is a reason, a housing need, why they need shared ownership, usually relationship breakdown), proof that they have sufficient funds for the deposit, landlord references showing not been in arrears in the last 12 months etc. They also tick off this list when contracts have been checked and signed, relevant fees paid etc.

When potential purchasers are ranked in terms of eligibility and housing need, if applicants displayed the same attributes, then the local authority was asked to prioritise the competing applicants. The governing criteria are translated into demonstrating "housing need"; as Alison was told by the officer, "[A]t the end of the day, that's what we're here for." As Cowan and McDermont (2006: 59; original emphasis) put it, "[N]eed is both a rationality and technology of social housing. ... It is also a wonderfully *obscure* device around which a variety of different expertise has coalesced." It is the manipulation of this device that enables social housing providers to demonstrate that they are meeting housing need. This is not (generally) housing need in the sense of otherwise having nowhere to live, although it may encompass insecurity, overcrowding, or the end of a private sector tenancy; but typically housing need was conflated with housing demand in the sense of an ambition, and unfulfilled need, for ownership.

Both Greendale and Fixham were required to ascertain eligibility of potential buyers and explain shared ownership to them, and had application forms for a property. Greendale had an interview checklist to be completed by the sales representative. However, the income-screening process was mechanical, gathering the details required to use the regulator's online affordability calculator, to explain the rudimentary basics of ownership, and to check the applicants had received the relevant brochures. Sometimes, these sales staff–prospective purchaser interactions were undertaken in the show home so that the home governed the interaction. Applicants also were given lists of suitable independent financial advisors who understood the demands of shared ownership, who would determine their creditworthiness. It was perfectly possible for such an advisor to be present on the site, for example, at launch events and the like, to determine financial eligibility for mortgages there and then. Names of solicitors who were said to understand shared ownership were also provided to applicants.

A rather different process was apparent in respect of re-sales—where a shared ownership property is sold on (assigned) to a new buyer. Of the buyer interviewees, 25 had bought on re-sale. We found that the relationship between shared ownership and housing need might become more strained in these transactions. The association had a right to nominate a new buyer within a certain period for the property at a price determined by an independent valuer. The model lease contained timescales within which the association had to nominate a new person (two months) and the nominated person had to enter into a contract of sale (12 weeks from the date on which the agreement was sent to them). Any buyer of a re-sale property would not receive the same level of information about shared ownership as a new-build buyer: "With resales the responsibility is left much more on [the buyer] and the solicitors as we don't do a viewing in the same way" (Greendale, Observation notes).

Both housing association providers charged fees in respect of re-sales. In Greendale, the fee to sell the property was 1 per cent of the value of the share being sold, and in Fixham, the fees for reselling shares ranged between £400 and 1.5 per cent of the full market value of the whole property depending on the date the lease was created; as Sam, one of our buyer interviewees put it, all of "which seems a little bit unfair when you're only selling 50 per cent; why do you have to pay 1 per cent of the full value of it?" The fees for selling are comparable with estate agent fees, but the service less so, as associations were not responsible for progressing the sale, as an estate agent often does. Fewer resources were expended in selling re-sale properties compared with new-build homes. The seller provided the photographs at Greendale and the surveyor was asked to provide photographs at Fixham, although sellers could also supply them. The presentation of re-sales was often of a poorer quality than new-build and other open market purchases.

The eligibility criteria for re-sales seemed much looser than the criteria for new-build buyers, presumably because there was less of a requirement to satisfy the regulator at this stage. Thus, the relationship between shared ownership and housing need became even more distant. The need of the association to satisfy itself of the housing need of the buyer was less constrained; indeed, if the association was unable to nominate a buyer within the relevant period, then the property could be sold on the open market, in which case any new buyer would not be required to demonstrate housing need at all. Finally, the government department responsible for shared ownership was consulting on whether to remove this nomination right (and, after our research had been completed, did so) (DCLG 2015).

Buying Shared Ownership

In this section, we discuss why our buyer interviewees bought their shared ownership property. Here, there was a mixture of reasons, some of which mirrored the private ownership market and some of which related to the buyers' own particular circumstances. This was the first phase of our interview schedule, as we discussed buyers' housing pathways with them, and how they alighted on this particular property and shared ownership in particular. As we noted in the introduction, our buyer interviewees tended to abstract themselves from social housing. They had various techniques for so doing, for example, through an expression of surprise that they had been selected. In this sense, our data is rather different from McKee's 14 shared equity/ownership interviewees in Glasgow and West Dumbartonshire (McKee 2011), perhaps because that research focused on areas with higher levels of poverty and deprivation, which were the subject of regeneration, and a larger proportion of the interview sample had previously been in the social rented sector.

Getting a Foothold

People's housing pathways and narratives are often riddled with metaphors and aphorisms (Gurney 1999). Our buyers' narratives were no different. Buyers talked about "getting a foothold on the property ladder", having a place that you could make your own, having security (usually in counterposition to the private rented sector), and having a "home". These were the most common narratives, alongside the possibility of capital growth. Paying rent in the private rented sector was "paying someone else's mortgage". As Smith (2008: 525) puts it, in the context of relating ownership to ethopolitics, "Not only does the investment component of owning render renting unwise, it also makes it seem unfair." Moreover, rather than seeing rent in exchange for housing services, the narratives reflected the creation of the "financialised citizen" or how ordinary people become the "investor subjects" within a financialised housing market (Langley 2006).

Ryan expressed this kind of narrative perfectly. He had just become a student when he and his wife bought their one-bedroom flat in 2009, but since then, he had completed his degree and a Master's. They had lived in private rented accommodation previously, which he described as "just a rented place". When asked why he registered with the housing association, he said:

Well, otherwise you pay the rent, it goes down the drain essentially, you pay the rent and you don't own anything and it's not a way to accumulate any wealth or whatever. So it was a way of sort of doing it differently, more wisely, spending our money on your day-to-day expenses.

Pete, who had been a "long-haired hippy" and refused ownership previously, had been persuaded by his wife as to the value of ownership:

My wife who is much more financially realistic than I am and more sensible generally had always been pestering me and saying why are we wasting money on rent you see. I said we don't have to bother about looking after the house and this, that and the other. I took the continental view because as you know on the continent a lot more people rent. She was saying we're going to have no equity and we won't have anything to pass on to our children and it's a big mistake. If there's any chance of getting any kind of shared ownership it would make sense, and I could not but agree.

Sam, whom we met in the previous section briefly, had previously been in a flat-share, which she described as "good fun", following an unsuccessful marriage. She and her ex-husband had been owners. She was registered disabled and a little bit older than other buyers. She did not want to return to renting "at my age" because "[i]t just kind of felt like I was going backwards instead of forwards". As she put it, "I'm quite prudent with my money, I'm quite shrewd and I just didn't want to really be throwing money down the drain on renting somewhere. I don't know, maybe it's just the way I've been bought up, I don't know. But it just seems a waste of money renting." Pamela expressed the same sentiments, but added the significance of having her name on the paper:

Because it meant that I could get my name on paper somewhere, and I wouldn't be stuck in the rental market paying those prices, and I'd have a bit of security at least. … The point of it was that I didn't want to be putting money into someone else's pocket any more, particularly hundreds of pounds every month. But to get this at least meant that I had my name on paper, and something on a property.

Another common trope was that the buyer was lucky in some way or another. They were lucky to find this particular property, or find shared ownership. That was how Sam described finding her property: "No one else was interested in it. It was just luck." Area and affordability were also key criteria for our buyer interviewees, as well as property condition and the possibility for capital appreciation.

Ade and Mel had lived in private rented accommodation for a considerable period. Mel worked in a city and Ade worked locally. Their daughter was born in around 2009. The area was expensive, but then, as they described it:

Ade: We were lucky: we found this. It's an ideal location, great for schools, for our daughter, facilities …

Mel: Also we had a budget limit, and it's very expensive here, so the chances that we were going to find a property we could afford were so slim, and so we were really lucky that this came up. And there was no chain or anything.

They were desperate to find somewhere because they had lived in their rented property for 3 or 4 years. Mel's maternity pay had come to an end. The landlady had never put the rent up, because they looked after the property. But, then, she needed to get possession because her business was going under. They could not find another rented property within their means. Their shared ownership property was cheaper and affordable. That rented property, they said, had felt like home because they had lived there for so many years (as Ade put it, it was a "big, creaky old home"). The shared ownership property, however, was something more to them:

Mel: The main thing for me is the fact that I feel more empowered because I know I can make changes to the property, whereas – I mean, the property we lived in was in a complete state, and she hadn't done anything to it. It was crumbling skirting – like, it was really bad. We made the best of it, but I was getting more and more frustrated, because I was at home all the time with my daughter: you notice it more. And it wasn't really practical for a child. And so in that way, this was better.

Ade: Moreover, by the end, because the rents were low we were excusing the state of the house, but then it was just – there was damp coming in, and there were so many repair issues that I just said to her, "Can you just please get it sorted out?" And then she put it up for sale. [Laughs] So by the end of it, it felt like we were almost sort of prisoners in the house, because we couldn't …

Mel: We couldn't afford to get out.

Ade: We couldn't get out, and we didn't want to ask her to do the work, because of the rents, but leaving it – not the rents, the repairs. But we knew they needed to be done, so we had to kind of pluck up the courage to ask for the repairs to be done, and then she put notice in.

Mel: It was a bit – because we were tight for money, and one of my jobs was doing childminding part-time, before and after school, which was at home, and obviously I was registered at that house, and I'd made it all safe and everything and done all the risk assessing and everything. So then to have to move, we were like, "Oh, crap, I'm going to lose my wage", so there was that thrown into it as well. So that wasn't great.

That sense of desperation was particularly felt by those who were moving from insecure situations, such as bed and breakfast (like Jim), or felt that they had a small window of opportunity. Paula was 3 months pregnant when her husband walked out on her. Rather than making an application for homelessness assistance, she went back to live with her parents. She did not want to rent again because her previous landlord had failed to pay the mortgage, which lead to her (and her then husband) getting a summons to court. Paula explained the predicament in which she found herself, once she had decided that shared ownership was her only option:

> If I wait until I've had the baby, I probably won't get a mortgage, this is my one small window, then I can buy a property, because they wouldn't give me a mortgage now based on me working three days a week and for childcare costs. So I just wouldn't have got it, so I was really panicking and stressed and hormonal anyway.

Moving from Social Housing

Eight of our buyer interviewees moved from social rented housing. We particularly focus on them here because, despite their small number, there were likely to be significant differences from our other buyers, because of the security of tenure in social rented housing. At that time, social renters had what came to be known, albeit through an inaccurate reduction, as a tenancy for life (DCLG 2010). They were not occupying insecure accommodation like those who had moved from private renting; for example, they could apply for a transfer to an alternative property (albeit that this could take some time in high-demand areas). They had what has been judicially described as a "status of irremoveability". There is, therefore, something potentially different and interesting about their stories.

And yet, there is little that is actually different. They sought the cloak of ownership; they were unhappy with their current accommodation, perhaps because it was overcrowded or they did not like the area, but that was not much different from the other buyer interviewees. They wanted choice and a bit more control, "fewer restrictions", as Jonelle put it. Joanne said:

> I didn't want to throw away rent just on a rented property, because the house I actually got on the housing association was actually a brand new house in [city], which was a lovely house and actually bigger than the one I [bought], but I actually wanted to have a stake in it. I think for me to look at – if I'm paying out every month, I want to have something at the end of it. I mean I was very driven by my parents as well that rent's throwaway money.

David and Michelle were exactly in that situation. They had grown out of their three-bedroom housing association rented property. They had sought a transfer or a swap unsuccessfully, as they were not sufficiently overcrowded to be a priority. They put their name on the list for shared ownership as a way out, not as a negative, but as a positive step in their lives. They recounted tales of neighbour nuisance and anti-social behaviour on their former estate as a reason to relocate further into the suburbs. Although their re-sale street property they had bought on a shared ownership basis was not in the best condition and they had incurred high repair costs, this had not dampened their enthusiasm for their move:

Michelle: We wanted to get on the property ladder. We were both working. We were both working full-time, we always have done, and especially in [city], it's just out of your range. We worked hard and it was hard to save.

David: We had quite a bit of money but we just couldn't get on the property ladder. It was the only way we could get on it.

Michelle: So this was our step on.

David: it was the only option [because we could not afford full ownership].

Aisling and her husband, for example, wanted to buy, as she had some savings, "but neither of us felt comfortable about the idea of buying a council flat, to be honest, disagreed with and then while we were just shilly-shallying, we got something in the post about [do-it-yourself shared ownership]". Some did try to obtain a swap or transfer, but without luck, or were able to move away from an expensive location to somewhere more affordable. This was what happened to Paul and his then partner. He described the serendipity with which a shared ownership leaflet for their chosen location came through their letterbox: "And then suddenly it was like that – it was like a missing bit of the puzzle just kind of fell into place and it was like, 'Oh, actually, that could be quite a good solution for us.'"

For two of our buyer interviewees, Claudia and Lois, shared ownership was a way out of a bad housing situation. We discuss Lois' interview in depth in Chap. 7. Claudia decided not to apply for a transfer from her council flat after she began a relationship and became pregnant:

[B]ecause, really, eventually I would have wanted to get a place of my own and I thought that was the way to go. I didn't want a council flat or to get another big council flat. I think this is more ideal, and, besides, I wouldn't have wanted to go to a council flat because you find there is a lot of violence sometimes, especially in this place and the place is dirty and all that. Where I used to live, there was mice all over the place so it was really disgusting in a way. [A] newly built place was very much appealing for all of us.

This kind of narrative about social rented housing estates, which was shared between Claudia and Lois, was unusual in our study among those who had lived at some point in social housing. For example, one of our interviewees who had lived in social housing previously felt that exercising the right to buy their social rented home was unethical.

Identity

Towards the end of our interview, we asked our participants whether they felt that they were part of social housing. This was, in a sense, a loaded question. We have already noted how shared ownership provided by housing associations is statutorily defined as social housing. Our question was not, however, a "knowledge of law" type of question. It was a question designed to elicit whether the participants felt part of social housing, or not. All of our data, like the sales material and many of our key stakeholders, had pretty much located shared ownership as private at the level of an idea or ideal. Some of the officers to whom Alison spoke in the observation phase of the research regarded shared owners as "see[ing] themselves as superior". We wondered the extent to which, if at all, that spectrum of private/social was reflected in their identities, as a kind of differentiation or selective belonging (Savage et al. 2005; Watt 2009).

The majority of our interviewees regarded themselves as "private" sector, and abstracted themselves from the social sector. There were two ways in which some of the shared owners to whom we spoke sought to differentiate themselves from others, notably social renters. First, they wondered why they had been eligible for shared ownership in the first place. Secondly, reflecting the design and layout of estates, some buyers sought to differentiate themselves from social renters, something that was particularly exaggerated. As Erving Goffman (1963/1990: 70) so neatly put it, "[F]amiliarity need not reduce contempt. For example, normals who live adjacent to settlements of the tribally stigmatized often manage quite handily to sustain their prejudices."

Eligibility

Michael is an exemplar of the first type of abstraction. Due to his schedule, we had to meet in a coffee shop. On arrival, he said that he thought that he would skew our data because he did not meet any of the eligibility criteria for shared ownership, although he accepted that he lived locally to the property and so had a local connection. It may well have been the case that he was accepted despite not being eligible because he bought his flat in 2009, and the flat had lain empty since the financial crisis: "[I]t was the last one in the building. It couldn't sell." Michael said that Greendale were at great pains to make him feel part of social housing, but this was an identity he rejected:

> So there's great emphasis on community support, and social support, and enabling people, so they run things like CV workshops and various other community action things, and they're quite big …. Yes, so they're at great pains to make sure that you understand you're part of some sort of social programme. Which is why I said I'm not a typical shared ownership, because I'm not a key worker, and I'm not a vulnerable person, I'm not a pensioner, most of the categories that that comes in. I'm not a single mother, you know, all those, I'm not a recovering alcoholic, substance abuser, any of things that seem to go along with social housing. Everyone I know in our building, they're just people whose incomes wouldn't enable them to buy 100 per cent of anything, really.

Tony made a similar argument, albeit without Michael's rhetorical flair:

> I think it was more kind of started the position of nothing ventured nothing gained, because I mean I guess one of notions that I'd had about shared ownership was that it was probably aimed at people on lower incomes than me, and kind of dare I say probably more deserving people than me. I mean I guess so half of [the city] people on kind of you know, good middle class incomes are priced out along with everybody else. So I didn't necessarily assume that it was something that I would be eligible for, kind of either key workers or people on low incomes would be the kind of people that I thought would be eligible. So actually, I was really surprised when I registered that kind of I would qualify on a solid but definitely not spectacular way.

Differentiation

The second method of abstraction was through a differentiation between self and others in the locality, particularly on mixed estates (such as at Hartford Meadows). This differentiation is what Paul Watt (2009) describes as "selective belonging". These were narratives in which our buyer interviewees tended to weaponise ordinary, everyday objects as symbols of their status against the social other. This stuff, like rubbish, was weaved into our interviewees' narratives about where they lived. They would not regard themselves as having "weaponised" that stuff because it was part of their everyday lives, and they had simply incorporated it into those lives. We use that descriptor because it gives life to those objects and, hard as it sounds, that was what it did.

Flo, for example, remarked on the layout of her property. There was a physical barrier between the shared ownership properties and the privately owned properties. She said that the shared owners were not allowed in the independently owned part. She went on:

> Yes, that's the bit that like people own 100 per cent. So they, when they built those I think they're—this is according to someone, … the guy that does some work for me. He said he's been over there and he said it's much higher spec. They've used better quality materials to build it. I don't think they're going to have any problem with their water just suddenly stopping, or their lift breaking. I think this one's slightly cheaper materials. So I think the fact that it's shared ownership.

There are overlaps here with our analysis in the next chapters, so we keep this section brief through one particular interview narrative, which ends with the weaponisation of sweet wrappers and airflow. It is a complex narrative, however, through which various tropes about the private and social were performed.

Jeannie's house was on an estate. It was in a cul-de-sac accessed off a long and winding road, with newly built properties on either side. Jeannie had mobility difficulties, which meant that her property had been adapted to her needs. There was a front door to the road, and her living accommodation, which was above her garage, was only accessible up a staircase. Jeannie's property was near open spaces and that was something that she loved about it. She had previously had gardens and when she realised that there was a strip of land at the end of the cul-de-sac, bordering on the open spaces, which had been left uncultivated and apparently without an owner, she began to use it (with permission from her neighbours) to grow flowers. She was proud of her flowers—when Dave met her, it was nearly spring time and she had two daffodils flowering, and she told him, "You've got to see them."

Jeannie explained the layout of the estate as part of her narrative because she had problems with both the "private houses" and the "social housing":

> [A private owner is] stressing me out, and it all got very unpleasant because I can't cope with that sort of stress. If I was a normal, healthy person I'd just shrug it off but when I live here on my own it's actually quite scary. Again, he's in private housing so I can't go through Fixham. The private houses at the back,

so even – yes, I suppose what I'm wittering on about is there are – there are certain problems with having social housing literally next door. Attached to me is social housing that side, and then the rest of that row, that direction, and opposite, and the other side I've got private, and the private have got some of the garages under me. They're a problem because they're private and you've got no leverage.

She had no leverage with the private owners at all, and had ended up squaring up with one because of their son's garage noise, which caused her nuisance. Fixham refused to help her, even though not causing nuisance was part of the leasehold agreement, and beyond that, "they're the people who should be showing respect in that direction, not I should be putting up with as much noise as they want to make". This caused her considerable upset, although they had finally moved on, but her division of the estate was also designed to establish her own identity and also to demonstrate that she had not expected to have problems with the owner-occupiers, who she believed would show more respect. As she put it later on in the interview: "I like to think having smarter people around does bring the people up a bit."

Jeannie tended to understand people through the way they kept their gardens. She was, therefore, able to differentiate between the social housing tenants:

> There are some lovely little front gardens along here, of people who are tenants who do look after their place. They're all polite to speak to, of the ones that I've spoken to, so the ones that I was having trouble with were at the far end. I didn't know them, and even they were fairly polite when I spoke to them and said would they tell their offspring off.

That this was to be remarked on performed two different roles in her narrative. First, it was to counterpose the social tenants against the private owners. Her surprise at a private owner being a nuisance, and refusing to ameliorate that nuisance, was matched with her surprise at the well-kept gardens and politeness of the social housing tenants. There was differentiation among both sets, which made the deviance worse. Secondly, Jeannie positioned herself as being in-between; she was a good person (although her experiences had made her "more severe" and "less smiley"); there were bad people on both sides of her.

The "trouble" to which she referred was with a "nuisance child" "at the far end" (i.e. the social housing end), who had been evicted subsequently. She counterposed herself, as a good neighbour, against that particular family. She continued:

Jeannie: They're [i.e. social housing tenants] not bad round here at all really. I think I only had one argument, which was a misunderstanding with one of the other neighbours about some of my plants going missing. They were kids, there used to be a nuisance child at the far end who used to – he was older than the other kids and he used to – he obviously got on with kids well and he'd club them all together, but then he'd get them all nicking stuff.

I: SO A MODERN-DAY FAGAN?

Jeannie: Yes, very much so, yes, and from what I can gather from residents' meetings we've had – luckily they lived at the far end of the road from me, but the people who were adjacent to them had terrible trouble with them, all sorts of threats to their life and all sorts of things from them. Somebody did say to me, "I so admire you! Do you know, you're the only person who's ever told that boy off?" [Laughing]

… Yes, he'd got these kids to nick – they would come round knocking on the door for money, and he'd come up with various moneymaking schemes. "What shall I do …?" I don't know, fine. Want to wash the car, yes, all right. You'd end up getting it washed afterwards. Yes, all right, okay. Yes, wash the car, but they had a carrier bag full of flowers, and they were out of my own garden, roots and everything. "Okay, yes, what's your name again? Let me just jot – where do you live?" So I got out there, got my mobility scooter out and went round to his mum. She was telling him off, "I told him to put those flowers in the bin, I told you not to go selling them." No, nothing about nicking them.

Jeannie continued her narrative and explained how there had been teething problems with the estate after she had moved in, which led to her complaining regularly about repairs which needed to be done—such as to the street lighting. Her narrative continued:

Jeannie: They came and changed the bulb a couple of times, and it still didn't work. So I did make a bit more effort to complain about that before. I was a bit worried it might be more of a problem once the council took over, but they did eventually come out with a lorry, dug up the road and fixed it. Yes, I always moaned about the rubbish. The rubbish is just terrible, but …

I: WHY IS THAT? …

Jeannie: Well, it's the children. It's all sweet wrappers, the kids up this end of the road. They all come out and go to the sweet shop on the way home from school, and it's nearly all sweet wrappers. An ice cream van comes every day in the summer and every weekend. He was over last weekend, so they just drop the wrappers in the street. Again, the social housing end of the street, you get that all the time. You don't get it the rest of the road. Just the way the wind blows unfortunately. Because … it all blows down this end. I get little whirlpools of wind outside my door, so – I mean I had to go out there this morning before you came. I thought I don't want him to see all these sweet wrappers.

These were throwaway lines in the middle of a lengthy interview, but they were meaningful, perhaps to us, more than to her. The sweet wrapper, combined with airflow, became a device through which Jeannie was able to mark herself out as different, as not part of the social. It was the kids from the *social housing end of the street*, and their refuse was blown down to the private part of the estate, thus dividing her part off. In these throwaway lines, the sweet wrapper and the airflow were a combination signifier of quite complex legal divisions. To put it another way, the stigmatised social was played out through the medium of the sweet wrapper.

Conclusion

In this chapter, we have demonstrated how the mere process of selling and buying shared ownership performs different representations of that product. We have opened out our analytical toolbox to demonstrate that aspects of the selling process, such as committing to a brochure, perform these differentiations. Buyers differentiated themselves; they tended to be aspirational and most had no experience of social housing at all. It was not surprising that they did not want to see themselves as part of the social housing estate, and that they were able to construct social housing tenants as different. They were educated and not vulnerable, they were houseproud and did not litter; they had morals and were nice people. They had got "a foot on the ladder" of ownership, and their talk about their pathways emphasised those distinctions, from insecurity to security, from paying somebody else's mortgage to their own stake. And then there is Jeannie's story, a story which fleshes out Hurdley's observation that "the meaning of things in the home is what gives home its meaning" (2006: 723), with a further thought that what goes on outside the home similarly gives home its meaning.

These are not just socio-legal representations of ownership/renting and social/private; they are also, in our rendering, expressions of a legal consciousness, translated into, and circulating around, objects and things. Whether told in a brochure or through weaponised sweetie wrappers, versions of legality were being created and transmitted, and cultural practices and divisions were being performed and translated. The sweet wrapper is emblematic of the division between the shared owner and the stigmatised social. In particular, the brochure has been a neglected, but rather important, facet of everyday life. It is the distillation of complexity into a market form. It is a product of successive translations, an attempt to simplify and convey the legal transaction through images and a little text. It is both the product of and produces its own legal consciousness. It is an in-between device, between seller and buyer, the market and other things, such as legality. It creates the image of the product which the social housing provider is seeking to purvey; it creates the image of the typical buyer which the social housing provider is seeking to attract; it must simplify the complex product into images and short text.

Bibliography

Callon, M. (1986), 'The Sociology of an Actor-Network: The Case of the Electric Vehicle', in M. Callon, J. Law and A. Rip (eds), *Mapping the Dynamics of Science and Technology: Sociology of Science in the Real World*, Basingstoke: Palgrave Macmillan.

Cowan, D. and McDermont, M. (2006), *Regulating Social Housing: Governing Decline*, London: Routledge.

Davies, S. and Sinn, C. (2016), *Shared Ownership 2.1: Towards a Fourth Mainstream tenure - Taking Stock*, Coventry: CIH.

Department for Communities and Local Government (DCLG) (2010), *Local Decisions: A Fairer Future for Housing*, London: DCLG.

Department for Communities and Local Government (2015), *Proposals to Streamline the Resale of Shared Ownership Properties*, London: DCLG.

Goffman, E, (1963) [1990], *Stigma: Notes on the Management of Spoiled Identity*, London: Penguin.

Gurney, C. (1999), 'Lowering the Drawbridge: A Case Study of Analogy and Metaphor in the Social Construction of Home-Ownership', 36(7), *Urban Studies*: 1705–22.

Hurdley, R. (2006), 'Dismantling Mantelpieces: Narrating Identities and Materializing Culture in the Home', 40(4), *Sociology*: 717–33.

Langley, P. (2006), 'The Making of Investor Subjects in Anglo-American Pensions', 24(5), *Environment and Planning D*: 919–34.

Law, J. (2002), *Aircraft Stories: Decentring the Object in Technoscience*, Durham: Duke UP.

McKee, K. (2011), 'Challenging the Norm? The "Ethopolitics" of Low Cost Homeownership in Scotland', 48(16), *Urban Studies*: 3399–413.

Osborne, H. (2014), 'Poor Doors: The Segregation of London's Inner-City Flat Dwellers', *The Guardian*, 25th July.

Savage, M., Bagnall C. and Longhurst, B. (2005), *Globalisation and Belonging*, London: Sage.

Sinn, C. and Davies, S. (2014), *Shared Ownership 2.0: Towards a Fourth Mainstream Tenure*, London: Orbit Group; Coventry: Chartered Institute of Housing.

Smith, S. (2008), 'Owner-occupation: At home with a hybrid of money and materials', 40(3), *Environment and Planning A*: 520–35.

Wallace, A. (2008b), *Achieving Mobility in the Intermediate Housing Market: Moving Up and Moving On?*, York: Joseph Rowntree Foundation.

Watt, P. (2009), 'Living in an Oasis: Middle-Class Disaffiliation and Selective Belonging in an English Suburb', 41(12), *Environment and Planning A*: 2874–92.

6

Experiencing Shared Ownership

Introduction

In this chapter, we focus on our buyer participants' data, and analyse their experiences of shared ownership. Our focus is on how they understand ownership and where they "fit" within it. As we demonstrated in Chap. 1, ownership is a complex and undulating concept in theory. One of the questions in our study was where it stopped and others' responsibilities started. Shared ownership is a complex product. As we noted in Chaps. 2 and 3, although buyers purchase a share in the property, they do so with strings attached. They are entirely responsible for their internal repairs and improvements; although the association or managing agent is responsible for conducting external repairs and improvements, shared owners are responsible for the entire share attributable to their property (whatever proportion they own); there are restrictions on what shared owners are entitled to do with their property—they are not entitled to sub-let it and, at the time of our research, there were restrictions on re-sale (the association had a limited period within which it could nominate a buyer at an independent valuation).

In this context, our buyer interviewees' engagement with questions around ownership and their fit with private or social ownership add to the developing literature about the porousness and fluidity of these concepts (see, e.g., Blomley 2016). In particular, in this chapter, we emphasise the interactive and situational aspects to ownership. That is, we argue that ownership is constructed through a mixture of interactions between people, and also between people and things, as an expression of their legal consciousness. This interactive aspect is inherent in much of the literature on property, of course;

© The Author(s) 2018
D. Cowan et al., *Ownership, Narrative, Things*, Palgrave Socio-Legal Studies,
https://doi.org/10.1057/978-1-137-59069-5_6

however, often, it is either implicit or ignored; when explicit attention is given to it, it tends to be around narrow issues, such as exclusion, without reference to the kind of softer attributes, which formed the central concerns of our buyers.

We begin this exploration with an analysis of how our respondents addressed our final question about whether they were owners or renters. This question was explicitly baldly framed as a binary, and most of our interviewees regarded themselves as owners as a result. However, reading back over the entire transcripts, we could see how their reasoning for ascribing that status to themselves was in tension with the rest of the interview. In the next chapter, we approach this tension explicitly through in-depth analysis of five interviews. Here, we do no more than draw attention to this tension. We then go on to consider certain dominant issues which arose in our interviews, and which threatened that ownership status. Key here were concerns over repairs, improvements, re-sale, and rent and service charges (although a puzzle emerges over the latter). Finally, we consider how the fact that their landlord was a housing association, a social housing provider, impacted on the interviewees' appreciation of their position. In short, the question here was whether the housing association should be expected to do more than a private landlord. Here, our buyers were explicitly addressing the question of the make-up of the social as an imaginary, a kind of deflection from their assumed status as owners.

Ownership?

The two principal metaphors used to describe ownership by our buyers were "freedom" and "control". Where they felt that they had freedom to control their environment, they felt more like owners. The formal legal basis of their occupation rarely informed buyers' thinking; rather, it was the feeling of control and responsibility over their home, particularly in terms of home decoration, and the lack of interference by the housing association, which was largely seen as a distant silent partner. As most of our interviews were conducted in shared owners' properties, we could see the real sense of pride they had in their homes, from feature walls through to extensions through to asking us to excuse the untidiness (which, it would be fair to say, we had not noticed). So, for example, as Nicki, Antonia, and Carl put it, respectively:

> It feels like it's mine. It always has been. I mean I know what you mean because I can't do anything – like I can't knock a wall down or do anything like that. Yes, but I think – I mean it's a bit limiting I suppose but it doesn't affect the way I feel about it, it still definitely does feel like my place.

I would not know the difference between owning outright and shared ownership. I would know the difference between private renting, I wasn't there for
very long but private renting I could tell the difference because I just didn't feel
like the house was mine. Here, I feel like the house is mine. I can do anything I
want to the garden.

I've spent a lot of money on doing it up and maintaining it and making it
look nice. So I feel like it is mine more than it isn't, yes.

However, this was not all one way, particularly where the buyer felt some
impediment on their freedom/control, expressed by Petra as, "I still feel some
breath on my neck, you know."

Arnold, who was retired, had bought a share in a new-build property, which
he loved. There had been some repair issues, in which he had felt that
Greendale had sat on their hands. As he put it, "I think they could help more
with problems. Not just say, you know, 'The rest is up to you. You've purchased this property.' That's all in black and white; they make it quite clear."
The following interaction occurred later in the interview:

I: I CAN SEE YOU OBVIOUSLY TAKE A GREAT PRIDE IN IT, OUT
THE FRONT, AND ALL THE PLANTS AND EVERYTHING, AND
IT'S IMMACULATE IN HERE. IT'S LOVELY.
Arnold: Yes. I mean, I've had coving put in. I mean, when you rent a place –
people say to me, "Why do you buy?" Because I want to live here probably
until I – whenever. So I'm gradually coving each room, because they do tend
to crack, at the ceilings. So that spoils it, so, yes, so I intend to do that.
...
I: SO IN THAT RESPECT DO YOU FEEL LIKE AN OWNER BECAUSE
YOU CAN DO ALL THOSE THINGS YOURSELF?
Arnold: Yes, I do. Yes, I do. I feel quite responsible for my property. But it's not
my property.
I: SO IN WHAT RESPECTS DO YOU MAYBE FEEL LIKE A TENANT,
THEN?
Arnold: [Hesitates] Basically all the work I've put into it is never going to be
mine. Which is – that's life, I suppose, isn't it?

Others expressed their ownership through what Cowan et al. (2009: 297)
described as "the power of the box"; that is, forms to be completed which have
boxes which operate as the kinds of binary codes which are assumed norms.
This was how Jude expressed her answer to the question:

Well, when you have to fill in forms, and they ask if you if you rent or whatever,
don't they, but there isn't actually a box on these forms for shared ownership,

so I put mine down as home owner, although I'm not fully. I often say that, and I say, "Actually, I'm none of these", and they go, "What do you mean?" I go, "Well, I'm part buy part rent", and they go, "Oh, that's private home owner", and I'm surprised that there still isn't a box on those types of forms. So I always just don't ask anymore, and tick homeowner, because for me that's what I am.

However, these kinds of observations were also tempered by our interviewees' senses of their interactions with others around them, such as how they were treated. This led to a sense of hesitation in answering this question, a reflection about their status which was derived from the way in which they had been treated. So, for example, this hesitation came across from our first interview, with Pamela, who, as we saw in the previous chapter, was concerned about having her name on "the paper", which made her feel like an owner. However, following leaks in her house in which there were issues over responsibility, she said that she felt that "[a]s long as they're getting their money, seriously, that is all they're bothered about". The ownership question came shortly after she expressed these concerns in the interview. Her response, in contradistinction to how she felt at the outset with the significance of her "name on paper", was as follows:

I don't know what I am. I don't know what they think I am. I think I'm the owner, but I'm also partly a tenant, but I'm a tenant that they don't really care about. But they'll look after their real – their tenants, who don't own their properties. They'll go and do everything for them. I don't get anything.

Similarly, Tony said:

It depends which bill comes through the post. I feel like an owner because, I mean I say it's mine, you know, the housing association largely keep out of our way; but I feel like a tenant when all the things that get frustrating turn up and our inability to control our own destiny in certain things like, you know, water pumps breaking and you can't just call a plumber and get him to fix the water pump. We have to phone somebody up. So, we had no water for a bank holiday weekend once because we couldn't get somebody to come and fix a water pump.

So, ownership was both interactional and situational. Sonia, for example, said that she did not think about whether she was an owner or a renter "until something happens like the service charge crops up". Susan related this to the market for her property:

It's weird, because it's one of those ones where I'm acutely aware where that the shared ownership question is really strange halfway house. I feel like I own the house and this is my flat, but that's where you appreciate you're not because you're just sitting in half of it, which is now worth a lot more. So kind of, give you a lot more latitude and the other half is just more unaffordable with a casting vote.

The market also affected how others related to their property. Here, the temporal location of the property in our interviewees' lives was significant. June's flat was not a "home for life" and her plan was to move in with her partner. She related the question to this kind of intermediate step in her housing pathway: "But this was important to do for myself, so I do see that I'm on the ladder if you put it like that and I've made a step, an inroad, a tiny one. I feel more secure than I would renting and I see it as a better investment, whatever that really means, but it's not just someone else's rent, at least some of it is going towards me." And, as Michael, who was in a similar position, said in response:

I don't know, is the honest answer. I already have kind of mentally left, because I was expecting to have been moved out and been in a new place now, and really this is all just, this is just part of a longer term plan, so it's not – although I'll own it financially, and it's property ownership, it's a big deal, and there's life change, it's never been an ambition of mine. As I said, I wanted to own the 50 per cent to make it easier to sell, that's really what it was.

Interrupting Issues

In this part, we analyse four particular issues which interrupted smooth narratives, and which caused our interviewees to think about their place on the spectrum: repairs, improvements, re-sale, and rent and service charges. In the first three situations, as we describe them, our interviewees felt out of control, lacked freedom to do as they wished, felt that they were treated poorly, and/ or felt categorised differently. In these kinds of issues, then, the interactional and situational analysis takes further root. However, as we describe it, a puzzle emerges regarding rents and service charges. Despite being told awful and emotional stories about effectively being forced out of their property by hikes in these charges, many of our buyers nevertheless kept the faith, regarding themselves as owners.

Repairs

Buyers told lengthy and involved stories about their repairs problems, some of which were long-running, often becoming emotional in their telling. Emma's story, which we tell in Chap. 7, reflects this deep emotional effect caused by dripping water. Many buyers found it difficult to appreciate how and why the housing associations were apparently disinterested in those repair problems when they owned a share of the property itself. This was particularly expressed by Emma: "They say, 'Absolutely nothing to do with us because you're a lease-holder'. Also at the time when it started, they owned 55 per cent of this flat, which I thought was incredible. Not a single person has come to visit me to see what the damage was at the time … – no-one was in the slightest bit interested in coming round to see what the damage was or how to get it rectified quickly."

And the line between the association's responsibility and that of the shared owner was a particular bone of contention. There was a simple rule of thumb that many of the people to whom we spoke understood, or came to understand: "As far as responsibility for things such as repairs were concerned, it was never spelt out to me, but I understood later on that internally is the resident's responsibility and the external structure, any faults or repairs, are down to Fixham" (Diane). Yet, this apparently sharp distinction also became porous at least for buyers, leading to the kind of ongoing conversations between the buyer and the association, which were of a regulatory character. This was what particularly impacted on Pamela's understandings about her identity on the spectrum. Hers was an emergency situation, which happened a few years after she bought the property:

> *Pamela*: The first thing that probably happened was about [c 2007]. … Middle of the night, the bathroom door was open, thankfully, and I was living here on my own at the time, and the bedroom door was open. About half past two in the morning, and I heard "drip, drip, drip". And there was water coming through the light in the bathroom.
> *I*: OH, NO! YES.
> *Pamela*: So I had a bit of a panic. Didn't even – I'd never had any reason to look for the stopcock, et cetera. So I had a bit of a panic. I rang Fixham up in the middle of the night, not realising that in actual fact it goes to [the] Council out-of-hours service.
> *I*: EMERGENCY SERVICE, YES.
> *Pamela* : So I rang them going, "Help, I've got a leak in my house. It's coming through the bathroom ceiling." They got somebody – so they got a plumber

to ring me back who talked me through what to do, and then they said they'd get someone out the next day. Well, okay, we got that bit sorted. What had happened was – I'll just explain quickly – the thermostat on the boiler had stopped working, so the water was heating up too high, so the tank in the loft was overflowing. In actual fact, when the plumber got up there, it had actually shrunk the whole ballcock, it was so hot.

I: OH, NO, BECAUSE IT WAS HOT!

Pamela: Then I rang up … Yes, but there was something else wrong, so I rang Fixham back during office hours, and they went, "Don't know anything about this." Looked into it, and they said, "Oh. You shouldn't have had any help at all. You're a shared owner." And I went, "Well, what else was I supposed to do?" They said, "Well, if you'd looked at your manual …" – I went, "It's half past two in the morning, and I have a leak coming through my bathroom. I was not going to start looking for my handbook. I expected somebody to be there to help me." And they said, "Oh, well, yes, but, I'm sorry, but you're not – it's only the tenants that should go to the out-of-hours service." And I said, "Well, that's not my fault, that I was put through to them and they sorted this for me." They then started to say to me that I had to pay for all the work. I can't remember exactly what happened then, but I did point out to them, if I hadn't been here – if I'd been on a night shift – I would have come home in the morning to no ceiling. But I don't know even if they would have been bothered then.

Simone, for example, had a range of teething problems with her new build, although the defects period (the period within which minor defects would be repaired free of charge) had passed by the time she moved in:

When I bought it I specifically said if there are any problems are we covered, and they said the guarantee's expired, but we have fully checked it, and we can tell you that it's all fine and that there aren't any problems. … Anyway, they basically turned round to me, when I initially spoke to them, and said well that's your problem, you bought it sold as seen. I said I haven't bought it sold as seen, because when I spoke to you, you said to me you'd checked everything, it's all fine, if there are any problems we'll deal with it. There was quite a bit of toing and froing, but because I stuck with it, and I eventually spoke to someone high enough up, said, "I'm so sorry, you shouldn't have had to go through that. We are responsible, we will send someone round to sort that out." They did sort it out, but that was only because I stuck with it and I spoke to the right person, because the people lower down were very rude to me. Told me it was my responsibility, and I had no legal right to change any of that.

Then, there was a problem when she came home from work one day:

Simone: The glass in the front door was shattered. We'd only been here a few weeks; it was very, very early on. It was probably about six or seven o'clock at night, so I phoned the emergency number…

I: WHAT, IT JUST HAPPENED OR…?

Simone: Well, I don't know. What we suspect had happened was that the grass had been cut that day, so I suspect something had been in the grass, a stone or something, and it shot up, because it was one of those little ride-on mowers.

[Interruption]

Yes, so I phoned up the emergency number because the buildings insurance, according to the rental contract, is part of the service charge, and the contents insurance, obviously we deal with ourselves. So I see a door as part of the buildings insurance, and I phoned up and I said, "The glass is broken." They sent someone round immediately to board it up, that was fine. They said phone back the next day, so I phoned back the next day, and they gave me the insurance details, fine. Twenty-four hours later, I got a very aggressive phone call, "Why have you phoned up to claim on the insurance? Glass in a front door is contents!" "Right, well I phoned up and you gave me the details, so I don't know why you've given me the details if you thought that that was the case, and I really can't see how glass in a front door is contents, because it really is the building." They were very, very aggressive. It was unbelievable. I'd never – I really couldn't believe it. I had a lot of – it went on for weeks, and in the end – I mean the claim's already going through, so they couldn't stop it, but they – a company that they got to deal with it were absolute cowboys and they couldn't get the right glass and I ended up with two different pieces of glass in the door, and it was just horrendous so yes.

I: DID YOU GET THE INSURANCE MONEY THROUGH?

Simone: Well, they all covered it in the end, through the insurance. I mean I had to pay an excess.

I: YES, BUT THEY PAID THE REST AND THINGS?

Simone: Yes, but again, this was one of these grey areas, which wasn't really covered very well. It looked quite clear from the paperwork, but because they'd not really established what was contents and what was buildings.

There was also a sense from our interviews that the participants' attitudes towards their repairing obligations changed over time. At the outset, they might have found themselves to be more naïve about the extent of their obligations, but, as their time in the property went on, their understandings developed, and they recognised the "weighted" nature of the bargain into which they had engaged:

It's a difficult one. I mean, I don't necessarily think – because from Fixham's point of view they're on a winner. I mean, if you're in rented accommodation it then becomes the responsibility of the landlord to actually do it, whereas with shared ownership the whole responsibility is down to the people who have taken on the shared ownership. I think it's a little bit much, because basically Fixham has nothing to do with it, so. (Jonny, 1995 purchase)

[A]t the beginning you understand, you think okay, fine, because you don't expect anything to go wrong. If anything does go wrong then that's when you think but hold on, this isn't fair. It's only then when you come to that then you think, hold on, this isn't fair. Then, of course, that's when you will try to challenge it but it's in the lease; "Yes, I know it's in the lease but come on." That's when, potentially, things can go wrong. (Carly, 2012 purchase)

This recognition had a particular effect on Jonny's behaviour, creating a sense of moral hazard. He simply decided not to make repairs to the property if it was not going to affect his share:

The way I look at it, more to do with now, if I want to buy a bigger portion of the property it's done on market value, so even though I've looked after the place and kept it up to standard or what have you, they don't take anything off. I mean, for instance, like the windows, they'll take a little bit off, because I've had those done, and any improvements, but if I was renting sometimes they'll give me a discount after, I think it's about, what, nine years or whatever; I would have got discounted if I was renting. So Fixham will make a huge profit out of investment, because they can basically walk away. All they've done is given me the money, I pay them rent for that section, so they're making money. Maybe not a lot, but the value of the house, I mean it's much better than having it in a bank or whatever, having that sort of money. So because I've got to buy at the market value, they make a huge profit out of it.

Fixham staff did note that the lease requires shared owners to keep the property in good repair, although Fixham did not inspect to ensure compliance. However, they could apply a penalty if, at re-sale, the property failed to reach the proper price because of disrepair, and staff were unsure to what extent shared owners appreciated this clause in the lease. This was not raised by buyers in older DIYSO properties who had experienced disrepair.

Improvements

The lease provided that buyers had to obtain approval from the housing association before the shared owner conducted any improvements to their property. There were two important reasons for this condition: first, anything which interfered with the structure of the property needed to be checked to ensure that it did not affect the building's integrity; and, secondly, the value of the improvements would be deducted from the value of the property if the shared owner decided to staircase. Nevertheless, there was considerable consternation about this requirement (if it was known—and, often, it was not), and particularly, the requirement to pay a fee to obtain the association's approval. As Joy and Ayaz put it:

> I thought it was just bizarre. I thought hold on, I have just paid over £1,000 to have new doors put on, of which 75 per cent are yours and now you want me to pay to register it as well. I just don't understand it at all.
>
> I would be very surprised if they ever turned round and said, "No, you can't do it", because obviously it's enhancing the value. I find it a bit cheeky they expect money every time you do something. I can't see why they're charging for anything like that.

For some, this requirement to obtain the association's approval interfered with their understandings of themselves as owners, and also about the association essentially freeloading. This was particularly expressed by Sara and Raj:

> *Sara*: Well, I think there isn't any comparison because before you knew that it was down to you, everything was down to you, whereas now it's not really, even down to having liked a tiled floor I should have got permission. I can't make changes without getting permission first.
>
> *Raj*: Yes, that's right. You've got all the responsibility and they take all the benefits basically because they don't seem to want to do any part of the maintenance and be responsible for it, yet they take the benefit for that when the house sells.

And Petra felt particularly antagonistic about this requirement:

> They of course need some plans, they need to contact the company who is going to do it, and they say, "Okay." But yes, you're going to feel like a homeowner if you need permission for that? No. No, you're not going to feel like a homeowner. … How am I going to feel? Like a loser really, like a loser, just a loser, yes.

Re-sale

The nascent market in shared ownership properties is difficult terrain (Wallace 2008b; CCHPR 2012). During 2014–15, re-sales comprised 38 per cent of the shared ownership market, up from 19 per cent during 2007–08, and so this market is not insignificant and growing (DCLG CORE Sales). During our research, there was a condition in the lease that required the shared owner to allow the housing association to nominate a buyer to the property at a price set by an independent valuer. However, it was also possible for sellers to circumvent this possibility by combining a sale of their property with staircasing up to 100 per cent of its value. This possibility was raised at the initial stakeholder focus group composed of shared owners. It positioned them as profit maximisers, and seeking to avoid the restrictive practices imposed by the housing association in selling their property. In 2015, the government decided to remove this clause from future leases, and varied existing leases to remove it.

In some cases, the right to nominate a subsequent purchaser has been raised as a barrier to selling on:

- by householders, who want their experience of selling a shared ownership or former shared ownership home to be as straight forward as possible; and,
- by lenders who view the Pre-emption Right as hampering the ability to realise the value of the home for the householder, or for themselves in the case of a repossession, and hence restrict their lending in this market. (DCLG 2015: para 8)

The latter point was something that had troubled lenders from the 1970s, although, over the next 40 years, it was unclear where this had come from, and certainly was not mentioned as an issue by any of our key stakeholders. The first point did not arise in our interviews either. However, what *did* arise in our interviews was a sense that the nominations and valuations process meant that the buyers missed out on one of the benefits of ownership; that is, an increase in the property's value and the fees charged by the housing association on sale.

An increase in value was particularly important because a profit would enable the buyers to move "up the housing ladder". Some of our interviewees had conducted their own market research with comparable properties, or had neighbours who, they felt, had been "stitched up" (as Emma put it). Market processes were raised, for example, by June and Carly, who said, respectively:

So it's not really like selling on the open market, because I'm assuming if you sell on the open market you can pretty much charge, if there's a bidding war the price can go up, which is not the case here ... because they'll probably buy it back first. They're going to want to keep it, so I don't really see that there's a huge benefit in being allowed to sell on the open market if you still have to offer it to them first.

This property won't be sold by an estate agent, this property will be valued according to what Fixham's agents think it's worth. So if I come along and if Fixham say it's worth £450,000 and I say I want to pay £550,000 for it, you wouldn't get £550,000 for it. You will get what Fixham feel it's worth.

This was Charlie's main complaint with Greendale:

Charlie: My one complaint with Greendale is they wouldn't allow me to sell on the open market. I would have to sell at the valuation price which is obviously lower than the open market. ...

I: HAVE THEY EXPLAINED TO YOU THE PROCESS?

Charlie: Not really, they just said that the housing association committee or whatever it's called, the government quango says that you can't sell [on the] open market if you're not [100 per cent] but I was arguing well actually it's in your interest because you'll get more money as well, 25 per cent, 75 per cent.

I: HAVE YOU GOT EVIDENCE THAT YOU GET ACTUALLY LOWER VALUATIONS?

Charlie: [X who] you'll see next for example, she had a valuation done which was significantly lower than the market value. This flat here sold for £625,000, a one bed flat.

I: IS IT THE SAME AS YOURS?

Charlie: It's slightly bigger but next door sold for £400,000 in February this year and it's the same size.

There was a difference between asking prices and surveyor valuations, but part of this concern arose as a result of the perception that shared owners would miss an opportunity to capitalise on their gains in rapidly rising markets.

The second issue concerned the fees charged. In Greendale, the fee to sell the property was 1 per cent of the value of the share being sold, and in Fixham, the fee for reselling ranged from a flat fee of £400 to 1.5 per cent of the full market value of the whole property depending on the date the lease was created: "Which seems a little bit unfair when you're only selling 50 per cent; why do you have to pay 1 per cent of the full value of it?"

(June). The fees for selling can therefore be comparable to estate agent fees, but the service less so, as housing associations were not responsible for progressing the sale in the same way as an estate agent often does. Fewer resources appeared to be expended in selling re-sale properties as new-build homes. For example, the seller provided the photographs at Greendale and the surveyor was asked for photos at Fixham, although sellers could also supply their own, with variable results in terms of quality.

Rent and Service Charges

One might expect that the payment of rent and service charges to a landlord or estate manager would be an interrupting feature in understandings about ownership. After all, the payment of rent has implications beyond the idea of ownership; and service charges, albeit a regular feature of a long leasehold agreement in England, were regularly equated with rent by our interviewees. That was, in general, not the case in our sample. What animated the interviewees, in general, were rises in rent over which they had no control (although they had signed up to a lease in which the rent rose annually by between 2 and 3 per cent above the retail price index)—and RPI had exceeded 3 per cent for most of the five years previous to our interviews, reaching 5 per cent during 2011 (Office for National Statistics (ONS))—and service charges which were inexplicable or for services which were either not done or inadequately done.

The issue about rent was particularly relevant for those who had been in shared ownership for some time. The assumption of those who devised the lease was that shared owners would staircase up to full purchase. Indeed, the shared ownership model and business planning is predicated on that basis (as discussed in Chap. 2). Rent rises, then, were set at levels that incentivise buyers to staircase. The security which shared ownership provided was, however, here a negative for Susan (who had been in her flat for five years), who compared private renting more favourably, as she was effectively stuck:

> I think the rent's gone up too much in the last five years. They did explain to me how they work the percentage of something, I don't know, I mean it's all above my head, I don't understand that sort of thing, I'm not a financial person, so you take their word for it. But I mean you can't argue it, so whereas in a private rented house if the landlord puts your rent up, the contract says in advance, and then if he decides to put your rent up, well if you don't like it you move on.

Private renting was the comparator used by many of our interviewees, who rated their rent against those values:

> The rent side hasn't changed that much. ... Well, it shouldn't have, because the prices were going down so rent should be geared to the price of the – the cost of the rateable value of the house. Well, if the price of the house is going down, then rent shouldn't go up, should they? Saying that, this year they did go up because that's the trend. You know, all private landlords are putting them up. Of course, not only did the rent go up, the service charge went up. (Colin c, 2010 purchase)

> If you look at these differences in prices, and if [Fixham], seven years later, they'd already had 15 grand in rent, they got an extra £41,250, so they'd already had £10,000 more than the investment. I haven't worked out what they would have got had they invested at ten per cent but I would guess that it's pretty similar. So, they'd had their capital back and now, admittedly, if they were buying, if they were using it to reinvest, to create more housing for more people, it wouldn't buy the same, it wouldn't buy the equivalent value. So, I can see that this is not strictly comparable but to have got to the point where they've already had almost double what they put in. (Aisling, 1992 purchase)

As regards service charges, although there was considerable consternation expressed about costs, particularly where these had risen steeply and rates over which the interviewees felt that they had no control, this tended not to interact with constructions of ownership. Aisha and Joe exemplify this kind of separation. Their service charge had increased from £80 per month to £230; in one year, "it went up a lot, like £90 a month in one fell swoop because they'd made mistakes". The mistakes had been made by a third-party managing agent, employed by the corporate builder, which had constructed the block of flats. Aisha and Joe had reconciled themselves to moving out as a result, because they could not afford the charge. They were both upset because they felt that shared ownership had been sold to them as a low-cost product (they were not alone in expressing this distinction—the cost of living expenses through the service charge made the property unaffordable to those on low incomes).

In response to the owner/renter question, Joe and Aisha said:

> *Joe*: I feel like an owner actually more than a renter but probably in law we're probably viewed...
>
> *Aisha*: Yes, I kind of do feel a bit like a renter. I think probably when we moved in I didn't. Obviously I understood the way it worked but I felt as if this was

our stake in ownership and obviously I do know that we would be selling and so in a sense I am an owner but I do feel that there has been a [point] where you might have that view and you might well be right but you have no voice so tough luck.

Mariam was in almost exactly the same circumstances. A third-party managing agent had increased the costs so that her continuing occupation of her flat was "economically unviable". The block was in a classic mixed tenure development: "[T]here's a property management company that manages the whole development and they provide different services, like concierge service and things like that, maintenance, that sort of thing in the communal areas and that's all fine." The private owners, as she put them, had the extra services of the concierge and other facilities. Over the years Mariam had lived in her flat, she had received salary increases, which enabled her to afford to continue living there. However, the service charges had increased considerably because of poor accounting. She wondered, "[C]oming back to the purpose of the [shared ownership] scheme, how is that right really?" Indeed, during the fieldwork, Fixham had unsold shared ownership properties in areas of high demand that were unaffordable to eligible people because of high service charges. In response to the owner/renter question, Mariam said:

It's a difficult one. I would say an owner primarily because, like I said, apart from paying the housing association every month, I don't have any dealings with that. I think you are treated slightly differently in that they won't support you in terms of getting repairs done and things like that, which I think is better and does make me feel more like an owner. Yes, I prefer it that way. I think if I still felt like a tenant that it would just completely defeat the whole object of doing it in the first place, not feeling that it was mine. Ultimately, I do own a bit of it so it is mine and, yes, that's always the way that I've seen it, it is mine. I don't even really think about the fact that they do own quite a big proportion of it. I don't know. I pay them that money but I just don't really think about it too much. I just think about the fact that it covers the property management, it covers the insurance.

One might postulate that the regularity of these costs, and their largely known value, meant that they did not interfere with our shared owner identities to the extent that an individual "incident" might: "[I]t's just something that you have to pay. I know some people complain, but life's a bit short I think" (Ryan, 2009 purchase). There is security in the routine. As Flo put it:

I feel like an owner, yes. I do, because obviously everything in it's mine. I can decorate. It's been quite frustrating – my old flat if there were holes in the walls from previous tenants where they'd put stuff up and taken it down – I've been able to decorate the whole thing the way I like it. Although like obviously I've had the problem with damp which I can't sort out myself, it does feel like my home. Even though I'm renting part of it, it doesn't feel like it at all. Actually the payments are quite straightforward. I found again [Fixham] are crap with the maintenance side. They're okay with like the general sort of getting it clean, it's always cleaned, it always smells of like bubble gum when I come back on a Friday.

We could argue that our data here speak to ownership because our interviewees related it to their security, and other tenures. However, that would not be doing justice to our interviewees' own narratives. If property and ownership are social constructions, and are developed from situational and interactional perspectives, we would be reading our understandings of property and ownership into the data. A puzzle emerges, in any event. All research in and of itself is situational and interactive. It may have been that were we to have conducted the research at the time this book is being written, our interviewees would have expressed themselves differently.

So, for example, our research was being conducted just as the "poor doors" trope was being publicised and interviewees as well as the housing associations related their narratives to those stories. Ade and Mel discussed the issue about rent rises in response to the owner/renter question:

I: DO YOU FEEL LIKE AN OWNER OR DO YOU FEEL LIKE A RENTER?
Mel: Feel like an owner.
Ade: Yes. The renting's the annoying part.
I: IN WHICH WAY IS IT ANNOYING?
Mel: It's annoying because it goes up every year. It goes up by 3 per cent every year. Well, it's below inflation – well, it depends on how high inflation is. I think RPI is, is it 2.8 per cent at the moment?
I: I'M NOT SURE.
Mel: Just slightly higher than RPI. Oh, no, no, hold on. I think it's RPI plus 3 per cent. I can't remember now. But it's definitely 3 per cent somewhere.
I: SO WOULD YOU FEAR THAT IT WOULD GO UP QUITE QUICKLY?
Mel: Yes, if you stayed here for a number of years, it would. When wages aren't increasing.

Social/Private

In previous chapters, we have drawn attention to the kind of tenure differentiation in which our interviewees engaged. Jessie's comment was typical of this kind of differentiation:

> Mostly the council renters who obviously didn't have quite the same pride of ownership as particularly the shared owners I think. Because we're all so like, oh my God we've finally bought somewhere, you know you really want to take care of it and some of the renters weren't.

In this section, however, our analysis moves on to consider how being in social housing affected our interviewees' everyday interactions with Fixham and Greendale. We consider whether, if at all, their expectations were different because they were social landlords. In essence, many shared owners felt that they could and should expect more from a social landlord than from a private landlord. We first noticed this particularly in Chap. 4, when we discussed our interviewees' comments about the landlord not coming to inspect the property or simply visiting, but that was in the context of the landlord's retention of a share in the property.

Some of our sample had little idea about the status of Fixham and Greendale—as Marley put it, "I had no idea who Fixham was. It was just pure chance." Having a landlord which was a social landlord affected how some of our interviewees' felt about each of the issues in the previous section. These issues went beyond simply the landlord–tenant relation; something more might have been expected of Fixham and Greendale because they were social landlords or because they were charitable. This "social mentality" meant that Ann-Marie decided to staircase rather than sell her flat. In response to a direct question as to whether she regarded the property as social housing, she rationalised her decision to staircase as follows:

> I do, and I still believe in it as a principle. It's just – if the purpose is just to have somewhere to live is your intention, then that's fine. But I think that one of the reasons why I wanted to staircase to 100 per cent was because I knew that Greendale would undervalue the property, because they would always try and maintain the ethos of the social housing, affordable element of it. So if Greendale had decided to put it on the open market – I felt it would have limited the people who would have applied for it and then secondly they would have undervalued it. So it wouldn't have been the market rate.

Emma, to whom we return in Chap. 7, had a major problem with water dripping into her flat from an unknown source. She felt that Greendale were obstructive: "I know it's their job to cover all their own backs, but they're not a private firm; they're a housing association offering affordable housing. You'd think they'd just be more supportive when something goes wrong and they really weren't at all." She went on:

> It was like three weeks after I'd bloody got married and we almost divorced two months later because the stress was hideous. But that's just the way it is but even though I am a leaseholder and I understand that, as I'm also a shared ownership buyer and it's a housing association, I'd expect them to just be a little bit more benevolent, I suppose, and help people out.
>
> ...
>
> maybe I'm feeling too much but this is a shared ownership property. They should step in and stand up for me and they didn't; I felt they sided with the contractors and not with me. The relationship is cosier with the contractors rather than the people that they're supposed to be in a relationship with.

Dave asked her whether she felt that it would have been different if the block had been owned privately. She responded:

> I probably would've expected less or about the same, but I would understand that because they're private and they're profit driven and I would expect that more. My expectations are different with the housing association; rightly or wrongly, my expectations are different. So probably if it was a private, I would've just left it at that and that's bad luck. But I'd like to think they would've been a bit quicker in helping me, they would've appreciated it more and realised that maybe I could make a claim against them. They would've taken it more seriously.
>
> I don't know whether it was just housing associations generally or this particular one, but they just weren't interested. I just felt as a housing association they should've been and they should've been supporting me.

Others suggested that Fixham and Greendale were more calculating in their roles. Indeed, rather than being a "social" landlord, they were business-like and profit driven; or, as Steven put it, "I'm just a cynic ... I think they run quite a tight ship, probably, as all housing associations do." Mohammed, who had bought a property in a s. 106 development, felt that Fixham had "made a killing":

> *Mohammed*: Well, the complaint we have is – you see, this is supposed to be social housing, and what those people did was, the housing association negotiated with the developer and actually bought the houses off-plan.

I: RIGHT.

Mohammed: Then they deliberately sat on those houses for about six to eight months, and they turned round and made a killing. They bought these houses for – mine, for example, for £215,000. And they sold it off to us at £315,000.

I: WOW.

Mohammed: You see? Which, you know, is unbelievable. I mean, legally whether there's a precedent, that's what we're checking on now, but it would seem like they would say, "Well, it was in the market", … Now, I think in the process they compromised in some of the amenities and fittings which should have gone with the houses. This is only eight out of, I think, possibly 300 in the block. And our neighbours, colleagues, who actually bought the house out-right without going through the housing association got a very good deal. Some of them paid even less than we paid, for better fittings. Like, they had kitchens and wardrobes all fitted in; better sanitary ware; the flooring was all wooden. Whereas for us we just had the basic lino and the carpet, which is basically social housing. And we had to pay £100,000 more.

Now, they have got entry – door entry system where automatically when there is a problem the concierge will tell which flat it is and it's on the screen and they have got direct communication. All the flats that were taken up by Fixham Housing do not have this. And we believe this was part of the deal that they negotiated with the owner, to take out all those other extras so that they just bought purely the skeleton of the house, and then fobbed it off to us at a colossal £315,000. Now, we are having a problem because we are say-ing that we think it was morally wrong, possibly even legally, because they were social housing, supposed to be helping people come up the ladder, and they actually turned it into a commercial entity: then it defeats the whole purpose of social housing.

Jessie was also sceptical, feeling that Fixham as social landlord was a kind of subterfuge:

I: YOU SAY … THAT FIXHAM ARE AN ORGANISATION WHICH ARE TRYING TO HELP PEOPLE. NOW IS THAT SOMETHING THAT WAS IN YOUR MIND WHEN YOU BOUGHT THE PLACE?

Jessie: Well you know I knew that they're not my financial advisors, they're not my parents, but the whole sort of ethos of shared ownership or the way it was marketed was, we are here to help people who are earning an okay salary, but cannot compete in the you know, housing markets like London to get onto the property ladder, and that you can increase your equity and build up your equity and it's here to help you become a home owner. So I think there is this subconscious thing of they are there to help me become a home owner, and I'm not sure they are. They are administering a scheme that might help me to, but they are property managers rather than here to help me become a home owner, and there's a difference. But I think you're encouraged to think that they're there to help you. They have a lot of social housing tenants, they are social housing landlords as well, so I think the shared ownership is almost like a bit on the side of the social housing stuff. You know if you look on their website, 80 per cent is social housing and tenants, and 20 per cent is shared ownership stuff. I don't know, I don't know how they make their money out of this, I don't know their business model, so yes.

Similarly, Mariam was sceptical about the "social" nature of Fixham's operation. This particularly came to light when she was discussing issues over valuation of her flat when it came to selling it. She began by recounting her neighbours' experiences:

So they called in the [valuers] that were recommended and they completely over-valued their flat and they knew that because they'd gone out to the market and got some other people from estate agents, etcetera, to come in, so they knew what roughly they should be looking at and actually it was completely over-valued. There's more than one person who's saying that so it then starts to raise questions around, well, why is that? Why would the housing association recommend people over-valuing your flat when you're looking to buy and extra proportion? So I think there's quite a bit of scepticism around … Again, it just all comes back to this idea that the housing association is a charity but there seems to be quite a few practices that are not in line with, a) charitable behaviour, or, b) kind of fair and transparent behaviour actually but it's very, very difficult to go into that. Unless you're a top lawyer or you've got access to that sort of advice, there's not a lot that you can do about it. You have to accept it because no one has the time or the capacity or the resources to look into things like that in a lot of detail.

These ideas about the meanings of social housing tie in with the broader academic literature to which we have adverted in earlier chapters. Here, however, we reflect on the meanings in relation to the kinds of differentiation we have observed. Shared owners differentiated themselves from social renters, on the one hand, but, on the other hand, some expected more from their housing association because it was a social landlord, and others felt duped in some way because their social landlord was running a profit-making business. Of course, a search for coherence between different interviews is not necessarily appropriate, but, equally, the lack of coherence in the often-assumed identity of the social landlord reflects a fracture at the heart of social housing, and particularly shared ownership, in the twenty-first century.

Conclusion

Previously articulated ambitions for shared ownership by policy-makers centred on asset accumulation and a range of factors that reduced public expenditure elsewhere, rather than on specific outcomes for buyers. One of the major achievements of shared ownership has been to make buyers feel that they are owners; that they have freedom and control, and security; and that, in the main, they are private, not social. However, as we have argued in this chapter, these ideas about ownership and the social are situational and interactive. There were issues, for example, which arose and which interrupted linear narratives, adding complexity and contradiction to those narratives. We see this, perhaps, most clearly when dealing with rent and service charges.

Our understandings of ownership being interactive and situational, as well as temporal, in that they alter over time and are dependent on events, challenge overly neat theories about ownership. Those theories cleanse property of its complexity. They do not recognise that in considering what property ownership means, it is always in action appearing in the mundane. Our buyers, we argue, were constantly engaging with this process, changing things, as they sought to establish their identities in the world both at the level of idea and relationally; and these ideas were inherently about legality as it was being constituted in their everyday lives. This is what we argue the narratives are telling us, through their complexity, contradictions, and richness of the interviewees' everyday lives.

So, for example, there were matters which were out of control, and which emphasised the shared owners' liminal status; but, even those who felt that they had lost their security, because they could no longer afford the service charges, felt that they were owners. To be sure, that feeling was more muted and hedged, but that identification was clearly important to them, in contradistinction to the on-the-ground facts. It may well be that the shared owners' problems were partly no different from other long leaseholders. However, some interviewees felt that their position was different because they were being helped into ownership by buying a share. This reflects the problematic at the heart of the shared ownership bargain—and one that was never satisfactorily explained to us by anybody during our research—that the shared owner is responsible for all repairs and service charges attributable to their property. Here, we think that it is worth playing with Blomley's ideas about ownership clusters, the recurring effects of performances around property in terms of their effects on legality. This ongoing process perhaps also explains why our buyers' narratives also perform a significant feat at the same time, of being contradictory to their everyday experiences, in which their struggles underscore their own lack of control. It is this contradiction which, we argue, underscores the mutually constitutive relationships in the triptych of law–property–society.

Bibliography

Blomley, N. (2016), 'The Boundaries of Property: Complexity, Relationality, and Spatiality', 50(1), *Law and Society Review*: 224–55.

CCHPR (2012), *Understanding the Second Hand Market for Shared Ownership Properties*, Cambridge: CCHPR.

Cowan, D., Morgan, K. and McDermont, M. (2009), 'Nominations: An Actor-Network Approach', 24(2), *Housing Studies*: 281–300.

DCLG (2015), *Proposals to Streamline the Resale of Shared Ownership Properties*, London: DCLG.

Wallace, A. (2008b), *Achieving Mobility in the Intermediate Housing Market: Moving Up and Moving On?*, York: Joseph Rowntree Foundation.

7

Assembling Shared Ownership

Introduction

In this chapter, we draw together our analysis of the key themes of this book around five randomly selected narratives provided by the shared owner buyers we interviewed. In these narratives, complex stories are told about ownership, as "merchants of morality" (Goffman 1956: 253), and about what Paul Watt has described as "selective belonging", a "spatially uneven sense of belonging and attachment" (2009: 2888; see also Jackson and Benson 2014). They are stories of differentiation, picking up on one of the themes of Chap. 5. They are narratives through which identities are performed and co-constituted with objects around the interviewees' homes, over time. As Benson and Jackson (2017: 6) put it: "The repeated and reiterative narration of negotiations in relation to housing – triumphs, anxieties and ambivalences – reveal differences in what people have, how they make sense of this and how they cope."

Rather than interspersing these narratives with our own analysis, we have taken the analytical step to set out relevant parts of our interviews directly from the transcript, with connecting sentences where we have moved on. We do this to enable as much of the stories to appear as they were told to us, and as we led in the interviews themselves. We recognise that our selection of "relevant" excerpts from the interviews reflects our choice, and our descriptions at the start of each story, as well as our linking sentences, are our words. However, these limits are placed on us, as authors, by the discipline of the textual form. In the concluding section, which we label "discussion", we analyse how these stories interacts with the themes of this book.

© The Author(s) 2018
D. Cowan et al., *Ownership, Narrative, Things*, Palgrave Socio-Legal Studies,
https://doi.org/10.1057/978-1-137-59069-5_7

The "triumphs, anxieties, and ambivalences" were narrated to us often through objects and about tenure. Neither of these was surprising. Housing/home researchers have adverted us to the significance of objects as transcending their status as objects, anthropomorphising and actively constituting identities and understandings of home (Hurdley 2006; Miller 2010). A generation of housing researchers have explained how tenure and identities are mutually constituting (see, e.g., Gurney 1999a, b; Rowlands and Gurney 2001).

Scholars have sought to bring these perspectives together. Jacobs and Smith (2008: 518) refer to an "assemblage of dwelling" as an attempt to capture the relation between home and housing. Cook et al. (2013: 295) refer to a housing assemblage denoting "home not as a place whose holism can be taken for granted and interrogated for its character and effects, but rather as a site of emergence, something which is produced, performed and in a state of always becoming through a seamless web of activity and engagement in a more-than-human world". While the focus of this work began with studies of indebtedness, others have, for example, used literature, photography, and art as agents of home (Blunt and Dowling 2006; Jacobs and Gabriel 2013; Jacobs and Malpas 2013). The reference points in this turn are the work of Bourdieu and Latour, because they work with non-humans, style, and aspiration. They are also quite radical in the housing studies tradition which has tended to focus on the consumption of housing, rather than on objects. As Jacobs and Gabriel (2013: 217) put it:

> Objects, people, ideas and things all make up the constituent components of housing. A material cultural approach represents a radical departure from past approaches in housing research in terms of its recognition of the hybrid nature of actors; relational understanding of phenomena; and recognition of the emergent and contingent nature of knowledge.

Our claim here is that this contributes to a better understanding of the ways in which people experience tenure as a kind of emotional rendition of property. This is where shared ownership becomes significant, because its nature requires buyers to position themselves; at least, it does when they are questioned about it by an intruding, errant researcher. At this point, objects which had no meaning, which were inanimate, become symbolic and take on meaning because that was the way that legality was experienced or, at least, explained.

So, for example, an external form which one has to complete that asks for your tenure—if you are a shared owner, do you tick the box for "owner", "private renter", or "social renter" because you are all three simultaneously.

Forms, however, generally require and are understood to require a binary response. Our interviewees uniformly ticked the owner box, but in this way, the form itself conspired to construct a property identity. Absent such binary responses, though, when they spoke about ownership/renting and social/private, they did so in terms which were complex and contradictory; they spoke of being owners whose lives were out of control and in different phases.

It is not surprising, therefore, that our buyers' narratives were internally contradictory, and that they told stories about things, which exemplified their sense of successful or partial control over their domain. They told stories which emphasised their sense of control, the mix of money and home, while at the same time effectively recognising that their control depended on others or things. And the narratives they told were temporally located to their experiences of ownership, as well as being temporally dislocated in the sense that they were taken out of time to provide illustrations of their positionality to the researcher sitting with them.

One of the keys to these narratives is also the version of legality being engaged. We did not ask our participants to provide "legal" narratives, and so we are reading legality into those narratives. Most of our interviewees did not have the economic capital to invest in bringing claims against others with whom they fought (and their income and/or capital was likely to put them above the rate to obtain legal aid). Their claims had not been forced through some law bottleneck. However, the stories we were told were legal in the expanded sense we described in Chap. 1, in which formal law may not be either approved or acknowledged.

Just like the chair in the snow, though, these stories are about property, ownership, exclusion, and control. So, for example, when Kleinhans and Elsingha (2010) operationalised empowerment for the purposes of their survey as operating along three dimensions (freedom, security, and privacy in the home; perceived control over one's life; and self-esteem), they were operationalising a set of legal understandings about ownership that have a certain interdisciplinary recognition. Our argument is that legality is part of this assemblage of dwelling as it emerges; it cannot be excluded because it is bound together with these triumphs, anxieties, and ambivalences.

Paul's Story, aka the Story of the Potted Plant

Paul was interviewed by Alison. He and his partner had lived separately in London. They wanted to move in together, but out of London, with their daughter. Paul had been a housing association tenant at that time (and the couple's decision to enter into shared ownership was discussed in Chap. 5). In 2007, the couple came across a shared ownership flat in Greendale's estate in Area 2 and decided to move there. In order to afford the property, Paul told what he described as a "white lie" on his mortgage application form about the amount he earned (this was 2007), and, fortunately, "they didn't ask too many questions to get the mortgage, so that was good".

The property they bought was in a mixed tenure block. They bought it off plan. Other residents were a mix of shared owners and social renters and their block sat behind the one that was for private sale. The private sale block had an internal courtyard and nice planting. On the other hand, Alison felt that the entrance to Paul's block was like a multi-storey car park entrance or a service entrance point. The block was organised by floor, so that shared owners were congregated on a particular floor above the social rented floor. Disaster struck almost immediately when they moved in—"Even the day we moved in, what is my daughter's bedroom had all mould and stuff in it."

Paul had understood the shared ownership bargain originally as follows:

> You know, if you're a tenant, if anything goes wrong you just ring up the housing association and they more or less come and fix anything. You know, like here, if the boiler breaks, that's on me to – I have to fix it. Or if there's issues, you take a greater responsibility as a homeowner, pretty much. And I think all of that was pretty clear, really.

He explained that he felt that Greendale had not really known how to manage the tenure mix:

> [O]bviously we sort of have different rights and responsibilities, and it kind of cuts both ways, because as a shared owner I think I have relatively more independence of the housing association, if you like, whereas if you're a tenant they sort of hold a power over you and can potentially evict you for antisocial behaviour or other things like that.

He provided two illustrations of this management problem. First, the block had not one but two residents' groups: "I was involved in, like a residents' group for the block, and basically the representation on that was – well, how it kind of ended up was there was one kind of rep for the tenants and one rep for the shared owners." This was not an uncommon happening in our case studies (as to which, see Chap. 6), in itself something redolent of difference and identity.

The second illustration concerned the quality of building (this was a new-build). There were various issues, one of which concerned smoke smells between flats. He complained to the housing association that there was "hard-core drug use" in the flat below his, the smells from which were so severe that the couple made a series of complaints:

> *Paul*: I think they made – [sighs] I think if they'd had a much stronger handle on it in the first place a lot of the things might have been more easily managed. It was not great. It was not great, and, you know, certainly …
>
> *I*: AND WHAT ABOUT THE SMELLS? HOW DID YOU RECTIFY THAT?
>
> *Paul*: It was – I mean, because of the nature of the problem, the guy doing hard drugs, we were literally waking up in the morning feeling nauseous, headaches, feeling really, really ill. You know, and you kind of start off going through the usual channels – I ended up just marching down to their offices and literally just demanding to see, like, whoever the most senior person was in that building at the time. I was like, "Give me the chief executive. Okay, if he's not in or can't see me, like, whoever." I was really, really angry about it, because it just took a long time and was really impacting on our quality of life.
>
> *I*: SO DID YOU THINK THE NORMAL WAY OF REPORTING IT WASN'T BEING EFFECTIVE, OR THEY WEREN'T LISTENING, OR …?
>
> *Paul*: Well, it was the sort of problem that was kind of hard to – doesn't fit into an easy – didn't really fit into any easy category for them to deal with. And even there were issues of having to prove it. So I had to – I think they might have facilitated it a little bit, but I had to get a police officer to come into our flat and confirm that the smells that were coming in were indeed drug-related.
>
> *I*: YES. [LAUGHS]
>
> *Paul*: Because you ring up and say, "Oh, there's smells in my flat", it can sound like you're being quite oversensitive or something like that … In the middle of winter, we had to sleep with the windows and doors open, just to let the smell out. It was horrible. So we had some issues there; other people also had some related issues, but we really copped that the worst, because we had this particular property.

Eventually, the household either moved on or was evicted; Paul was not sure which.

The basic point was that, in these dealings, Paul felt out of control. He had to rely on the housing association, but that reliance was shaky. Yet, he felt like an owner. As he put it:

I pay a mortgage every single month and, you know, ever so ever so gradually, each passing month, I own a teeny bit more. And that, yes, that is – yes, the first time I ever experienced that, and probably the only way I was going to experience that, given the other circumstances of my life and the relationship that I was in. So it was the only way I was going to do that, and so, yes, I feel like it because I get a mortgage statement every year and I get to pay the mortgage every month, and, yes, fundamentally it is my space to do what I want. And mostly the housing association doesn't interfere and doesn't bother us, and you can sort of ignore them, as well.

Paul gave examples about his sense of being an owner, one of which was about flue vents, and the other, flowerpots. The flue vents were "part of this ongoing issue about smoke and things not working properly, and at some point they wrote and said, like, all these flats, for some health and safety regulation, need to have a load more squares cut into their ceilings, so what they've been proposing is, like, making at least, maybe another two of those in the ceiling, which just looks quite ugly, to be honest with you". Paul had exercised his ownership right through ignoring the association's request to create the "ugly holes": "I think it's different for the tenants. This is where the tenants maybe have a little bit less scope, or maybe feel a bit less empowered to actually challenge what the housing association might say to them."

The flowerpot example was, in many respects, the perfect example of the performative properties of things, as well as about the interactive nature of the interview process. Paul began the story of the potted plants, like many of our interviewees, as an example of his control over the properties of his property and because it differentiated him from the social tenants downstairs:

> *Paul*: This is, like, another issue: if you saw outside my flat and some of the others, people have got some potted plants and stuff?
> *I*: OH, YES, I THOUGHT THAT WAS NICE.
> *Paul*: Yes, I think it's nice, and it's one of the things – and also, the lower floors from here are tenants; the upper floors are shared owners. One of the differences between the floors is the shared owners have more of that kind of … decoration and sort of personalisation, a sense of making it a nice environment. Because we've all got a stake in it and it's our flats, and maybe some of the social problems that exist in some of the other properties aren't – you don't get that with the shared owners. I'm talking, like, people out of prison, I'm talking about people with drug habits and so on and so forth. So looking after some nice flowers outside their front thing may not be their priority.
> *I*: NO, FAIR ENOUGH.

Paul: But for the shared owners it's like, we don't have gardens here, and that is just one nice thing to do, to sort of take care of the thing and have a bit of pride in it, and try and make it a nice environment for everybody.

So, for Paul, then, the potted plants performed ownership through caring about his property and its environment, and distinguished his property holding from the social tenants, who would not prioritise making the outside of their flats nice. However, Paul's story was also a story about resistance against the housing association and being out of, but then in, control. The provider constructed the potted plants as a health hazard and required their removal. Paul and Jill, another resident, resisted the requirement to move them:

Paul: And then at some point, they started – you know, they really started saying to me and [Jill], on the far end, like, "You can't have those. They're a fire issue. If there is an emergency, that could obstruct the emergency services, or they could be a hazard to other people." And me and [Jill], being on the far ends of the block …
I: YES. WELL, YOU'LL HAVE NO ONE GOING PAST YOUR PLANT POT, WOULD YOU?
Paul: There's no – yes. No one's going to be going past, because there's no exit there. And so we've both stood our ground and fought it, and they were really – you know, they were getting quite insistent, and, you know – I can't remember what kind of actions they were threatening to take against us, but they were sort of – you know, there was a little bit of a confrontation between us as …, those with the plants, versus the housing association. And because what they were saying was just ridiculous, and they were saying, …, "Oh, well, there's been cases in other places where children have stepped up onto the plants and fallen" – you know, and toppled down and fallen three storeys. And I said, "Well, I'm the only person on this floor with a child. I can live with the – you know, like, I'm prepared to be a grown-up and take the risk and live with the risk." Because it's not a real issue. It's a non-issue. And the idea that it might somehow obstruct the emergency services if there was a problem: again, a completely, completely ridiculous objection. And so, yes, we ended up basically saying, "Well, no", basically, "and if you want to escalate it, we will be kind of talking to, like, the local media", and actually saying, "Look at this housing association with their ridiculous rules who don't want people to have a nice quality environment", and at some point they sort of backed down and we heard nothing more. But we had to have a bit of a battle with them about that.
I: RIGHT.
But I'm glad we did, and as you say, it looks nice.
I: YES, I LIKE THE NASTURTIUMS. THEY'RE NICE. [LAUGHS]

The provider backed down but only by omission, as Paul thought about it, because of his strategies for dealing with their objection and threats. His approach was about claiming control and ownership not through the law of property, but in the ways that owners make such claims of resistance, through entreaties against their "ridiculous objection" and threats.

Emma's Story, aka the Story of the Nightmare Leak

Emma was a civil servant who was Dave's first interviewee on this then new project. She had a doctorate and had conducted academic fieldwork, including interviews. We met Emma in Chaps. 4 and 7, when discussing her solicitor and the conveyancing documentation. Emma's flat was on the top floor of a new-build block in a "horse-shoe" arranged development. Her block was on the right as you looked at it, there was a block of owners in the middle, and on the left was the social housing block.

The "main issue" with shared ownership for her was that, although you only buy a share, "if you're a leaseholder you're liable for anything that happens inside". Emma's story was of a "nightmare leak" which actually affected both her property and her neighbour downstairs:

> The issue we had and continue – well, had at the time – was that there was a leak coming from somewhere that looked like it was coming from my flat. But there was no evidence for an entire month that it was coming from my flat. So we were trying to rule out all possibilities. All [the housing association] would do was, "It's nothing to do with us; it's coming from your flat". I'm like, "Well, how do you know it's coming from my [flat]" – it's a vicious circle thing.
>
> ...
>
> Fortunately for them [i.e. her neighbours], theirs is mainly cosmetic [damage] but it was incredibly stressful for the month of October last year. I'd be lying there in the morning at half seven in the morning; my phone would be pinging. There'd be a photo if the leak had got bigger and bigger and bigger. I was doing everything humanly possible to work out where it was coming from. They were on the phone. Because I'd only just started a new job recently and I was on probation and she was at home, she was doing all the phone calls. Both of us were in tears most of the time because of [the housing association's] attitude and how long it takes to get through to speak to anybody.

Her housing association, she felt, had been obstructive—"They wouldn't help us at all so that delayed everything by much longer":

Their issue for all of us was, "You're the leaseholder; you're responsible for what's going on". The view I take is, fine, unless it's a latent defect – which this is – and it's been proven that it's down to the construction company then it's not my fault. That's how I would see it, but it's up to me; the onus is on me to prove otherwise. Even when there's been an expert's report – we had forensic engineers in doing all that – they've all agreed on that and I'm not allowed to see that report. But this is another issue that's interesting with shared ownership. If you have an issue, under your buildings insurance because it's a group buildings insurance policy, I have to pay the excess to start everything off. I had to pay the excess to get some-one out to see if there was a pipe in my flat. There was no evidence it was even coming from my flat but I had to initiate that process just to prove that.

Emma and her partner had spent hours on the telephone to the provider's repairs service over a period of around eight months.

Then, in the middle of her story, she broke off and told a different story, which, for her, was about a similar issue to do with her service charge but which also, for us, was used by her to illustrate her own positionality:

> *Emma*: Another issue with shared ownership which, I understand why it hap-pens – well, I don't really understand why, it's annoying – is that we're obviously in a so-called affordable housing, although it's not really very much. We pay a service charge and this block is a mixture of privately-owned tenants, shared ownership and social housing. I completely agree with that principle; it means you don't always get the greatest neighbours and a big mix of neighbours but I understand the importance behind it. But I presume the social housing side of it doesn't pay any service charge. I don't know how that works exactly.
> We've had a couple of incidents with people in the social housing side that have been fly-tipping and causing a lot of rubbish. There was a Roma family over there but there were others as well that they have since been kicked out. But during that time – and I complained about this a few years back to the housing association – shared ownership people and I presume the private, our service charge goes up because it's the general maintenance. Our propor-tion goes up and it went up by something like £100 each a year for an issue that is nothing to do with us. I remember going to – we had a residents' forum and I was saying, "Why is our service charge coming up because we're not doing anything wrong, but other people are?" Everyone else was there; it was only me from the shared ownership side. Everyone else was saying, "Oh, we're really happy that our rent has gone down."
> Although I'm shared ownership and affordable housing, I know it's probably unavoidable but we do feel that we're subsidising other parts when actually we can't really afford to do that. We're trying to be good tenants and maintain things and report things if things are fixed so they get it all done. Other people aren't playing their side of it. I know that's probably unavoidable but I just think

that's unfair for people that are on only 25, 30, 40 per cent ownership that it really went up a lot. Then when this particular family moved, you saw how much it went down because they itemise the amount. So you know that rubbish clearance – and it was obvious because there were rats and we had a lot of problems, luckily on that side. But it was down to that particular family so …

I: SO WHEN YOU SAY THAT SIDE, HOW IS IT ORGANISED HERE? SO ON THE OTHER SIDE OF THE CORRIDOR YOU'VE GOT FULLY OWNED?

Emma: They're fully owned and on that side they're fully owned. These are shared ownership. I'm not really sure. Then there's a mixture of private ownership, I think. I think it's changed a bit but more on that side – there's like a horseshoe shape – are more social housing tenants or privately-owned social rented, I think. But there's definitely a mix. I'm not sure exactly but I know that there is a difference in the way that people – well, obviously how they pay – but the service charge issue and how that is sorted out because I know that ours has gone up at times when other people's has gone down and we thought that was unfair and nobody …

[telephone rings]

I agree with that, but I don't think it should be for people on affordable housing to be subsidising and it was quite a lot; we felt the subsidy was quite a lot that we were subsidising each year so.

After all this out of controlness, Emma still felt that she was an owner. She hived the issue off to a feature of the leaseholder relationship; whereas, if her boiler or a radiator had "gone", "I have no question at all on that [i.e. it was her responsibility] and I never queried it throughout the whole thing and that's fine".

Pat and Reena, aka the Story of the Cigarette Butt

We met Pat and Reena in Chap. 5, when we described how the block in which their flat was located was off the main street containing the owner blocks. We explained that their block was down a flight of stairs, with another flight leading down to the social rented housing block. We mentioned that the windows in their flat were closed. It was one of the hottest days of the year. The windows were closed because of some trouble that Pat had with a neighbour in the social rented block. Their story is, in a sense one of being in control and out of control; about the porousness of physical boundaries, as well as social boundaries. His was a story in which noise and anti-social behaviour had particularly inflected his appreciation of ownership. Pat was, in fact, a housing worker with a local authority. The couple had bought the flat in part because it was convenient for their son to commute to school and because it was close to Pat's football team's stadium.

They had been very happy in the flat, and recognised (and valued) the tenure mix that made up the area. Pat felt that they had "done very well". However, there had been an incident, which Pat rationalised to himself as being about him "being a bit Victor Meldrew-ish in terms of the noise". But,

I think you could get that anywhere, couldn't you? You could live down a million pound [house], you know, and you could have a neighbour who perhaps wasn't considerate. What's heightened it for me recently, … that a few weeks ago we were sitting here relaxing, we had a houseguest and one of the neighbours downstairs falsely accused us of throwing cigarette butts down out of our window into his front garden. We don't smoke, but he was so irate and wound up about it that he wasn't listening, and he was quite confrontational about it, and the fact that he threw a rolled up thing of tin foil, ball of tin foil, I initially thought, "Is there a drug deal going on there? You know, what's going on?" So, I called the police and they spoke to him and he was, you know, not listening to them and shouting, "Oh, you know, they're number [X]", and the police were saying, "Well they're not number [X]." Thankfully [our son] was asleep and we had another neighbour who lived in the Housing Association who then stuck her head out of the window and was shouting at us and, probably, they're probably very frustrated because I imagine somebody here on this block is being very inconsiderate and smoking and throwing cigarettes, but we don't smoke, you know. So, that, I'm quite hypersensitive at the moment to any noise, to anything, because it's just what's happened. So, I'd imagine before that I was feeling more in love with it and I am, but it's just tainted it a little bit for me at the moment, you know, that's all, as, yes.

Dave asked him whether he felt like an owner. His response at first was as follows:

Yes, I do, … yes, in the sense that, well, in the sense that I want to take care of it and I think that that is probably, rightly or wrongly, a characteristic of people that own things, but no, we're very aware that it's shared ownership and I think that we would like to, at some stage, own something.

He went on,

Without shared ownership I would be feeling that living somewhere like here and renting, and paying £1300, £1400, £1500, that would be eating, the sort of person I am, that would be eating away at me because I would be thinking, "What am I building here? What am I building for the family?" What are we building here? We're building something, yes, we're building 25 per cent of something and also, as long as the rent's paid, as long as the mortgage is paid, there's some security, yes? The landlord won't just turn round to us and say, "Leave." Obviously it's always compulsory orders and nothing's for life, but, you know, as much as anyone, there's some security, but that's the sort of person I am. I like to try and have things, you know, quite ordered.

Had he now felt differently about the place?

When we moved in here it was the winter, and it was October, and the windows were shut, and we didn't have any problems with neighbours and I suppose I thought, "Great, I love this, this is what housing should be, you know, it should, be everybody together and this is what makes London so great, that it's not like Paris", or something like that. … A little bit of that shine has gone off, but what I'm hoping is that once I've sort of calmed down from it, because I felt a bit violated when he threw something through the window and [our son] was asleep, which was great, and he didn't wake up and he wasn't there. I felt perhaps as a man or, you know, or I don't know, I felt very angry and thankfully it didn't result in us having a – you know, the next day I woke up and [Reena] sort of calmed it down and I'm thankful that she did because, you know, who knows what could have happened. I could have gone out there, we could have a physical altercation, I could have ended up arrested, that would have had massive impacts on my job, my life. I'm not – I can't have a criminal record or anything like that. And the noise element, it's annoying, but that being said, I feel that he, you know, I deal with people, I feel he was probably really wound up. Maybe he's reflecting on it now.

What I wanted to do is try and do mediation afterwards, but also a part of me afterwards, a day or two, really wanted to try and punish him, yes? So, I discussed with my wife that I wanted to like ring his housing association because I knew who it was, and I did, but I didn't give my name because Reena said, "Look, let's talk about this when we get home." She said to me, "Look, you know, let's just leave it now, the police have spoken to him. If there's any other things, we'll call his housing association and we'll call ours."

And then, Pat opened up, about how his work affected him:

I put the people in, and they are the most vulnerable people, and that's sad, you know, they've had their troubles in life, but I don't want to be around it after work, quite frankly. I don't want to be around people who are smoking weed, or playing loud music, or do everything in aggressive [ways]. I want to be around middle class people, yes, quite frankly, you know, whether that sounds snobbish or not, ...

Lois' Story, aka the Story of the Good Neighbour

Lois was interviewed by Alison. Like Jeannie, whom we met in Chap. 5, Lois constructed herself as a good neighbour. She had been a housing association social rented tenant in "a bit of a deprived area" for 15 years prior to buying a 40 per cent share in her house in 2013 with her husband. It was a little further out from her previous accommodation, but it was on a leafy estate, next to open spaces in an area that she would otherwise have been unable to afford: "I was scared about coming further out and then when I saw it that was it! I would have done anything to get one. … To be honest, we didn't go too much into the rates and things because we were just, I would have done anything, even if it was a higher rate. I would have sold my puppy!" The estate was a mixed tenure estate, with blocks of flats and individual houses, some of which were shared ownership and some of which were ownership. The estate was managed by a third-party agent.

Her description of the buying process began with her description of the conveyancing process:

> *Lois*: They just sent you loads of paperwork to read, so no, I never met a solicitor at all. The housing association did do an interview and went through some of the things.
>
> *I*: WHAT SORTS OF THINGS DO YOU RECALL THEM …?
>
> *Lois*: You tend to pick out things that stick in your mind. I mean I picked out that in this property with this lease, we're not allowed, even though someone has, to have Sky dishes; we're not allowed to change the fronts of our house.
>
> *I*: NO, YOU'RE LIKE THE ENTRANCE TO THE ESTATE, QUITE GRAND AND LANDSCAPED AND EVERYTHING ISN'T IT?
>
> *Lois*: Yes. You're not allowed to have a vehicle over a certain weight, like you can't have a massive caravan; people in flats here I know can't have pets – birds I suppose they could have, or fish, but dogs or cats, no. I suppose you can't change the exterior, but the thing that sticks in my mind is that even if you buy it, you're still a leaseholder.
>
> *I*: DID THEY EXPLAIN ABOUT YOUR RIGHTS AND RESPONSIBILITIES OF BEING IN SHARED OWNERSHIP?
>
> *Lois*: Yes, to a certain extent, but shared owners get very confused where their part ends and the bit they rent begins. We were on full repair lease, which means this is our house. If the gas heating goes wrong or any other defects, we repair it. A lot of people miss that. For example, our bell went wrong and my husband said, "Oh, should we ring Fixham, the bell …." I said, "No, the bell's ours. That's our bell."

Alison arrived for the interview in a car, and Lois began a discussion about the car parking problem on the estate. This discussion about parking prompted the following interaction, in which she divided herself off:

Lois: We've got a car port at the back and we own one under the car port and one behind that. There are three spaces in the car port and three spaces behind. So we've got two spaces each; they serve the three houses that are our sister houses there. Everyone else has got one space, but most people in this day and age have more than one car. They gave us a shed and we thought to have a bike, which would be more eco-friendly. But there were people parking in other people's spaces. So now we've got permits. So even though I own that, I have to have a permit to park in my own drive and the green one is to park on the estate because you could get a ticket. I haven't got a problem with the parking because I have enough parking.

I: ARE THERE FLATS ON THE ESTATE?

Lois: Yes, there are flats here.

I: PRESUMABLY THEY JUST HAVE ONE SPACE?

Lois: Yes, they've just got one, but some people in flats haven't got a car. But say you came today, you couldn't just park in any bay or you'd get a ticket. You can only park in the bay that's yours, or in a visitor's bay. But if you're in a visitor's bay you have to have a visitor's pass which is red; if you're in the road you've got to have a green one. It is quite complicated, but I wouldn't like to see anyone get a ticket. They've bumped up the pavement and we're trying to get the Residents' Association to see if the council will make a lay-by because it's just a bit of a wasted pavement.

I: WHAT PROMPTED YOU TO SET UP THE RESIDENTS' ASSOCIATION?

Lois: Where I lived before, it was horrible. You see benefits people, that kind of environment. I go to work and I look after my home and I look after my garden and when you come home and there are people out in the street … The thing I always say: there was a woman in the street and it was summer and she was sitting on the curb while her neighbour dyed her hair, while drinking from a neat bottle of vodka and later on in the evening – I didn't witness it but my neighbour said that the woman who was drinking the vodka had a wee in the street. She was wearing a maxi dress and she didn't take anything off, just stood there and had a wee. You just think, "I don't want to live in this any more." People have babies in the streets in nappies running around. You just get in your car, you go to work, you come home and you shut your door. When I moved here, I was like, "Oh my, I've got community; I've got people all in the same boat, the bulk of us are shared owners. There are private houses and some of the houses on this estate are pretty nice. My neighbours are shared owners; we're all in the same boat, we've all got to go to work, we're all on the budget. I just thought, because I'm not into picking up litter and I'm a bit sad and old, ... , we did a bit of door-knocking, I and the community development lady for the area and we decided to set up a Resident's Association."

I: IS THAT JUST FOR THE GENERAL NEEDS OF THE SHARED OWNERS?

Lois: Well, we invited everybody and no one came except our Fixham people, but none of the private people came. We all pay our service charge to the same company. I pay mine and the house that's private next door pays theirs. They made a Residents' Association and didn't invite us. The managing agents didn't think to invite any of us.

I: SO THE MANAGING AGENTS AREN'T FIXHAM THEN?

Lois: No. We pay, I think they're called []. We pay our service charge through Fixham but it goes to []; they pay their's direct to []. But they excluded us.

I: OH NO! SO HOW DID YOU MANAGE THAT? DID THEY CHANGE THEIR MINDS?

Lois: No.

I: SO YOU'VE GOT TWO RESIDENTS' ASSOCIATIONS?

Lois: Yes. Theirs is yearly; ours is proper and is called the [] Residents' Association, but I do know some of the private residents just from walking around, really and they were invited initially. When we had our first meeting I gave minutes to every single house on this estate; I posted them through the door and said when the next meeting was. But now I won't because if they were interested, well, they've all got the address if they wanted to contact the team and we've got our own email address.

I: YES, WELL, OBVIOUSLY YOU WOULD BE RAISING THE SAME THINGS LIKE THE PARKING OF THE ESTATE UPKEEP.

Lois: Well, the parking is probably peculiar to us because the big houses have big drives, so they've got two- and three-car drives. It's hard, but it's almost better that it's separate because our issues are probably different. Someone in a general-needs home who's not working, the things they're interested in or want clarification on might be different from someone living in a £600,000 house, who's a doctor. So we're looking at ways of saving money on bills and things like that but some other people don't care or don't need to bother with so much. But we're all on a budget ...

Lois   : Also, now I know all the residents, so there are couple of those, for example, there's a gentleman who lives in one of the general-needs, and he looked pretty scary from the outset. If you saw him walking along the road you've probably cross over to the other side, trying not to look scared. He's actually lovely. He's very quietly spoken but he looks quite decent. So now I say hello and I know most people by name. So at least now if there was a problem like someone parking in someone's space, now we've got it all out there, people can be a bit more – they don't realise sometimes that they're being antisocial but not being good neighbours maybe. So yes, I think it helps.

Alison subsequently asked Lois if she felt like an owner. Her answer was positive:

Even though I can't change the outside – it's new, so I wouldn't want to change the outside anyway – I can do, you know, I wouldn't be asking Fixham permission to … I know you're meant to …, but pretty much I feel I can do what I like. If I wanted to change my bathroom suite tomorrow I'm going to change it but also I'm adding value to my property. When you're renting all you want to do is pay. You don't really want to add value to a housing association property that isn't yours because you can't take it with you. So you wouldn't necessarily want to put a new kitchen in. For example, in our kitchen, we've been saving up and we're going to get one of those glaze splash-backs and they are really, really expensive. If it were my other house, no, but here I'm going to have what I want. Even if I have to wait, I will have what I want, rather than what I think will just do, now I'm at the stage where I think I'll wait to get the thing that I actually want. So I'd rather go with that and get the thing I want. I suppose it's like the house I want. My other house was an okay house inside, but I suppose I have had to wait for the thing I want.

As the interview drew to a close, Alison asked about service charges. Again, Lois divided herself off, this time from her neighbours:

Lois: It's £50 a month. But we got a refund this year because the person who handed the estate over from Fixham gave everyone the wrong information and it was shocking. He doesn't work for Fixham anymore. My house ends at my front door, so my front garden isn't actually mine; it's meant to be maintained by Fixham. When it was all set up, all the front gardens are like no-man's land. So this bit's meant to be maintained by a company called [] but the bit at the side of the part is the managing agent's and no one knows whose bit belongs to who and it's been like that ever since. So I do my own front garden, but the residents were kindly told by this guy that yes, they were going to maintain the front gardens. No, they don't. They cut the bushes down once a year if they get above your window sill; they're not going to come out and plant pansies and make it look pretty in your front garden but they will in the main area.

I: IS THAT BECAUSE YOU'RE ON THE SORT OF ENTRANCE AND THEY WANT TO BE ABLE TO HAVE SOME CONTROL OVER WHAT THE ENTRANCE TO THE ESTATE LOOKS LIKE?

Lois: Yes. I mean they've done a little playground over there. But I think that's why we got a refund because everyone was going mad. We weren't even getting – a bit more round there it's not as nice because a couple of people in there don't really look after their gardens because they're paying for it. The lady opposite to me, we've got trees down the side of the house, lovely little Christmas trees; I think they're yew. Because she was paying her service charge, last summer she had weeds coming above her window. She would not touch those weeds because she was paying. Now my perception is yes, I know I'm paying, but I can see weeds so I'll pull them up myself. Her perception is that she's paying for it so she's not going to do it.

I: SO DID PEOPLE GET ONTO FIXHAM AND WHAT WAS THEIR RESPONSE?

Lois: When we got our service charge statement we were given a refund and it was the fact that everyone said, "Do you think I'm paying for gardening when you haven't done any?"

I: SO HAVE THEY PUT SOMETHING IN PLACE NOW TO DEAL WITH THOSE THINGS THIS YEAR?

Lois: I never see [Fixham's gardening contractor] here. I see the estate manager gardeners but I don't ever see [Fixham's] gardeners.

I: WHO ARE THE ESTATE MANAGER GARDENERS?

Lois: They've got a van and they mow out the front there and they mow down here, and they'll mow the grass there but won't touch the bushes. We do the bushes. Now I've got all this lovely row of little green trees, which look beautiful; her trees are all dead because she left them.

Jeanette and Zach, aka the Story of the Charter

So far, the stories we have told are of those people who constructed themselves as owners. We noted in Chap. 6, however, that this construction was not uniform among our participants. Our final story is of Jeanette and Zach, whom we met in Chap. 4. Jeanette and Zach there expressed different views about contact with Fixham. On the one hand, they said that they had never had any contact with Fixham; one the other hand, they were pleased that was the case. They had bought their house in 2003 through a DIYSO scheme, having previously been living with Jeanette's parents. Jeanette had resisted rented accommodation because "[b]asically you don't get anything out of it. You know, you are paying the money to somebody else". Zach had owned a property with a previous partner.

They wanted to make a long-term investment and buy a property into which they would grow. They bought a house which was 33 years old that nobody else wanted: "I think the lady actually turned round and more or less said to us, not straight out, but you're at the bottom of the list for potentially any housing and the only reason we got this house is because nobody else wanted it." Their understanding of property as an investment was a key factor in their explanation of the shared ownership transaction. They purchased their house for £105,000: "We have seen a house go a couple of streets away exactly the same mid-terrace. It was in better condition because our kitchen and our bathroom need updating, but that went for £167,000." They wanted to buy the rest of their house from Fixham, but their salaries were too low to do so.

Alison, who conducted the interview, asked whether they felt that they had enough information when they bought the property:

Zach: Definitely it was there, but it was like jargon. It wasn't simplistic.
Jeanette: No.
Zach: [The previous owner, who had a particularly severe disability], although he could read and write, it must have been very difficult for him to understand jargon because we are quite numerate and we had a devil of a job.
Jeanette: We were given reams and reams of paperwork.
Zach: It was legal jargon you might say.
Jeanette: Yes, and we had to just sit down and after a little bit we're just like, "What?" Yes, we really didn't understand what was going on.
I: DID FIXHAM OR THE SOLICITOR EXPLAIN ALL THE KEY FEATURES OF IT WELL?
Jeanette: The key points that I knew was explained to us, was that we owned half of the building and Fixham owned the other half of the building and the land.
Zach: And the land it is built on, thus the freehold, you are just the tenant.
Jeanette: That was explained, but anything else, and it wasn't until we actually purchased the house that we found out that we were responsible for everything inside the house.
Zach: The total upkeep if you like.
Jeanette: Because we've got an issue at the moment where our boiler needs replacing, we can't afford to do it, but Fixham refuse to help us with it.
...
I: YES, AND DO YOU FEEL THAT THAT WASN'T MADE CLEAR TO YOU WHEN YOU PURCHASED THE PROPERTY?
Zach: Definitely not.
Jeanette: No.
Zach: And bearing in mind not just the boiler, the total upkeep. I mean the only thing, because I have friends in the building trade and occasionally dabbled in the building trade away from my own business, I was aware that you'd have to fix the roof. What definitely wasn't made clear to us was if say there was a leak on the roof you were to inform Fixham immediately and one of their nominated tradesmen builders fix it on your behalf and you are to pay them. You have no choice of builder.

I: REALLY, IS THAT THE CASE?

Jeanette: Yes.

Zach: Yes, that is very bad and to consolidate the point … Because of the mortgage, and you're probably aware, by law we have to have the minimum building survey on this property to acquire the mortgage offer from Nationwide. It falls upon you. You have to pay for it. It's £200 odd quid, £250 I believe. We were offered a basic survey, an intermediate and a high survey typically in £250 increments. We chose the lowest £250 rather than the £500 or in-depth survey of £750 at our own expense. What wasn't found by the surveyor, to my disgust even at the low end of £250 survey, this house had three leaks; one on the toilet, one on the installed shower at the time and one on the roof. We moved in only to find out all three leaks, which absolutely upset and worried us because we'd spent a lot of our savings. How we're going to pay for all these leaks? … Although the charter with Fixham says we are to inform them immediately, no, I'll be damned if I phone someone, whether they are the landlord or not, for me to incur great expenses from a tradesmen which they will initiate. My best friend is a builder. I got my best friend to immediately repair, and I mean immediately, practically the next day or the next available day, the defects leaks in the roof which were to do with the leaded flash band had come loose between our roof and next doors, my friend fixed it at my cost without any interference from Fixham and the repair has remained for 12 years. Then progressively, as we found out, the two other leaks later on, firstly the shower was leaking onto the ceiling boards behind the bath. One couldn't see it. To be fair to the surveyor obviously it was a low key survey. You'd have to literally pull the bath panel out to look at the bath to see the shower is leaking. We found out from damp that it was leaking and we had to have that removed by a qualified plumber rather than inform Fixham because the leak was something that had to be addressed straight away, immediately once we'd located it. That was the second leak. The third leak, and the final kick in the teeth, was the toilet decided to leak. A qualified tradesman came and fixed that, yet again our own expense.

I: YES.

Zach: Although I broke the charter rules, I chose to do so because I knew it would take much longer to fix them and at greater cost.

…

Zach: Yes, inform them immediately. Basically, by their own definition, allegedly you are not allowed to carry out or get anyone to carry out any interior work without their consent, and basically nominate any tradesmen. They have the right to take over the whole business and initiate the repair when they feel fit, and by which trader they nominate. That is totally unacceptable because all the time it takes to call out someone the leak could get worse and bring the ceiling down. The only, what shall we call it? The only nicety of this in our rent, which hasn't been mentioned and we need to mention it, there is a subsidiary paid towards building, not contents insurance, but building insurance, which obviously Fixham would get reimbursed from. We actually pay that out of our rent, so I believe, although officially by their own charter we broke their charter rules, my wife and I are covered legally because we actually pay for the building insurance out of our rent to them. That's why I feel if we were chastised by them anyway, we cannot be chastised legally because my wife is actually paying for that in her ground rent.

Their dismay about being responsible for the repairs to the property was matched by a further issue over making improvements to the property. They wanted to "update" the kitchen and the bathroom:

Jeanette: Well, we want to do it, but our main bugbear with Fixham is the fact that they dictate to us what we do in our home. We pay them rent, yet they won't help us with anything. The problem with shared ownership is you are a home owner and you're a tenant, but you've got no rights as the homeowner and you've got no rights of the tenant, because normally, if you were a tenant, you pay rent and the …

Zach: Landlord.

Jeanette: Landlord, that's the word, has the obligation to fix any faults so what my problem is why are we paying them rent? What is the rent for? I know the building insurance is there. They own the land so, of course, we've got to pay them rent, but surely if we are paying them rent then there is money there for them to assist us with any problems with the house?

I: I SEE, AND THIS IS SOMETHING THAT YOU DON'T FEEL YOU WERE MADE AWARE OF WHEN YOU BOUGHT IT?

Zach: Definitely not.

Jeanette: No, they don't say oh if there is any problems with the house, you have to tell us, we dictate to you what building person tradesmen you use and you have to pay for it.

I: SO THEY SENT THIS INFORMATION LIKE, WHAT, IN A HANDBOOK OR A LEAFLET?

Zach: I always think back to John Major when he initiated his charter. It was very sort of like legal jargon presented actually ironically, if I recall, in A5 as well as in A4 format on coloured paper the do and don'ts.

I: I SEE AND THAT WAS APPLICABLE TO SHARED OWNERS SPECIFICALLY, WAS IT?

Zach: Definitely yes, for what our case was, well it is still.

Jeanette: So if we wanted to do a new bathroom, like we wanted to update our bathroom, we'd have to tell Fixham that we want to update our bathroom, they'd have to approve everything that we want to do in the bathroom so they then ultimately have the say of what we can and can't do, and then they'll tell us who they want us to have as a tradesman or we have to tell them who we want, and they have to approve that tradesman and then we have to pay for the whole lot.

Zach told another story to nail the point home, much later in the interview:

Zach: There is one other sort of practical problem, which we may have sort of glossed over to do with the repairs, but I do find with definitely our charter through and through, something which really aggravates me is, and the hypocrisy with it, as a tenant for Fixham we are allowed to construct or re-landscape the property outside; the exterior, the garden, the grounds, whichever way you want to put it, anyway we like within council parameters. In other words, I'm a reasonable bricklayer, I could build a brick wall at my own expense and cost and effort anywhere on the property or a pond or a new fence, or a fountain, anything like that, a major improvement of re-landscaping which would increase the value of the property and make it more pretty for everyone, if not really for ourselves. I can't see how I can be given the total free hand to do anything on the ground, yet a porch on the front of this property, which has been on here since its foundations, it's halfway built, it's very easy for my best friend and I to fully enclose the porch, it's a canopy porch which can be bordered up, bricked up and bordered, totally improved at my own expense and logic because I'm a capable tradesman, legitimate building friends, okay I would have to ask local government permission i.e. [] Borough Council, but it clearly says in the charter with Fixham that you'd be in absolute breach, possibly a legal breach, obviously I'd be aware it would a legal breach if we didn't have local government authority permission.
I: RIGHT.
Zach: But they'd be really agitated and annoyed, and consequently could sue you if you built a new porch without their permission.
I: HAVE YOU ASKED THEM TO BUILD A PORCH? ARE YOU SURE THEY'D BE ANNOYED AT YOU?
Jeanette: The reason why we say this is because when we were in the process of going through purchasing the property, it then come to light that the previous tenant to us replaced the doors and the windows and Fixham were thinking of taking legal action against them because they did not seek their permission.

Jeanette and Zach's responses to Alison's question about whether they felt that they were owners or renters was similarly revealing, particularly when it went on to the discussion about what might be changed about the share ownership bargain:

I: OKAY, BEFORE YOU MENTIONED THAT YOU WERE AN OWNER AND A RENTER, BUT YOU FELT LIKE YOU DIDN'T GET THE BENEFIT OF EITHER, IF THAT'S A CORRECT CHARACTERISATION.

Jeanette: Yes.

I: WHICH ONE OF THOSE CARRIES THE MOST WEIGHT FOR YOU? DO YOU FEEL MORE LIKE AN OWNER OR A RENTER?

Zach: No, definitely feel like a tenant.

Jeanette: Yes.

Zach: Always.

Jeanette: Because you don't have the freedom. We are classed as a homeowner, but we can't do what we want with our own home. We are not a tenant because we don't get help. We don't get maintenance of the property. We pay rent so we are kind of in limbo. We are not really either.

I: YOU'RE A SHARED OWNER?

Jeanette: We're a shared owner. We've not got rights to do what we want with our own house, but we've not got assistance of the perks of being in a rental property.

I: AS I SAID, IF YOU HAD THE POWER TO CHANGE THINGS, WHAT WOULD BE THE KEY THING YOU WOULD WANT TO CHANGE?

Zach: Definitely a subsidy towards major repairs, a subsidy of some kind, a percentage if you like towards repairs. That's all I ask.

Jeanette: Yes.

Zach: Because the rent is lowly, I think it should be means tested so if you were paying a higher rent then the subsidy should be 50 per cent towards the repairs, but to be fair and in Fixham's defence, because our rent is lowly and has always been increased in very small increments, I think it should be say 25 per cent paying towards repairs.

Jeanette: Because it is to their benefit as well because any improvements to the property will increase the value of the property.

Zach: Maintain or increase value, yes.

Jeanette: So at the end of it, they will see the benefit.

Zach: They will be reimbursed. They are being reimbursed in the long-term.

Discussion

Our purpose in letting our participants' tell their narratives largely uninterrupted was to enable them to explain their own everyday lives as they see them, without being interrupted by our analysis. Their narratives are clearly purposive and dialogic, in the sense that they are explaining to somebody (Alison or Dave, in these interviews) whom they have not met before about their everyday lives, and experiences, of shared ownership. As we noted in Chap. 1, interviewees were not told in advance about our knowledge or expertise, or our disciplines, although they were told about our institutions and the funding source, as well as why we were contacting them: "This research project uses qualitative research methods like interviews to look at the everyday lives of shared owners and how shared ownership is perceived. We are looking at how problems arise and are dealt with by policymakers, providers, lenders and consumers by these actors." As a result, in these stories, we have not hidden the interviewer's prompts for more information about a particular event, or turn of events, or the more directed questions asked by the interviewer. Equally, we did not ask our interviewees any "law" questions, although we did ask them about the nature of the transactions into which they entered, as it emerged in the interviews, as this was the project's focus.

In this section, we reflect on these narratives against the themes of this book. We re-tell those narratives against the themes which we have highlighted consistently in this book. In telling their stories, we argue that the narrators were constructing their own sense of coherence against a fundamentally bi-tenurial thing, which is largely incapable of categorisation against our normal taken-for-granted understandings about tenure. As we have argued in previous chapters, shared ownership operates in complex ways along two particular spectra: owning/renting and social/private.

We argue that these spectra are situational, in the sense that individual aspects of shared owners' everyday lives lead to different positions on those spectra. To be sure, the shared owners divided themselves off from social rented housing and they did so by expressing their distaste in symbolically violent ways, to adopt the Bourdieu frame. Other scholars, in a more Foucauldian frame, might suggest that these expressions reflect an affective governmentality expressed through disgust of the *other* (Ghertner 2010; Ashworth 2017). Even though the two interviewees here who expressed this kind of disgust of social rented housing had previously lived in that tenure, this was not a uniform expression among previous social renters in our study, and was expressed by others with no such experience. We might postulate that this kind of expression of disgust is a kind of socialised knowledge, but one which was drawn upon to divide off the shared owner so that they could make sense of the distinctions between themselves and others. Recall, for example, Jeannie's narrative from Chap. 5, in which she differentiated herself from the good/bad in expectations around others' tenure. These stories are examples of the kinds of selective belonging in which our interviewees engaged.

In these stories, the narrators in this chapter ascribed characteristics to the social other, in what Mary Douglas (1966: 2) described as "a positive effort to organise the environment", and "positively re-ordering [their] environment, making it conform to an idea". In other words, we see this particular frame as a cultural construction, and one that is inherently legal in its ordering, in which the spectra of social/private and owning/renting are purged so that they become binaries, and conform to pre-existing categories.

That is certainly the case in four of the stories in this chapter. The odd one out was Jeanette and Zach's story. This was a story in which they set themselves up as owners—their principal rationale for entering shared ownership was to avoid paying rent to a landlord and to engage in a profit-making enterprise. They framed their house/home in this talk as a business-like transaction; they actively compared their property value against the market, which made them feel better, like they were earning capital (albeit "cybermoney", as Zach put it). However, it was their obligations, as they constructed them, which made them feel othered. Their lack of "freedom" meant that they could not do what they wanted with their home. They were unable to upgrade their bathroom or kitchen, and couldn't complete the porch. They were out of control as a result. This led them on to asking questions about the nature of their obligations and the full repairing lease.

The other four stories contain complex narratives about the shared owners' being out of control, but then describe themselves as owners through what they did actually have control over. In other words, their stories performed a kind of rhetorical trick by, at once, explaining the issues that they had with shared ownership and being out of control in dealing with those issues, but at the same time diminishing the significance of those issues in answering the "owner" question. As Jane Bennett (2010: 23–4) puts it, in discussing assemblages "of diverse elements, of vibrant materials of all sorts":

> Assemblages are living, throbbing confederations that are able to function despite the persistent presence of energies that confound them from within. … Assemblages are not governed by any central head: no one materiality or type of material has sufficient competence to determine consistently the trajectory or impact of the group.

It is precisely this sort of oscillation we have in mind when we think about our data; it suggests that rather than looking for coherent accounts and perhaps even being surprised at their apparent incoherence, we should embrace the fractures in these accounts. The warm embrace of *home*ownership, against the stickiness of renting, meant that perhaps particularly for shared owners, in their liminal state, ownership was the sought-after characteristic of the relationship—so, for example, Lois' discussion of the cold shoulder that she was given by the owners' residents' association but her subsequent neighbourly discussions with all the residents, which established her place on the estate.

We do not suggest that these stories are particular to shared ownership—indeed, we think that they may be relevant to the leasehold relation more generally—but our point is that the liminality of shared ownership is likely to make buyers more acutely aware of their circumstances, and their narrative then becomes more significant in the telling.

Each of the stories concerns property, and in each, property is an active relationship, or, as we would prefer to describe it, process. The descriptions of property were told through tales of action and resistance. These were tales about legality, and employed expressions of power/resistance. They were about the form of the transaction—as Zach put it, the "Charter"—and its consequences. They were about using property as a form of identity and place-making.

Stories of power/resistance were not of the dissident type, but of the inclusive type; indeed, they emphasised the teller's place in their construction and constitution of society. Paul's story about the potted plants, constructed by the housing association, in Paul's words, as a health and safety issue (thus tapping into the discursive narratives around wastefulness and regulation—see, e.g., Cabinet Office 2015), was a story in part about how he overcame the housing association (in a kind of David and Goliath way) through his strategies of resistance against "their ridiculous rules who don't want people to have a nice quality environment". Emma's story was, in part, similar about her attempts to face up against the bureaucracy, to find the leak and to recognise where her property rights stopped and started. The simple question was, from where did that water leak spring? That simple question was met with the association's response that it was Emma's responsibility. Emma was simply trying to find the leak so it could be stopped and everybody would then be happy. She faced pressure from her neighbour. Pat and Reena's resistance was of a different type—a conscious omission to open the windows in order to avoid a further altercation with their neighbour.

Most of all, these were stories about things, stuff. What was notable in each story presented here was the ways in which the shared owners weaved things around their narrative, not just as some sort of optional extra, but as the centrepieces of their stories. From the maxidress to the dripping water to the mythical cigarette butt to the rubbish to the Charter, things were central to these property stories. In doing so, the shared owners anthropomorphised things, giving them life and letting them translate their hopes, anxieties, and concerns. Lois, for example, used rubbish (specifically picking it up) to emphasise the place-making role in her understandings about property (which were linked to neighbourhood), counterposing her green Christmas trees with her neighbour's dead ones. Paul's nasturtiums emphasised the extent of his ownership rights.

Remember the wonderful turn of phrase used by Rachel Hurdley (2006: 723), "[T]he meaning of things in the home is what gives home its meaning." That somewhat allegorical phrase allows us to argue that property talk is an ongoing process through which one's relationship with property is given meaning. However, our data also draw attention to the problematic of house/ home existing not just around things in the home, but also things outside. The red pass that Lois' visitors would have to put in their cars to denote outsider's parking right.

More than this, though, it was the extent of the property, which our data both confirm and challenge. Of course, property was related to its exclusive capacity, which, of course, Pat and Reena performed by the act of closing their windows. However, these stories demonstrate property wandering outside the confines of exclusivity and the home. So, when Paul put his flowerpots outside his front door on the walkway, this was a statement about personalising the outside as not just his territory, but about the environment of the (shared) owner. It was because he had "a stake in it and it's our flats" that enabled him to construct property in this way, and, particularly, as a counterposition to the social other. The construction of responsibility for the outside—indeed, where the boundaries lay, if anywhere—was central to the stories told by Emma, Lois, and Jeanette and Zach. Further, the stories were about security both inside and outside the home. In this way, Pat and Reena's story, which, on its face, appears to be a straightforward story about property exclusion, was a story about property transcending boundaries, about safety and security (something which proved problematic for them when there were issues over the front-door lock to the building) beyond the home, and about concerns regarding neighbours and the neighbourhood. It was a story in which, effectively, Pat's work came home (or was brought home) with him.

Property lawyers and economists are inclined towards enabling their doctrines and laws to produce neatness through binary divides, and they are really rather good at that, even with things that are on the cusp. Our data, on the other hand, challenge these kinds of devices through the ways in which everyday practices—we would say, of legality—of property disrupt these artificial boundaries. In our data, what is particularly interesting is the reproduction of these ideas, through things; so, with the anthropologists, we argue that us and things, property and legality, are mutually constitutive of the house/home. As Clarke (2001: 42) puts it,

> The house objectifies the vision the occupants have of themselves in the eyes of others and as such it becomes an entity and process to live up to, give time to, show off to. ... So the proliferation of home decoration and the popularization

of design that has become a key, contemporary component of a relationship that was never simply between an internal private sphere and an external public sphere, but a more complex process of projection and interiorization that continues to evolve.

This ongoing process perhaps also explains why these narratives also perform a significant feat at the same time, of being contradictory to the participants' everyday experiences, in which their struggles over things, dealings with problems in the home or with their housing association underscore their own lack of control and, conversely, control.

Bibliography

Ashworth, M. (2017), 'Affective Governmentality: Governing Through Disgust in Uganda', 26(2), *Social and Legal Studies*: 188–207.

Benson, M. and Jackson, E. (2017), 'Making the Middle Classes on Shifting Ground? Residential Status, Performativity and Middle-Class Subjectivities in Contemporary London', online first, *British Journal of Sociology*.

Bennett, J. (2010), *Vibrant Matter: A Political Ecology of Things*, Durham: Duke UP.

Blunt, A. and Dowling, R. (2006), *Home*, London: Routledge.

Cabinet Office (2015), *The Red Tape Challenge Reports on Progress*, available at http://webarchive.nationalarchives.gov.uk/20150522175321/ http://www.redtapechallenge.cabinetoffice.gov.uk/home/index

Clarke, A. (2001), 'The Aesthetics of Social Aspiration', in D. Miller (ed), *Home Possessions*, Oxford: Berg.

Cook, N., Smith, S. and Searle, B. (2013), 'Debted Objects: Homemaking in an Era of Mortgage-Enabled Consumption', 30(3), *Housing, Theory and Society*: 293–311.

Douglas, M. (1966), *Purity and Danger: An Analysis of the Concepts of Pollution and Taboo*, London: Routledge & Kegan Paul.

Ghertner, D. (2010), 'Calculating Without Numbers: Aesthetic Governmentality in Delhi's Slums', 39(2), *Economy and Society*: 185–217.

Goffman, E. (1956), *The Presentation of Self in Everyday Life*, London: Random House.

Gurney, C. (1999a), 'Lowering the Drawbridge: A Case Study of Analogy and Metaphor in the Social Construction of Home-Ownership', 36(7), *Urban Studies*: 1705–22.

Gurney, C. (1999b), 'Pride and Prejudice: Discourses of Normalisation in Public and Private Accounts of Home Ownership', 14(2), *Housing Studies*: 163–85.

Hurdley, R. (2006), 'Dismantling Mantelpieces: Narrating Identities and Materializing Culture in the Home', 40(4), *Sociology*: 717–33.

Jacobs, J. and Smith, S. (2008), 'Living Room: Rematerialising Home', 40(3), *Environment and Planning A*: 515–9.

Jacobs, K. and Gabriel, M. (2013), 'Introduction: Homes, Objects and Things', 30(3), *Housing, Theory and Society*: 213–8.

Jacobs, K. and Malpas, J. (2013), 'Material Objects, Identity and the Home: Towards a Relational Housing Research Agenda', 30(3), *Housing, Theory and Society*: 281–92.

Jackson, E. and Beson, M. (2014), 'Neither 'Deepest, Darkest Peckham' nor 'Run-of-the-Mill' East Dulwich: The Middle Classes and Their 'Others' in an Inner-London Neighbourhood', 38(4), *International Journal of Urban and Regional Research*: 1195–1210.

Kleinhans, R. and Elsingha, M. (2010), '"Buy Your Home and Feel Control": Does Home Ownership Achieve the Empowerment of Former Tenants of Social Housing', 10(1), *International Journal of Housing Policy*: 41–61.

Miller, D. (2010), *Stuff*, Cambridge: Polity.

Rowlands, R. and Gurney, C. (2001), 'Young Peoples' Perception of Housing Tenure: A Case Study in the Socialization of Tenure Prejudice', 17(2), *Housing, Theory and Society*: 121–30.

Watt, P. (2009), 'Living in an Oasis: Middle-Class Disaffiliation and Selective Belonging in an English Suburb', 41(12), *Environment and Planning A*: 2874–92.

8

Messiness and Techniques of Simplification

Although shared ownership remains a marginal tenure in terms of the wider housing market, and is dwarfed by other policy interventions (such as the right of many social housing tenants to buy their home or the large-scale sell-off of much council housing), it has been tasked with exponential growth because it primarily addresses those locked out of ownership. Shared owners were encouraged into the sector to take advantage of at least part of the aspirations resulting from ownership—such as asset accumulation, security, and engaging in the values of homeownership. One of the major achievements of shared ownership for the shared owners interviewed, who were formerly private renters, was an opportunity to obtain quality accommodation with long-term security of tenure at a price comparable to, or often less than, their previous accommodation—a "no brainer", as a couple of shared owners described their decision. The actual or perceived insecurity, lack of control, and the constant churning of tenancies and disrepair in the private rented sector were important factors for many to access shared ownership.

Nevertheless, this has been a project which has challenged our assumptions about ownership and sociality. We have argued for that curious, and uncomfortable, sense of in-betweenness that comes from a recognition that apparently polar opposites (ownership/renting; social/private) are actually not so; instead, they exist on scales. Or, perhaps, a better way of thinking about this is that the mundane experience of ownership exemplifies its messiness. So, rather than thinking about property as owned or rented, as either private or social, as being characterised by exclusion or other monochrome notions, through the course of our project, we have come to see it as involving a messy, dynamic set of processes and practices.

© The Author(s) 2018   **207**
D. Cowan et al., *Ownership, Narrative, Things*, Palgrave Socio-Legal Studies,
https://doi.org/10.1057/978-1-137-59069-5_8

Fig. 8.1 Participants' experiences of shared ownership

The messiness of shared ownership can be characterised by a word cloud from our interviews with buyers about their experiences. We asked buyers to summarise their experiences in five words. The word cloud provides a graphic summary of those words (Fig. 8.1).

This word cloud reflects that messiness through the contradictory words used by our interviewees to describe their experiences. Our buyer participants spoke of the opportunity, its affordability, the security, and independence that they were able to get out of their home. They were lucky and happy. At the same time, one can see contradictions appearing here—their experiences had caused frustration and disappointment.

In order to make sense of that messiness, we all need techniques of simplification. We have seen these techniques operate in different ways in the course of this study (just like the property theorists). The very reduction of something as messy as shared ownership to a mantra of "part own, part rent" or as "a foot on the ladder" is part and parcel of that simplification. Rather than adopt such slogans, John Stanley used the metaphor of the technicalities of passenger aircraft and argued that those technicalities did not stop people from flying—in other words, we are surrounded by technical complexity, but this does not stop us from going outside.

At a time when we are apparently in need of short descriptions, "literally" (a word which we discussed in Chap. 5 and evidently dislike!), to describe things, these phrases have taken on a life of their own. They are trotted out as descriptors, apparently without much thought now, yet they have also become powerful mediators, with an agency of their own. Their power as marketing slogans for this product is that they exhort action and enable potential buyers to "see" the product. Indeed, when we talk of the housing crisis, these slogans are spoken of themselves as being part of the solution. They involve no threat to the status quo; they are consumption oriented in the sense that they reinforce the ownership value in consuming housing and take the focus away from its production; and, because they are cheaper, they sell the shared ownership offer as low-cost homeownership.

What emerged from the policy primeval soup—a phrase borrowed from Kingdon's classic on policy-making—was a hybrid scheme designed to mediate between different markets at a moment when there was a sharp division between owning and council housing. Private renting was regarded as a dead tenure. However, this hybrid was problematic in concept, design, and execution. That it survived at all was by no means inevitable. This messiness had to be resolved, and specific units within the government department responsible for housing became engaged in developing the ideas. Yet, the process of enrolling others and resolving the messiness was undoubtedly engaged through a quite simple rendering of the idea as producing ownership, and tying this idea to a politics which valued ownership *uber alles*. The valorisation of ownership in this way "is a combination of class prejudice and myth" (Madden and Marcuse 2016: 79), which relies on a construction of housing tenure that has been itself constructed to valorise ownership.

This messiness and simplification is translated into the everyday lives of shared owners and shared ownership. The management of shared ownership, characterised by absence because it is equated with ownership, and the selling of shared ownership as mirroring the private sector are part and parcel of these processes. They are also insidious in that they involve processes of division and further stigmatising the stigmatised. We can see this most clearly in the asides to the narratives of our buyers—the self-interruptions to their narratives which divided themselves off from social rented housing. Yet, the messiness remains in their narratival conflicts: they felt in control, but, at least at times (and, for many, most of the time), they were out of control; they were not part of the social, but, at least at times, wanted its embrace.

And when we had completed all but this chapter of this book and reflected on it, Helen wrote to Alison and Dave:

> My biggest concern is the way in which I think the text essentialises shared ownership. Surely our argument is that [ownership] is essentially a strategy that is aided by property law … Shared ownership challenges this essentialism by lying at the margins. This is managed by the housing associations by making huge efforts to fit shared ownership into ownership … I think the shared owners are resisting this essentialising in a multiplicity of ways … I worry that the way in which the fieldwork is presented confirms rather than unpicks the essentialising … So they [the shared owners] become complicit in the hierarchy of property etc … I would prefer us to concentrate on conflicts and nuance, … At the moment, there is a tendency of the field work to replicate the essentialising logic.

Helen's comment reflected the uncomfortable proposition that, in our focus on shared ownership, we had ourselves engaged in our own techniques of simplification, and abstracted it. In a way, it is difficult to get away from this essentialism when one is writing a book about shared ownership as a thing, having spent quite a lot of our time researching it. Yet, one of the points Helen was making is that many of the problems highlighted by our shared owners are characteristic of ownership more generally. That feeling of being in control and yet out of control is something which those of us who have been owners know all too well. Beyond our own experience, we have no data with which to contrast or compare our buyer interviewees' experiences. In many respects, this is to our advantage, because we can suggest implicitly that our findings extend beyond our subject matter. That is probably what we want you to think, although we know that we can't actually write that explicitly because we are limited by our data and by our methodological perspective, which entreats us not to be expansionist. What we can say, however, is that we have presented a view of a hybrid form of ownership and property from the margins. We think that this is probably unlikely to be unusual, but that will take a further project.

And, in any event, without that essentialism, it is unlikely that shared ownership would have survived beyond the 1970s, let alone been the recipient of such enormous amounts of public money. Nevertheless, the sense of awkwardness engendered by Helen's comment has resulted in overwriting and editing, to the extent that we hope that at least some of this clumsiness and simplification has been rectified. Part of our fascination with this subject lies in its complexity as a hybrid thing, its anomie within the law of property, and the ways in which different constituent agents (things) made sense of it, co-constitute it, and co-produce it. There is plenty further research that needs to be done around this subject—our data did not account for ethnicity or gender, for example—in the context of the low-cost homeownership offer.

We also recognise—and hope that our text brings out—that shared ownership has occupied a pivotal and trailblazing role in the financialisation of housing, which housing itself can now not do without. This is the new(ish) political economy of social housing, in which—mirroring the private sector—large-scale private finance machines, ratings agencies, and the like congeal around, and produce, a social that is far removed from its forebears. The whole design of shared ownership was manipulated to bring private finance into the social housing sector, in terms of mixing public grant with private finance to deliver units of shared ownership in the first place, and, then, in using the lease as a way of bringing in more private finance into the consumption of those units.

More than this, though, it enabled housing associations to cross-subsidise their social rented activities because shared ownership created a surplus for re-distribution into their activities. And we can see the effects of this financialisation in our study, whether it be through marketing leaflets or the architecture of our case study housing associations' offices; and this runs through to the expectations of our buyer participants of their respective housing association provider. More broadly, shared ownership represents one of the original and sharpest ends of the commodification of social housing. One egregious consequence of this development has been the cost of some shared ownership properties. For example, *The Guardian* drew attention to a £1 million three-bedroom shared ownership property for sale in the London Borough of Hackney (Osborne 2015):

> The flat is in a new development called The Cube, which is described as "a contemporary development of stylish apartments, in a location that offers the opportunity to live London life to the full". The cross-shaped building has won several awards for its innovative design and look. A two-bedroom property in the same development being offered through a normal sale is on the market at £1.3m, but the housing association is offering three three-bedroom properties at rents of less than £200 a week.

The Chief Executive of the housing association offering the property, the Islington and Shoreditch Housing Association, was cited as justifying the sale of the property at this price as follows:

We recognise that the home highlighted by the Guardian is out of reach to many of the households we prioritise to assist.

It does still, however, meet our objective of assisting people who would otherwise not be able to purchase in that area. The proceeds from shared ownership are invested in providing low-cost rent homes in the same area.

This kind of development represents the almost-inevitable corruption of the concept of shared ownership in this financialised world. The loosening of the eligibility criteria following the Cameron government's intervention is likely simply to exacerbate this trend.

All of this demonstrates that shared ownership is not so much about meeting housing need, but about producing subsidy; to the extent that organisations and policy-makers are able to argue that it is about meeting housing need represents the malleability of that concept, which now becomes the "objective of assisting people who would otherwise not be able to purchase in that area". When Tom Murtha (2014; Murtha is a doyen of social housing, and who, coincidentally, was involved in the original NFHA Working Group discussed in Chap. 2) wrote ironically, "Don't worry[,] our values will save us", he drew attention to the flexibility inherent in the term "social business", which both our case study housing associations sought to operationalise. We drew attention to the different ways in which they did so. However, more generally, the real question for associations is, as Murtha suggested, "Are some housing associations being dazzled by 'being commercial' to the detriment of their social ethos. If this is the case who will save us?"

All the way along, underpinning these relationships and twists lies the lease. This has been the central object of our study. It is here that what we referred to as a "methodological footnote" has guided our understandings—the legal consciousness of things. It was the lease that made shared ownership knowable and legible, precisely because it was known to the law of property and, slightly more mundanely, to mortgage lenders. All the understandings of the key players congealed into its terms, so it spoke for those key players. It was the lease that streamlined this messiness, and made it seem smooth through, for example, manipulating its terms to provide succour to those same mortgage lenders and to make it the equivalent of (if not exactly like) ownership. And, in our study, it was the lease that structured and produced action.

Yet, it was also the lease that produced further messiness. Some of this messiness came to the fore in shared ownership's own crisis moment, the law case of *Midland Heart v Richardson*. In judging the long lease to be nothing more than an assured (probably shorthold) tenancy, the case laid down a challenge to the progenitors of the concept; the translation can be regarded as treasonous to their intentions and desires, but it was produced out of their document and the general law. Yet, that case was itself marginalised because it challenged the simple, linear narrative of shared ownership as ownership. In doing so, policy-makers failed to see that the lease itself, and the way in which it was translated, was the issue. Others spoke for and about Ms Richardson as some sort of unusual character, deflecting attention from the thing that caused the issue, and failed to appreciate that the judge's interpretation in that case now enables housing associations to use this mandatory ground for possession more generally. That mandatory ground for possession is in strong contrast to the law and practice governing the right of lenders to take possession of mortgaged property.

From the outset, the lease has been a problematic thing. It was the lease that many complained (bitterly) about during our study as creating complexity from identifying responsibility for problems through to removing the relationality of the landlord–tenant relation. To be sure, our research participants sought to bring order to that everyday, and explained its messiness by reference to other actors (such as the failure of the conveyancer to provide proper advice to the buyer). But this is precisely the point—it had to be explained away. People had to be implicated in the failure, so the thing lost its explication.

It was the lease that structured the organisation and responses of our case study housing associations as ownership and enabled them to draw on the *caveat emptor* idea. We recognise that many of the issues that our shared owners told us about were issues that could just as easily have existed in any long leasehold relationship. Indeed, the long leasehold remains one of the most problematic relations that the limited property law foists on people. It may well be that our sample of buyers felt these problems more than others because of their marginal status and incomes. Exercising rights under leasehold law is a challenging process on which few leaseholders embark. In that sense, the shared owners may not be disadvantaged in comparison with the providers' other leaseholders, but may be more so if the development is managed by a third party, where the provider may also carry little weight or influence with the management company. It was often the case that charges here more frequently lacked transparency and were high, occupying a greater proportion of housing costs than in other provider-controlled development.

The lease was by no means the only thing, although we might say that it was the most significant. The stories we were told were imbricated with, and implicated, many things in their telling. Potted plants, flowers, and sweet wrappers were perhaps the most memorable things for us. On the shelf, these things lack meaning; they are passive. Yet, when placed in a garden or outside a front door or on a pavement, we argue that they come to have rather more complicated meanings; in this book, they have many meanings—about ownership and its divisibility from the social. They enmeshed law, legalities, the material, and the ideational. They do rather more work than passively representing ownership or aesthetic beauty. As Daniel Miller (2010: 94) puts it, "Objects can be obdurate little beasts, that fall from the mantelpiece and break, that refuse to grow in shady spots in the garden, that cause us to trip, and that crash their systems just as we were about to type something genuinely interesting. If, in all such cases, they are clearly not reflecting the agency that is represented by us, then it seems reasonable to start talking in terms of the agency represented by them – the gremlins."

And here, we return to the question of property. This book has been about property, and its relationship with law and society. We originally proposed a triptych of law–property–society, which is mutually constituting. Our book offers a critique and a challenge to the dematerialised and monochrome thesis of the property theorists who insist on exclusion and placing law first. Our work, just like that of Blomley, points to the everyday elasticity of boundaries—physical as well as conceptual. Of course, part of our appreciation about ownership is that it emphasises control over the inside to the best that we can. Feature walls and other aspects of the personalisation of property are what might make house home, at least partially. However, our data also demonstrate that property is porous and flexible, a process in its own right, which must take into account the financialisation of housing and its critique. And our data suggest that this process has, at its heart, belonging, a sense of one's identity in relation to, and connection between, the home as well as to the outside. So much of our data addressed this ontology of property.

In our insistence on the law–property–society relationship, we are seeking to open up investigations, and to open our eyes to the wealth of material which is all around us and in which this relation is drawn. We have, for example, drawn attention to a particular socio-legal object—marketing materials—which we have not ourselves seen analysed in this way, but which properly should be regarded as a site in which law–property–society coalesces. However, the home itself is also something which moulds us, through our constant engagement with it. For our buyer interviewees, there was that sense of aspiration and home-making, which they felt unable to do in the private rented sector, but which was constantly in process. So, rather annoyingly, albeit in tune with our methodological bent, our conclusion is that law–property–society is nothing more (and nothing less) than a set of processes, which change tack over time.

Bibliography

Madden, D. and Marcuse, P. (2016*), In Defense of Housing: The Politics of Crisis*, New York: Verso.

Miller, D. (2010), *Stuff*, Cambridge: Polity.

Murtha, T. (2014), 'Don't Worry Our Values Will Save Us', *Inside Housing*, 26th August.

Osborne, H. (2015), '"Affordable" Shared Ownership Flat in Hackney on the Market for £1m', *The Guardian*, 24th August.

Erratum to: Ownership, Narrative, Things

Erratum To:

© The Author(s) 2018
D. Cowan, et al., *Ownership, Narrative, Things*, Palgrave Socio-Legal Studies,
https://doi.org/10.1057/978-1-137-59069-5_1

The original version of the book contained an error that has been corrected. The book title in the below reference has been corrected to *"Routledge Handbook of Law and Theory"*.

Cloatre, E. and Cowan, D. (forthcoming), 'Materialities and Legalities: Some Observations', in A. Philippopoulos-Mihalopoulos (ed), *Routledge Handbook of Law and Theory*, London: Routledge.

The updated original online version for this chapter can be found
https://doi.org/10.1057/978-1-137-59069-5_1

© The Author(s) 2018   **E1**
D. Cowan et al., *Ownership, Narrative, Things*, Palgrave Socio-Legal Studies,
https://doi.org/10.1057/978-1-137-59069-5_9

Appendix: Summary of Buyer Interviews

© The Author(s) 2018
D. Cowan et al., *Ownership, Narrative, Things*, Palgrave Socio-Legal Studies,
https://doi.org/10.1057/978-1-137-59069-5

10.1 Greendale

Interview number	Name	Area	Gender	Occupation	Previous tenure
1	Pamela	2	Female	Police	Private renting
2	Emma	1	Female	Civil Servant	Private renting
3	Joshua	1	Male	Economist	Flat share
4	Aisling	1	Female	n/a	Council tenant
5	Flo	1	Female	Teacher	Private renting
6	Agnes	1	Female	Secretary	Private renting
7	Don	1	Male	Airport	Private renting
8	Ben	2	Male	Retired	Owner-occupier
9	Paul	2	Male	n/k	Housing association tenant
10	Pete	2	Male	Retired/p-t	Private renting
11	Jim	2	Male	Student/youth worker	Bed and breakfast
12	Bethany	1	Female	Media	Living with parents
13	Arnold	2	Male	Retired	Private renting
14	Elsie	2	Female	Retired	Council tenant
15	Nicky/ Norm	2	Female/Male	Carer	Owner-occupier
16	Sonia	2	Female	n/k - f-t	Private renting
17	Susan	1	Female	Customer service	Private renting
18	Tony	1	Male	n/k	Private renting
19	Bob	1	Male	IT	Flat share
20	Jill	1	Female	HR	Owner occupier
21	Sam	1	Female	Publishing	Flat share
22	June	1	Female	Sports	Living with parents
23	Ann-Marie	1	Female	Local authority	Living with parents
24	Antonia	1	Female	Teacher	Private renting
25	Nik	1	Male	LA contractor/ unemployed	Private renting
26	Michael	1	Male	TV	Private renting
27	Pat and Reena	1	Male & Female	LA	Shared ownership/ private renting

When bought	Property type bought	Percentage share bought (+ = staircase)	Re-sale?	Issues
2005	Two bed house	50	Yes	Leak
2007	Two bed flat	45 + 45	No	Leak
2011	One bed flat	25	No	None
1992	Two bed flat	50 + 25	No (DIYSO)	Rent /sc
2013	Two bed flat	30	Yes	Leak
2000	One bed flat	25	Yes	Repairs/bad deal
2004	Two bed flat	25	Yes	Repairs/responsibility/ management/ communication
1994	Two bed house	50	No (DIYSO)	Improvements/ communication
2007	Two bed flat	50	No	New build
2010	Three bed house	25	No	Car parking
2009	Two bed house	25	No	Background/arrears
2003	One bed flat	50	Yes	Service charges
2009	Two bed house	25	No	New build quality/ repairs
1994	Two bed house	25	No (DIYSO)	Rent
2007	Two bed house	35	No	Repairs/responsibilities
2008	Three bed house	50	No	Service charge/ affordability
2009	One bed flat	50	No	New build/repairs
2007	One bed flat	25	Yes	New build/repairs
2004	One bed flat	65 + 35	No	New build/repairs
2012	Two bed flat	30	No	New build/service charge/affordability
2012	Two bed flat	50	Yes	Noise/length of lease/ communication
2014	Two bed flat	25	Yes	Car parking; communication
2007	Two bed flat	50+50	No	Affordability/staircasing
2006	Two bed flat	25	Yes	Affordability/disrepair/ rubbish
2006/2007	One bed flat	25	No	Maintenance
2007	One bed flat	50 (+50 currently)	No	Staircasing/gripes
2013	Two bed flat	25	Yes	Noise; ASB

(continued)

Interview number	Name	Area	Gender	Occupation	Previous tenure
28	Emily	2	Male	Self-employed	Private renting
29	Petra	1	Female	n/k	Private renting
30	Nicki	2	Female	Nurse	Shared house
31	Jude	2	Female	Estate agent	Private renting (family separation)
32	Colin	2	Male	n/k	Living with family

10.1.1 Fixham

Interview number	Name	Gender	Occupation	Previous tenure
1	Justin	Male	Charity day worker	Owned/private rented
2	Marisol	Female	Education/building	Parents
3	Clare	Female	Teacher	Private rented
4	Lois	Female	Housing	Housing association
5	Paula	Female	Social worker	Parents
6	Simone	Female	Homemaker	Private rent
7	Aisha and Joe	Male & Female	Self-employed/ musicians	Private rent
8	Derek	Male	n/k	Private rent
9	David and Michelle	Male & Female	n/k	Housing association
10	Carl	Male	n/k	Parents
11	Andrew	Male	p/t worker	Private rent
12	Ryan	Male	Unemployed (ex-student)	Private rent
13	Joanne	Female	Bank	Parents – Housing association
14	Jonny	Male	n/k	Private rent
15	Sofia	Female	Housing association	Private rent
16	Ade and Mel	Male/Female	Council/homemaker	Private rent

When bought	Property type bought	Percentage share bought (+ = staircase)	Re-sale?	Issues
2009	Two bed house	25 or 30	No	Rent, service charge, repairs
2004	Two bed flat	70	No	Service Charge, Disrepair
2008	Two bed house	50	No	ASB, service charge
C 2008	Two bed house	50	No	ASB, repairs
C 2010	Two bed house	40	Yes	Area/planning, maintenance

Flat/house	When bought	Percentage share bought (+ = staircase)	Re-sale?	Issues
One bed flat	2014	25	Yes	Communication; security
House	2008	25	Yes	Improvements; staircasing
Two bedroom flat	2009	25	Yes	Repairs/improvements, staircasing
Three bed house	2012 (off plan)	40	No	Parking, new build
Flat	2013	25	Yes	Parking, ASB
Two bed house	2011	33	No	New build, resale
Two bed flat	2007	30 (+45)	Yes	Service charge, management company
Three bed house	2009	50	Yes	Improvements, insurance
Four bed house	2008	25	Yes	Disrepair
Two bed house	2012	50	Yes	
House	1999	75	Yes	Affordability/repairs
One bed flat	2009	40	No	Affordability/moving
House	1996	50 (+50)	No	Subletting, improvements
Three bed house	1995	40	No	Improvements, repairs, resale
Four bed house	2014	50	Yes	Defects/repairs, central heating
Two bed house	2014	50	No	Moving

(continued)

Interview number	Name	Gender	Occupation	Previous tenure
17	Steven	Male	Unemployed	Friends
18	Jeanette and Zack	Male/Female	Self-employed/small business	Parents
19	Diane	Female	Outreach worker	Private rent
20	Jonelle	Female	Administrator/carer	Social rent
21	Bobby	Female	NHS worker	Private rent
22	Albert and Julie	Male/Female	Retired	Private rent
23	John	Male	Self-employed	Private rent
24	Jo	Female	Retired	Shared ownership to private rent
25	Carly	Female	Housing association	Family breakdown/ private rent
26	Ross	Male	Charity	Private renting (non-UK)
27	Niamh	Female	Unemployed	Private rent
28	Claudia	Female	Nurse	Council rented
29	Mariam	Female	Social Work	Private renting
30	Karisma	Female	Teacher	Private renting
31	Jessie	Female	HR	Shared renting
32	Jeannie	Female	Unemployed	Private renting
33	Sian	Female	Low wage	Rent-a-room
34	Donna	Female	Social worker	Private renting
35	Marley	Female	Employed	Living with parents
36	Janine	Female		Living with parents
37	Alicia	Female	Bank	Private renting
38	Rachel	Female	Company	Shared ownership

Flat/house	When bought	Percentage share bought (+ = staircase)	Re-sale?	Issues
Three bed house	2002	50	Yes	Affordability
Two bed house	2003	50	Yes	Disrepair/improvements/resale/ communication
Two bed flat	2006	50	No	New build/communication/ staircasing
Four bed house	2014	30	No	Repairs/new build
Two bed house	2012	25	Yes	
One bed flat	2012	25	No	Repair, new build, service charge
Three bed flat	2014	30	No	Communication
Three bed house	2003	30 (+10)	No	
Four bed house	2012		No	
Three bed flat	2004	30	No	Service charge, lease
Three bed house	2009	50	Yes	Repairs, improvements
Three bed flat	2011	25 (+ considering 75%)	No	New build, restrictions
Two bed flat	2005	35	No	Service charges, rent, resale
Two bed flat	2014	30	No	
One bed flat	2005	30 (+70)	No	Staircasing, new build
Two bed flat	2011	40	No	ASB, new build, noise
Three bed house	2004	25	Yes (DIYSO)	Affordability, communication, resale
Two bed house	2004	60	No	Managing agent, communication, social
Two bed flat	2011	30/33?	No	Service charge, new build
Two bed house	2009	25	No	Service charge, communication
One bed flat	2006	50	No	Staircasing, noisy neighbour
Four bed house	2014	30	No	ASB

Bibliography

Alexander, G., Panalver, E., Singer, J. and Underkuffler, L. (2009), 'A Statement of Progressive Property', 94(4), *Cornell Law Review*: 743–4.

Allen, P. (1982), *Shared Ownership: A Stepping Stone to Home Ownership*, London: HMSO.

Apps, P. (2017), '25,000 Shared Ownership Homes Under Construction', *Inside Housing*, 19th January.

Atkinson, R. and Blandy, S. (2007), 'Panic Rooms: The Rise of Defensive Homeownership', 22(4), *Housing Studies*: 443–58.

Atkinson, R. and Blandy, S. (2016), *Domestic Fortress: Fear and the New Home Front*, Manchester: MUP.

Belsky, E., Retsinas, N. and Duda, M. (2003), 'The Financial Returns to Low Income Homeownership' Paper Presented for the Affordable Homeownership: Critical Perspectives Symposium, University of North Carolina, March 6–8, 2003.

Benson, M. and Jackson, E. (2017), 'Making the Middle Classes on Shifting Ground? Residential Status, Performativity and Middle-Class Subjectivities in Contemporary London', online first, *British Journal of Sociology*.

Birmingham Mail (1975), 'Half and Half Homes Plan Is Launched', *Birmingham Mail*, 17th September 1975.

Battye, F., Bishop, B., Harris, P., Murie, A., Rowlands, R. and Tice, A. (2006), *Evaluation of Key Worker Living: Final Report*, London: DCLG.

Bennett, J. (2010), *Vibrant Matter: A Political Ecology of Things*, Durham: Duke UP.

Birch, J. (2017), 'The Trouble with Leasehold', *Inside Housing*, 13th April.

Blackstone, W. (1765), *The Commentaries on the Laws of England*, London: Dawsons.

© The Author(s) 2018
D. Cowan et al., *Ownership, Narrative, Things*, Palgrave Socio-Legal Studies,
https://doi.org/10.1057/978-1-137-59069-5

Blandy, S. and Goodchild, B. (1999), 'From Tenure to Rights: Conceptualising the Changing Focus of Housing Law in England', 16(1), *Housing Theory and Society*: 31–42.

Blandy, S. and Robinson, D. (2001), 'Reforming Leasehold: Discursive Events and Outcomes, 1984–2000', 23(3), *Journal of Law and Society*: 384–408.

Blessing, A. (2012), 'Magical or Monstrous? Hybridity in Social Housing Governance', 27(2), *Housing Studies*: 189–207.

Blomley, N. (2003), 'Law, Property, and the Geography of Violence: The Frontier, the Survey, and the Grid', 93(1), *Annals of the Association of American Geographers*: 121–41.

Blomley, N. (2013), 'Performing Property: Making the World', 26(1), *Canadian Journal of Law and Jurisprudence*: 23–48.

Blomley, N. (2016), 'The Boundaries of Property: Complexity, Relationality, and Spatiality', 50(1), *Law and Society Review*: 224–55.

Blunt, A. and Dowling, R. (2006), *Home*, London: Routledge.

Boeger, N. (2017), 'The New Corporate Movement', in N. Boeger and C. Villiers (eds), *Shaping the Corporate Landscape: Towards Corporate Reform and Enterprise Diversity*, Oxford: Hart.

Boehm, T. and Schlottmann, S. (2008), 'Wealth Accumulation and Homeownership: Evidence for Low-Income Households', 10(2), *Journal of Policy Development and Research*: 225–56.

Bowes, A. and Sim, D. (2002), 'Patterns of Residential Settlement among Black and Minority Ethnic Groups', in P. Somerville and A. Steele (eds), *'Race', Housing and Social Exclusion*, London: Jessica Kingsley.

Bramley, G., Dunmore, K., Durrant, C. and Smart, G. (1995), *Do-It-Yourself Shared Ownership: An Evaluation*, London: Housing Corporation.

Bramley, G. and Dunmore, K. (1996), 'Shared Ownership: Short-Term Expedient or Long-Term Major Tenure?', 11(1), *Housing Studies*: 105–31.

Bramley, G. and Morgan, J. (1998), 'Low Cost Home Ownership Initiatives in the UK', 13(4), *Housing Studies*: 567–86.

Bramley, G., Morgan, J., Cousins, L., Dunmore, K., Three Dragons Consultancy and MORI Social Research (2002), *Evaluation of the Low Cost Home Ownership Programme*, London: ODPM.

Bright, S. and Hopkins, N. (2009), 'Low Cost Home Ownership: Legal Issues of the Shared Ownership Lease', 73(4), *Conveyancer and Property Lawyer*: 337–49.

Bright, S. and Hopkins, N. (2011), 'Home, Meaning and Identity: Learning from the English Model of Shared Ownership', 28(3), *Housing, Theory and Society*: 377–96.

Brown, A. (2004), 'Anti-social Behaviour, Crime Control and Social Control', 43(2), *Howard Journal of Criminal Justice*: 203–11.

Building Societies Association (BSA), Council for Mortgage Lenders (CML), Homes and Communities Agency (HCA) and National Housing Federation (NHF) (2014), *Handling Arrears and Possession Sales of Shared Ownership*

Properties, London: CML. https://www.cml.org.uk/policy/guidance/all/guidance-for-handling-arrears-and-possession-sales-of-shared/

Bumiller, K. (1988), *The Civil Rights Society: The Social Construction of Victims*, Baltimore: Johns Hopkins University Press.

Burgess, G., Crook, T. and Monk, S. (2013), *The Changing Delivery of Planning Gain through Section 106 and the Community Infrastructure Levy*, Cambridge: Cambridge Centre for Housing and Planning Research.

Burridge, A. (2010), 'Capital Gains, Homeownership and Economic Inequality', 15(2), *Housing Studies*: 259–80.

Cabinet Office (2015), *The Red Tape Challenge Reports on Progress*, available at http://webarchive.nationalarchives.gov.uk/20150522175321/http://www.redtapechallenge.cabinetoffice.gov.uk/home/index/

Cairncross, L., Clapham, D. and Goodlad, R. (1997), *Housing Management, Consumers and Citizens*, London: Routledge.

Callon, M. (1984), 'Some Elements of a Sociology of Translation: Domestication of the Scallops and Fishermen of St Brieuc Bay', 32(1), *The Sociological Review*: 196–233.

Callon, M. (1986), 'The Sociology of an Actor-Network: The Case of the Electric Vehicle', in M. Callon, J. Law and A. Rip (eds), *Mapping the Dynamics of Science and Technology: Sociology of Science in the Real World*, Basingstoke: Palgrave Macmillan.

Callon, M. and Latour, B. (1981), 'Unscrewing the Big Leviathan: How Actors Macro-Structure Reality and How Sociologists Help Them to Do So', in K. Knorr and A. Cicorel (eds), *Towards and Integration of Macro and Micro Sociology*, London: Routledge.

Cameron, D. (2015), 'This Is a Government that Delivers', 7th December, https://www.gov.uk/government/news/prime-minister-this-is-a-government-that-delivers

Carr, H. (2010), 'The Right to Buy, the Leaseholder, and the Impoverishment of Ownership', 38(4), *Journal of Law and Society*: 519–41.

Christie, H., Smith, S. and Munro, M. (2008), 'The Emotional Economy of Housing', 40(1), *Environment and Planning A*: 2296– 312.

Clarke, A. (2001), 'The Aesthetics of Social Aspiration', in D. Miller (ed), *Home Possessions*, Oxford: Berg.

Clarke, A. (2010), 'Shared Ownership: Does It Satisfy Government and Household Objectives?', in S. Monk and C. Whitehead (eds), *Making Housing More Affordable: The Role of Intermediate Tenures*, Oxford: Wiley Blackwell.

Clarke, A., Heywood, A. and Williams, P. (2016), *Shared Ownership: Ugly Sister or Cinderella? The Role of Mortgage Lenders in Growing the Shared Ownership Market*, London: CML.

Cloatre, E. (2013), *Pills for the Poorest*, London: Palgrave Macmillan.

Cloatre, E. and Cowan, D. (forthcoming), 'Materialities and Legalities: Some Observations', in A. Philippopoulos-Mihalopoulos (ed), *Routledge Handbook of Law and Theory*, London: Routledge.

Cohen, M. (1927), 'Property and Sovereignty', 13(1), *Cornell Law Review*: 8–30.

Cole, I. and Robinson, D. (2000), 'Owners, Yet Tenants: The Position of Leaseholders in Flats in England and Wales', 15(6), *Housing Studies*: 595–612.

Conservatives (2015), *The Conservative Party Manifesto*, London: The Conservative Party.

Cook, N., Smith, S. and Searle, B. (2013), 'Debted Objects: Homemaking in an Era of Mortgage-Enabled Consumption', 30(3), *Housing, Theory and Society*: 293–311.

Cooper, D. (2007), 'Opening Up Ownership: Community Belonging, Belongings, and the Productive Life of Property', 32(3), *Law and Social Inquiry*: 625–64.

Council of Mortgage Lenders (CML), Homes and Communities Agency (HCA) and National Housing Federation (NHF) (2014), *Guidance for Handling Arrears and Possession Sales of Shared Ownership Properties*, London: CML.

Cousins, L., Ledward, C., Howe, K., Rock, G. and Taylor, G. (1993), *An Appraisal of Shared Ownership*, London: HMSO.

Cowan, D. and McDermont, M. (2006), *Regulating Social Housing: Governing Decline*, London: Routledge.

Cowan, D., Pantazis, C. and Gilroy, R. (2001), 'Social Housing as Crime Control: An Examination of the Role of Housing Management in Policing Sex Offenders', 10(4), *Social and Legal Studies*: 435–57.

Craig, P. (1986), 'The House that Jerry Built? Building Societies, the State and the Politics of Owner-Occupation', 1(2), *Housing Studies*: 87–108.

Crook, T. and Whitehead, C. (2010), 'Intermediate Housing and the Planning System', in S. Monk and C. Whitehead (eds), *Making Housing More Affordable: The Role of Intermediate Tenures*, Oxford: Blackwell.

Crook, T., Bibby, P., Ferrari, E., Monk, S., Tang, C. and Whitehead, C. (2016), 'New Housing Association Development and Its Potential to Reduce Concentrations of Deprivation: An English Case Study', 53(16), *Urban Studies*: 3388–404.

Daily Telegraph (2013), 'John Coward—Obituary', *Daily Telegraph*, 21st November, http://www.telegraph.co.uk/news/obituaries/politics-obituaries/10481998/John-Coward-obituary.html

Davey, F. and Bates, J. (2014), *Leasehold Disputes*, 3rd ed, London: Legal Action Group.

Davies, M. (1997), *Property: Meanings, Histories, Theories*, London: Glasshouse.

De Botton, A. (2007), *The Architecture of Happiness*, London: Penguin.

De Santos, R. (2013), *Homes for Forgotten Families: Towards a Mainstream Shared Ownership Market*, London: Shelter.

Department for Communities and Local Government (DCLG) (2007), *Homes for the Future: More Affordable, More Sustainable*, Cm 7191, London: DCLG.

Department for Communities and Local Government (DCLG) (2010a), *The Coalition: Our Programme for Government on Communities and Local Government*, London: DCLG.

Department for Communities and Local Government (DCLG) (2010b), *Local Decisions: A Fairer Future for Housing*, London: DCLG.

Department for Communities and Local Government (2015), *Proposals to Streamline the Resale of Shared Ownership Properties*, London: DCLG.

Department for Communities and Local Government (CLG) (2017), *Fixing Our Broken Housing Market*, London: DCLG.

Department of Environment (1971), *Fair Deal for Housing*, Cmnd 4728, London: HMSO.

Department of the Environment (DoE) (1977), *Housing Policy—A Consultative Document*, London: HMSO.

Department of the Environment (DoE) (1995), *Our Future Homes: Opportunity, Choice and Responsibility*, Cm 2901, London: DoE.

Douglas, M. (1966), *Purity and Danger: An Analysis of the Concepts of Pollution and Taboo*, London: Routledge & Kegan Paul.

Dowling, R. (1998), 'Gender, Class and Home Ownership: Placing the Connections', 13(4), *Housing Studies*: 471–86.

Easthope, H. (2004), 'A Place Called Home', 21(3), *Housing, Theory and Society*: 128–38.

Easthope, H. (2014), 'Making a Rental Property Home', 29(5), *Housing Studies*: 579–96.

ECOTEC (2008), *Evaluation of the HomeBuy Agents in the Delivery of the National Affordable Housing Programme 2006/08*, London: ECOTEC.

Elsinga, M., Hoekstra, J. and Dol, K. (2015), 'Financial Implications of Affordable Home Ownership Products: Four Dutch Products in International Perspective', 30(2), *Journal of Housing and the Built Environment*: 237–55.

Engel, D. and Munger, F. (2003), *Rights of Inclusion: Law and Identity in the Life Stories of Americans with Disabilities*, Chicago: University of Chicago Press.

Ewick, P. (2008), 'Consciousness and Ideology', in A. Sarat (ed), *The Blackwell Companion to Law and Society*, Oxford: Blackwell.

Ewick, P. and Silbey, S. (1998), *The Common Place of Law: Stories from Everyday Life*, Chicago: University of Chicago Press.

Financial Services Authority (FSA) (2013), *Building Societies' Sourcebook*, London: FSA.

Flint, J. (2002), 'Social Housing Agencies and the Governance of Anti-social Behaviour', 17(4), *Housing Studies*: 619–37.

Flint, J (2004), 'Reconfiguring Agency and Responsibility in the Governance of Social Housing in Scotland', 41(1), *Urban Studies*: 151–72.

Ford, J., Burrows, R. and Nettleton, S. (2001), *Home Ownership in a Risk Society*, Bristol: Policy Press.

Forrest, R. and Hiroyama, Y. (2015), 'The Financialisation of the Social Project: Embedded Liberalism, Neo-liberalism and Home Ownership', 52(2), *Urban Studies*: 233–44.

Forrest, R., Lansley, S. and Murie, A. (1984), *A Foot on the Ladder? An Evaluation of Low Cost Home Ownership Initiatives*, Working Paper No 41, Bristol: School for Advanced Urban Studies, University of Bristol.

Forrest, R., Murie, A. and Williams, P. (1990), *Home Ownership: Differentiation and Fragmentation*, London: Unwin Hyman

Fox O'Mahony, L. (2014), 'Property Outsiders and the Hidden Politics of Doctrinalism', 67(1), *Current Legal Problems*: 409–45.

Freeman, R. and Maybin, J. (2011), 'Documents, Practices and Policy', 7(2), *Evidence and Policy*: 155–70.

Fritsvold, E. (2009), 'Under the Law: Legal Consciousness and Radical Environmental Activism', 34(4), *Law & Social Inquiry*: 799–824.

Giuliani, M. (1991), 'Towards an Analysis of Mental Representations of Attachment to Home', 8(2), *Journal of Architectural and Planning Research*: 133–46.

Goffman, E. (1956), *The Presentation of Self in Everyday Life*, London: Random House.

Goffman, E. (1958), *Stigma: Notes on the Management of Spoiled Identity*, London: Penguin.

Grabham, E. (2016), *Brewing Legal Times: Things, Form and the Enactment of Law*, Toronto: University of Toronto Press.

Graham, N. (2011), *Lawscape: Property, Environment, Law*, London: Routledge.

Gurney, C. (1999a), 'Lowering the Drawbridge: A Case Study of Analogy and Metaphor in the Social Construction of Home-Ownership', 36(7), *Urban Studies*: 1705–22.

Gurney, C. (1999b), 'Pride and Prejudice: Discourses of Normalisation in Public and Private Accounts of Home Ownership', 14(2), *Housing Studies*: 163–85.

Halliday, S. and Morgan, B. (2013), 'I Fought the Law and the Law Won? Legal Consciousness and the Critical Imagination', 66(1), *Current Legal Problems*: 1–32.

Hamnett, C. (1999), *Winners and Loser: Homeownership in Modern Britain*, London: Routledge.

Hargreaves, J. (2014), *Mr Messy*, London: Egmont.

Haworth, A. and Manzi, T. (1999), 'Managing the "Underclass": Interpreting the Moral Discourse of Housing Management', 36(1), *Urban Studies*: 153– 65.

Herbert, C., McCue, D. and Sanchez-Moyano, R. (2013), 'Is Homeownership Still an Effective Means of Building Wealth for Low-Income Households? (Was It Ever?)', Joint Centre for Housing Studies, Harvard University, http://www.jchs.harvard.edu/sites/jchs.harvard.edu/files/hbtl-06.pdf

Heywood, A. (2016), *From the Margins to the Mainstream: A Study of the Prospects for Shared Home Ownership in the North West*, London: The Smith Institute.

Hills, S. and Lomax, A. (2007), *Whose House Is It Anyway? Housing Associations and Home Ownership*, London: Housing Corporation/Coventry: CIH.

Hillyard, P. and Watson, S. (1996), 'Postmodern Social Policy: A Contradiction in Terms?', 25(3), *Journal of Social Policy*: 321–46.

Holmes, C. (2005), *The Other Notting Hill*, Studley: Brewin Books.

Homes and Communities Agency (HCA) (2010), *Updated Consultation Note for Stakeholders Following Informal Consultation Process*, 29th January 2010, available at https://www.gov.uk/guidance/capital-funding-guide/1-help-to-buy-shared-ownership

Homes and Communities Agency (HCA) (2011), *Affordable Homes Programme 2011 to 2015: Guidance and Allocations*, London: HCA.

Homes and Communities Agency (HCA) (2013), *Shared Ownership Model House Lease*, available at https://www.gov.uk/guidance/capital-funding-guide/1-help-to-buy-shared-ownership#section-11

Homes and Communities Agency (HCA) (2016a), *Shared Ownership and Affordable Homes Programme 2016–21: Prospectus*, London: HCA.

Homes and Communities Agency (HCA) (2016b), *Capital Funding Guide*, London: HCA.

Homes and Communities Agency (HCA) (2016c), *2015 Global Accounts of Housing Providers*, London: HCA.

Homes and Communities Agency (HCA) (2016d), *Shared Ownership: Joint Guidance for England*, London: HCA.

Homes and Communities Agency (HCA) (2017a), *Shared Ownership and Affordable Homes Programme 2016–21: Addendum to the Prospectus*, London: HCA.

Homes and Communities Agency (HCA) (2017b), *2016 Global Accounts of Housing Providers*, London: HCA.

Homes and Communities Agency (HCA), Council of Mortgage Lenders (CML) and National Housing Federation (NHF) (2010), *Shared Ownership: Joint Guidance for England*, London: CML.

Honore, A. (1961), 'Ownership', in A. Guest (ed), *Oxford Essays in Jurisprudence*, Oxford: OUP.

Hull, K. (2016), 'Legal Consciousness in Marginalized Groups: The Case of LGBT People', 41(3), *Law and Social Inquiry*: 551–72.

Hunter, C. (2015), 'Solar Panels, Homeowners and Leases: The Lease as a Socio-Legal Object', in D. Cowan and D. Wincott (eds), *Exploring the 'Legal' in Socio-Legal Studies*, London: Palgrave Macmillan.

Hurdley, R. (2006), 'Dismantling Mantelpieces: Narrating Identities and Materializing Culture in the Home', 40(4), *Sociology*: 717–33.

Jackson, E. and Nemson, M. (2014), 'Neither "Deepest, Darkest Peckham" nor "Run-of-the-Mill" East Dulwich: The Middle Classes and Their "Others" in an Inner-London Neighbourhood', 28(4), *International Journal of Urban and Regional Research*, 1195–210.

Jacob, M-A. (2017), 'The Strikethrough: An Approach to Regulatory Writing and Professional Discipline', 37(1), *Legal Studies*: 137–61.

Jacobs, J. and Smith, S. (2008), 'Living Room: Rematerialising Home', 40(3), *Environment and Planning A*: 515–9.

Jacobs, K. and Gabriel, M. (2013), 'Introduction: Homes, Objects and Things', 30(3), *Housing, Theory and Society*: 213–8.

Jacobs, K. and Malpas, J. (2013), 'Material Objects, Identity and the Home: Towards a Relational Housing Research Agenda', 30(3), *Housing, Theory and Society*: 281–92.

Jacobs, K. and Manzi, T. (2017), '"The Party's Over": Critical Junctures, Crises and the Politics of Housing Policy', 32(1), *Housing Studies*: 17–34.

Johnson, J. (1988), 'Mixing Humans and Nonhumans Together: The Sociology of a Door-Closer', 35(3), *Social Problems*: 298–310.

Jorgensen, C. (2016), 'The Space of the Family: Emotions, Economy and Materiality in Homeownership', 33(1), *Housing, Theory and Society*: 98–113

Karn, V., Kemeny, J. and Williams, P. (1985), *Home Ownership in the Inner City: Salvation or Despair?*, Aldershot: Gower.

Keenan, S. (2013), 'Property as Governance: Time, Space and Belonging in Australia's Northern Territory Intervention', 76(3), *Modern Law Review*: 464–93.

Keenan, S. (2015), *Subversive Property: Law and the Production of Spaces of Belonging*, London: Routledge.

Kennett, P., Forrest, R. and Marsh, A. (2013), 'The Global Economic Crisis and the Reshaping of Housing Opportunities', 30(1), *Housing, Theory and Society*: 10–28.

King, P. (2010), *Housing Policy Transformed: The Right to Buy and the Desire to Own*, Bristol: Policy Press.

Kingdon, J. (2011), *Agendas, Alternatives and Public Policies*, Boston: Longman.

Kleinhans, R. and Elsingha, M. (2010), '"Buy Your Home and Feel Control": Does Home Ownership Achieve the Empowerment of Former Tenants of Social Housing', 10(1), *International Journal of Housing Policy*: 41–61.

Langley, P. (2006), 'The Making of Investor Subjects in Anglo-American Pensions', 24(5), *Environment and Planning D*: 919–34.

Latour, B. (2000), 'When Things Strike Back: A Possible Contribution of "Science Studies" to the Social Sciences', 51(1), *British Journal of Sociology*: 107–23.

Latour, B. (2005), *Reassembling the Social: An Introduction to Actor-Network-Theory*, Oxford: OUP.

Latour, B. (2010), *The Making of Law: An Ethnography of the Conseil d'Etat*, Oxford: OUP.

Latour, B. and Woolgar, S. (1986), *Laboratory Life: The Construction of Scientific Facts*, Princeton: Princeton UP.

Law, J. (1996), 'Traduction/Trahison: Notes on Actor-Network Theory', TMV Working Paper Number 106, Oslo, Norway: University of Oslo.

Law, J. (1999), 'After ANT: Complexity, Naming and Topology', in J. Law and J. Hassard (eds), *Actor-Network Theory and After*, Sociological Review Monographs, Oxford: Blackwell.

Law, J. (2002), *Aircraft Stories: Decentring the Object in Technoscience*, Durham: Duke UP.

Law, J. (2004), *After Method: Mess in Social Science Research*, London: Routledge.

Law, J. and Mol, A. (1995), 'Notes on Materiality and Sociality', 43(2), *The Sociological Review*: 274–94.

Law, J. and Singleton, V. (2000), 'Performing Technology's Stories: On Social Constructivism, Performance, and Performativity', 41(5), *Technology and Culture*: 765–75.

Low Cost Home Ownership Task Force (2003), *A Home of My Own*, The Report of the Government's Low Cost Home Ownership Task Force, London: Housing Corporation.

Lupton, M., Hale, J., Sprigings, N., and Chartered Institute of Housing (2003), *Incentives and Beyond? The Transferability of the Irwell Valley Gold Service to Other Social Landlords*, London: ODPM.

Malpass, P. (2000a), 'The Discontinuous History of Housing Associations in England', 15(2), *Housing Studies*: 195–212.

Malpass, P. (2000b), *Housing Associations and Housing Policy: A Historical Perspective*, Basingstoke: Macmillan.

Malpass, P. (2005), *Housing and the Welfare State: The Development of Housing Policy in Britain*, Basingstoke: Palgrave Macmillan.

Manzi, T. and Morrison, N. (2017), 'Risk, Commercialism and Social Purpose: Repositioning the English Housing Association Sector', forthcoming, *Urban Studies*: 1–18.

McDermont, M. (2007), 'Mixed Messages: Housing Associations and Corporate Governance', 16(1), *Social and Legal Studies*: 71–94.

McDermont, M. (2010), *Governing, Independence, and Expertise: The Business of Housing Associations*, Oxford: Hart Publishing.

McKee, K. (2011), 'Challenging the Norm? The "Ethopolitics" of Low Cost Homeownership in Scotland', 48(16), *Urban Studies*: 3399–413.

McKenzie, D. (2006), *An Engine, Not a Camera: How Financial Models Shape Markets*, Cambridge, Mass: MIT Press.

Mercer, P. (2016), 'Could Shared Ownership Help Sydney's Housing Affordability Crisis?', *BBC Online News*, http://www.bbc.co.uk/news/business-37116439

Merrill, T. and Smith, H. (2000), 'Optimal Standardization in the Law of Property: The Numerus Clausus Principle', 110(1), *Yale Law Journal*: 1–70.

Merrill, T. and Smith, H. (2001), 'What Happened to Property in Law and Economics?', 111(2), *Yale Law Journal*: 357–98.

Merry, S. (1990), *Getting Justice and Getting Even: Legal Consciousness among Working-Class Americans*, Chicago: University of Chicago Press.

Miller, D. (2010), *Stuff*, Cambridge: Polity.

Morrison, N. (2016), 'Institutional Logics and Organisational Hybridity: English Housing Associations' Diversification into the Private Rented Sector', 31(8), *Housing Studies*: 897–915.

Mullins, D., Czischke, D. and van Bortel, G. (2014), *Hybridizing Housing Organisations: Meanings, Concepts and Processes of Social Enterprise*, London: Routledge.

Murie, A. (1975), *The Sale of Council Houses: A Study in Social Policy*, CURS Occasional Paper No 35, Birmingham: University of Birmingham.

Murie, A., Niner, P. and Watson, C. (1976), *Housing Policy and the Housing System*, London: Allen & Unwin.

Murie, A. and Williams, P. (2015), 'A Presumption in Favour of Home Ownership? Reconsidering Housing Tenure Strategies', 30(5), *Housing Studies*: 656–76.

Murtha, T. (2014), 'Don't Worry Our Values Will Save Us', *Inside Housing*, 26th August.

Murtha, T. (2015), 'The Housing Association that Will No Longer Build Homes for the Poor', *The Guardian*, 7th August.

National Audit Office (2006), *A Foot on the Ladder: Low Cost Home Ownership Assistance*, HC 1048 Session 2005–2006, London: NAO.

National Federation of Housing Associations (NFHA) (1978), *A Handbook for Community Leasehold*, London: NFHA.

Nedelsky, J. (1990), 'Law, Boundaries, and the Bounded Self', 30(1), *Representations*: 162–89.

Nielson, L.B. (2000), 'Situating Legal Consciousness; Experiences and Attitudes of Ordinary Citizens about Law and Street Harassment', 34(4), *Law and Society Review*: 1055–90.

Office of the Deputy Prime Minister (2005), *HomeBuy—Expanding the Opportunity to Own*, Consultation Paper, London: ODPM.

Osborne, H. (2014), 'Poor Doors: The Segregation of London's Inner-City Flat Dwellers', *The Guardian*, 25th July.

Osborne, H. (2015), '"Affordable" Shared Ownership Flat in Hackney on the Market for £1m', *The Guardian*, 24th August.

Osman, A. (1975), 'A New Kind of Owner-Occupier', *The Times*, 18th September.

Page, D. (1993), *Building for Communities*, York: Joseph Rowntree Foundation.

Parkinson, S., Searle, B., Smith, S., Stokes, A. and Wood, G. (2009), 'Mortgage Equity Withdrawal in Australia and Britain: Towards a Wealth-Fare State?', 9(4), *European Journal of Housing Policy*: 363–87.

Pawson, H. and Mullins, D. (2010), *After Council Housing: Britain's New Social Landlords*, Basingstoke: Palgrave Macmillan.

Peaker, G. (2013), 'The Hidden Dangers of Shared Ownership', *The Guardian*, 3rd September.

Penner, J. (1996), 'The "Bundle of Rights" Picture of Property', 43(3), *UCLA Law Review*: 711–820.

Penner, J. (1997), *The Idea of Property in Law*, Oxford: OUP.

Pharoah, R, Holland, J. and Wootton, R. (2015), *A Fair Share? Understanding Residents' Experiences of Shared Ownership*, London: Viridian Housing.

Piketty, T. (2015), 'Property, Inequality, and Taxation: Reflections on *Capital in the Twenty-First Century*', 68(2) *New York University Tax Review*: 631–47.

Price, S. (1958) *Building Societies: Their Origin and History*, London: Franey.

Radin, M. (2012), *Boilerplate: The Fine Print, Vanishing Rights, and the Rule of Law*, Princeton: Princeton UP.

Resolution Foundation (2013), *One Foot on the Ladder: How Shared Ownership Can Bring Owning a Home into Reach*, London: Resolution Foundation.

Riles, A. (2006), 'Introduction: In Response', in A. Riles (ed), *Documents: Artifacts of Modern Knowledge*, Ann Arbor: University of Michigan Press.

Riles, A. (2011), *Collateral Knowledge: Legal Reasoning in the Global Financial Markets*, Chicago: University of Chicago Press.

Robertson, D. (2006), 'Cultural Expectations of Homeownership: Explaining Changing Legal Definitions of Flat "Ownership" Within Britain', 21(1), *Housing Studies*: 35–52.

Rose, C. (1985), 'Possession as the Origin of Property', 52(1), *University of Chicago Law Review*: 73–88.

Rose, C. (1994), *Property & Persuasion: Essays on the History, Theory, and Rhetoric of Ownership*, Boulder, Col: Westview.

Rose, N. (1999), *Powers of Freedom: Reframing Political Thought*, Cambridge: CUP.

Rowlands, R. and Gurney, C. (2001), 'Young Peoples' Perception of Housing Tenure: A Case Study in the Socialization of Tenure Prejudice', 17(2), *Housing, Theory and Society*: 121–30.

Royal Commission (1885), *Royal Commission on the Housing of the Working Classes*, vol II: Minutes of Evidence, London: HMSO.

Sarat, A. (1990), '"The Law Is All Over …": Power, Resistance and the Legal Consciousness of the Welfare Poor', 2(2), *Yale Journal of Law and the Humanities*: 343–79.

Sassen, S. (2014), *Expulsions: Brutality and Complexity in the Global Economy*, Cambridge, Mass: Belknap Press.

Saunders, P. (1990), *A Nation of Home Owners*, London: Allen and Unwin.

Savage, M., Bagnall, G. and Longhurst, B. (2004), *Globalization and Belonging*, London: Sage.

Savills (2016), *Spotlight Shared Ownership*, London: Savills. http://pdf.euro.savills.co.uk/uk/residential---other/spotlight-shared-ownership-2016.pdf

Searle, B. (2012), 'Recession, Repossession and Family Welfare', 24(1), *Child and Family Law Quarterly*: 1–23.

Shelter (2010), *The Forgotten Households—Is Intermediate Housing Meeting Affordable Housing Needs?*, London: Shelter.

Silbey, S. (2005), 'After Legal Consciousness', 1(1), *Annual Review of Law and Social Science*: 323–68.

Silbey, S. (2010), 'J. Locke, op. cit.: Invocations of Law on Snowy Streets', 5(2), *Journal of Comparative Law*: 66–91.

Silbey, S. and Cavicchi, A. (2005), 'The Common Place of Law: Transforming Matters of Concern into the Objects of Everyday Life', in B. Latour and P. Weibel (eds), *Making Things Public: Atmospheres of Democracy*, Cambridge, Mass: MIT Press.

Silbey, S. and Ewick, P. (2003), 'Narrating Social Structure: Stories of Resistance to Legal Authority', 108(6), *American Journal of Sociology*: 1328–72.

Sinn, C. and Davies, S. (2014), *Shared Ownership 2.0: Towards a Fourth Mainstream Tenure*, London: Orbit Group; Coventry: Chartered Institute of Housing.

Smith, S. (2015), 'Owner-Occupation: At Home with a Hybrid of Money and Materials', 40(3), *Environment and Planning A*: 520–35.

Spenceley, J. (2008), *Trends in Housing Association Stock in 2007*, A Dataspring Briefing Paper on Behalf of the Housing Corporation, Cambridge: Dataspring.

Stanley, J. (1974), *Shared Purchase: A New Route to Home-Ownership*, London: Conservative Political Centre.

Stewart, A. (1981), *Housing Action in an Industrial Suburb*, London: Academic Press.

Tang, C., Oxley, M. and Mekic, D. (2017), 'Meeting Commercial and Social Goals: Institutional Investment in the Housing Association Sector', 32(4), *Housing Studies*: 411–27.

Tenant Services Authority (TSA) (2009), *Existing Tenants Survey 2008: Shared Owners*, London: TSA.

Teruel, R. (2015), 'The New Intermediate Tenures in Catalonia to Facilitate Access to Housing', 2, *Revue de Droit Bancaire et Financiere*: 115–8.

Underkuffler, L. (2016), 'A Theoretical Approach: The Lens of Progressive Property', in S. Blandy and S. Bright (eds), *Researching Property Law*, London: Palgrave Macmillan

Valverde, M. (2003), *Law's Dream of a Common Knowledge*, Princeton: Princeton UP.

Valverde, M. (2005), 'Authorizing the Production of Urban Moral Order: Appellate Courts and Their Knowledge Games', 39(2), *Law and Society Review*: 419–56.

Van Oorschott, I. and Schinkel, W. (2015), 'The Legal Case File as Border Object: On Self-Reference and Other-Reference in Criminal Law', 42(4), *Journal of Law and Society*: 499–527.

Wallace, A. (2008a), 'Knowing the Market? Understanding and Performing York's Housing', 23(2), *Housing Studies*: 253–70.

Wallace, A. (2008b), *Achieving Mobility in the Intermediate Housing Market: Moving Up and Moving On?*, York: Joseph Rowntree Foundation.

Walker, R. (2000), 'The Changing Management of Social Housing: The Impact of Externalisation and Managerialisation', 15(2), *Housing Studies*: 281–99.

Walt, A van der (2009), *Property in the Margins*, Oxford: Hart.

Warnock, M. (2015), *Critical Reflections on Ownership*, London: Edward Elgar.

Watson, S. (1999) 'A Home Is Where the Heart Is: Engendering Notions of Homelessness', in P. Kennett and A. Marsh (eds), *Homelessness: Exploring the New Terrain*, Bristol: Policy Press.

Watt, P. (2009), 'Living in an Oasis: Middle-Class Disaffiliation and Selective Belonging in an English Suburb', 41(12), *Environment and Planning A*: 2874–92.

Whitehead, C., Spenceley, J. and Kiddle, C. (2005), *The Role of Housing Associations in the Intermediate Market*, London: Housing Corporation.

Index

© The Author(s) 2018
D. Cowan et al., *Ownership, Narrative, Things*, Palgrave Socio-Legal Studies,
https://doi.org/10.1057/978-1-137-59069-5

Printed by Printforce, the Netherlands